Out of the Red

What strategies could governments use to build capitalism under democratic rules of the game?

Development and Inequality in the Market Economy

The purpose of this series is to encourage and foster analytical and policy-oriented work on market-based reform in developing and postsocialist countries. Special attention will be devoted in the series to exploring the effects of free market policies on social inequality and sustainable growth and development.

Editor:
Andrés Solimano

Editorial Board:

Alice Amsden	Patricio Meller
François Bourguignon	Vito Tanzi
William Easterly	Lance Taylor

Titles in the Series:

Andrés Solimano, Editor. *Road Maps to Prosperity: Essays on Growth and Development*

Andrés Solimano, Editor. *Social Inequality: Values, Growth, and the State*

Lance Taylor, Editor. *After Neoliberalism: What Next for Latin America?*

Andrés Solimano, Eduardo Aninat, and Nancy Birdsall, Editors. *Distributive Justice and Economic Development: The Case of Chile and Developing Countries*

Jaime Ros. *Development Theory and the Economics of Growth*

Felipe Larraín B., Editor. *Capital Flows, Capital Controls, and Currency Crises: Latin America in the 1990s*

Mitchell A. Orenstein. *Out of the Red: Building Capitalism and Democracy in Postcommunist Europe*

Ricardo Ffrench-Davis. *Economic Reforms in Chile: From Dictatorship to Democracy*

Stephanie Griffith-Jones, Ricardo Gottschalk, and Jacques Cailloux, Editors. *International Capital Flows in Calm and Turbulent Times: The Need for New International Architecture*

Carol Wise. *Reinventing the State: Economic Strategy and Institutional Change in Peru*

Out of the Red

Building Capitalism and Democracy in Postcommunist Europe

Mitchell A. Orenstein

Ann Arbor

THE UNIVERSITY OF MICHIGAN PRESS

Published in the United States of America by
The University of Michigan Press
Manufactured in the United States of America
⊚ Printed on acid-free paper

2004   2003   2002   4   3   2

A CIP catalog record for this book is available from the British Library.

Library of Congress Cataloging-in-Publication Data

Orenstein, Mitchell A. (Mitchell Alexander)
    Out of the red : building capitalism and democracy in
    postcommunist Europe / Mitchell A. Orenstein.
        p.   cm.
    Includes bibliographical references and index.
    ISBN 0-472-09746-6 (cloth : alk. paper) —
    ISBN 0-472-06746-X (pbk. : alk. paper)
        1. Poland—Economic policy—1990–   2. Czech Republic—
    Economic policy.   3. Czechoslovakia—Economic policy—
    1945–1992.   4. Poland—Politics and government—1989–
    5. Czech Republic—Politics and government—1993–
    6. Czechoslovakia—Politics and government—1945–1992.
    7. Post-communism—Poland.   8. Post-communism—Czech
    Republic.   9. Post-communism—Czechoslovakia.   I. Title.
    HC340.3 .O73 2001
    338.947—dc21   00-012902

Grateful acknowledgment is made to Cambridge University Press
for permission to reprint figure 1 (from Adam Przeworski,
*Democracy and the Market: Political and Economic Reforms in
Eastern Europe and Latin America* [New York: Cambridge
University Press, 1991], fig. 4.1, p. 163. Reprinted with the
permission of Cambridge University Press.) and to Albert O.
Hirschman for permission to reprint figure 8 (from Albert O.
Hirschman, A Dissenter's Confession: The Strategy of Economic
Development Revisited. In *The Strategy of Economic Development*
[Boulder, Colo.: Westview Press]. Reprinted with permission.).

For Martine

Contents

Figures

Tables

Acknowledgments

This book represents the culmination of many years of research and writing, during which I enjoyed the assistance of numerous individuals and institutions. Yale University's Center for International and Area Studies (YCIAS) got the project started with a dissertation research grant. I received additional research support in the dissertation phase from the International Research and Exchange Board (IREX), the Institute of International Education (IIE), and the Woodrow Wilson International Center for Scholars. The American Council of Learned Societies–Social Science Research Council (ACLS-SSRC) Joint Committee on Eastern Europe provided funding for language training. I thank all of these institutions for investing in this research.

I owe a great debt to my dissertation adviser, David Cameron, and other faculty in the Departments of Political Science, Sociology and History at Yale University, especially to Ian Shapiro, Sylvia Maxfield, Robert Jenkins, and Piotr Wandycz, for steering me in the right direction at crucial moments and helping me shape the questions addressed in this work. I also cannot imagine having completed this project in the same way without the input, support, and friendship of Yale graduate student colleagues Jonathan Stein and Mark Weiner, who served as great interlocutors and comrades over the years.

Most of the writing, however, took place at institutions other than Yale, and I am much indebted to them as well. The first draft was written in Oxford, while I was a visiting scholar at Nuffield College, and finished in 1996. As time and events moved on in postcommunist Europe, the manuscript required substantial revision. I completed one set of revisions while a postdoctoral fellow of the Thomas J. Watson Jr. Institute for International Studies at Brown University from 1996 to 1998. I began a second set at Harvard University's Center for European Studies in summer 1999 and finally completed the work while an East European Studies Research Fellow at the Woodrow Wilson International Center for Scholars in Washington, D.C., in summer 2000. I owe all three institutions my warmest thanks and appreciation for opening their excellent facilities to me and providing me with wonderful colleagues and many new insights. I also thank my colleagues at the Maxwell School of Citizenship and Public Affairs, Syracuse University, for their faith in, and support of, this project. Finally, how could I ever forget the Institute for EastWest Studies, now the EastWest Institute, New York, which provided beautiful offices, great friends and colleagues, and numerous adventures in Prague, Warsaw, and beyond. Thanks also to the American Political Science Association for judging "Out of the Red" the best doctoral dissertation in comparative politics in 1997 and the winner of that year's Gabriel A. Almond Award. And thanks to Ellen McCarthy of the University of Michigan Press for her trust and for stewarding the manuscript to publication.

I feel greatly indebted to the numerous friends and scholars who have taken a significant amount of time to read earlier drafts and sections of this manuscript and discuss the core issues with me. Although I will inevitably fail to name everyone, I would like especially to thank Robert Anderson, Hilary Appel, Karla Brom, Wlodzimierz Brus, Ingrid Buxell, Michael Cain, John Campbell, Ellen Comisso, Linda J. Cook, Stephen Crowley, Jean de Fougerolles, John Gould, Carol Graham, Anna Grzymala-Busse, Jerzy Hausner, Stephen Heintz, Joel Hellman, Kristin Hohenadel, Robert Jenkins, Daniel Jowell, Tadeusz Kowalik, Gerald McDermott, Robert Mickey, Joel Migdal, Kálmán Mizsei, Witold Morawski, Krzysztof Ners, Joan Nelson, David Ost, Martin Potůček, Dietrich Rueschemeyer, Marilyn Rueschemeyer, Andrzej Rudka, Peter Rutland, Andy Schwartz, Marc Skapof, Joel Turkewitz, Andrzej Tymowski, Milada Vachudova, Jiří Večerník, Kieran Williams, Rick Woodward, and Alan Zuckerman. John Birkelund, chairman of the board of the Watson Institute, deserves special mention for both pinpointing errors in an earlier version and appreciating the finer qualities of the manuscript at the same time.

Special thanks go to Alexander Russo, who provided invaluable research assistance in the final stages of manuscript preparation, to Rita Mesias for her work on chapter 4 and to Ilean Cashu, for his help with the references. I am also indebted to the many government officials, scholars, trade unionists, and enterprise managers in East Central Europe who agreed to be interviewed for this project and supplied me with a mountain of research materials and insights. I hope that the publication of this book goes some of the way toward repaying the debt I have incurred to them.

Finally, my deepest appreciation goes to Martine Haas, who offered valuable insights and lived through the highs and lows of this project with great charm and enthusiasm. And to my parents, Phil and Joyce Orenstein, who educated and inspired me through their example of hard work and artistic dedication. It is to them and their parents and grandparents, who came from Central and Eastern Europe under often very difficult conditions, that I owe my fascination with and concern for the politics of the region.

Introduction

When Central and Eastern European countries emerged out of the red in 1989, they fell into a world dominated by liberal and, in economics, neoliberal discourse (Ackerman 1992; Szacki 1995, 6).[1] Backed by powerful international organizations, private capital, and the mainstream of the Western economics profession, the neoliberal "Washington consensus" on reform in the developing world was at its height in the late 1980s (Williamson 1990, 1997; Naím 2000). Developed countries themselves had just been swept by neoliberal reforms, epitomized by the "Reagan revolution" in the United States and Margaret Thatcher's remarkable attempts to remake British economy and society. Left parties and social democrats were in disarray around the world, largely because the fall of communism made the left confused about its prospects for the future. In postcommunist Europe in particular, neoliberal economic ideas enjoyed a dramatic and sudden ascendancy, while early advocates of social democracy or a third way were rapidly shunted aside (Szacki 1995, 2–3). Neoliberal reformers seemed to rise to the top of new democratic governments by an unwritten law of gravity. Soon neoliberalism, the most unfamiliar of economic theories in the lands of Marx, Engels, and Lenin, dominated public policy discourse throughout the region.

Neoliberal economists who rose to power after 1989 quickly developed radical programs for economic reform with the support of Western advisers and Washington-based international organizations. They thought hard about how to adapt standard neoliberal economic programs to the postcommunist context. This meant addressing the unusual structural economic conditions of socialism. It also meant developing strategies for economic transformation that would work under democratic rules of the game.

Democracy First, Reform Later

Democracy was a central feature of the revolutions of 1989 in Central and Eastern Europe. While Chinese communists were implementing market economic reforms without granting political rights and freedoms, Central and Eastern Europe experienced a reform sequence of "democracy first, reform later" (Haggard and Kaufman 1992). Analysts quickly identified this sequence as a potential source of strategic problems. Social democratic theorist Ralf Dahrendorf worried that new democracies in Central and Eastern Europe would not be able to tolerate the political pressures generated by radical economic reform. He wrote in 1990:

Basic constitutional changes can be introduced in a matter of months. . . . On the contrary, economic reforms will without fail lead through a valley of tears. Things are bound to get worse before they get better. . . . It is hard to tell how long the trek through the valley will take, but certain that it will take longer than the lifetime of the first parliament and always likely that it will engender a degree of disillusionment which will threaten the new constitutional framework along with the economic reforms, which promised so much but could not deliver in time. (1990, 83–84)

Governments that came to power after 1989 in Central and Eastern Europe would struggle to build prosperous capitalist economies at the same time as democratic political institutions. Striking a balance between these two goals proved difficult at times. Democracy as a political system seeks to involve the widest possible spectrum of organized political forces. Yet in Central and Eastern Europe, some of these forces, particularly those tied to the communist economic system or those harmed by the sudden plunge into market competition, might oppose radical economic reforms. Would new democracies be able to generate the political authority to implement radical economic change over the protests of powerful vested interests and discontented losers of transition? What would reformers do if major political forces turned against the market revolution? Some worried that zealous economic reformers might overturn democracy in order to follow through with the transition. Would this not be a rational response to the likelihood of a populist democratic threat? Alternately, if economic reforms enriched a small elite of "winners," might this elite undermine democracy in order to preserve its advantages? Could new democratic political institutions avoid being overwhelmed by the unleashed forces of a market economy?

These questions became crucial to the Central and East European transformations, for these countries were attempting something few had ever tried: to build capitalism under conditions of political democracy. There were reasons to think this task difficult or even impossible. Few advanced countries experienced their initial period of capitalist development under conditions of democracy. In the traditional development literature, democratic governance was supposed to come after capitalist economic development and the creation of a large middle class (Lipset 1960). In Western Europe, the usual pattern was for capitalism to develop under authoritarian or feudal rule, and then foster demands for greater political representation as the urban middle classes grew (Moore 1966). Capitalism and democracy were widely viewed as compatible in the later stages, but not at first. Successful newly industrialized countries in East Asia followed a similar pattern of capitalist development under authoritarian rule, until finally democracy movements blossomed in the 1980s and 1990s, along with the rise of a sizable middle class.

Many analysts believed that authoritarianism facilitated the early stages of economic development (Maravall 1995, 13–14). The argument for developmentalist authoritarian regimes was simple: the disjunctures and social upheavals caused by rapid capitalist development required political stability that only authoritarian regimes could provide. It was illogical to expect the majority of people to vote for a capitalist system that in the short run would cause great increases in inequality, a massive reallocation of resources, painful shifts in employment, and stressful individual transitions of all types. Such transformations required a firm hand. Analysts believed that new democracies were particularly vulnerable to immediate consumption demands and therefore unlikely to make the difficult economic decisions required for development (Maravall 1995, 14). Thus, much of the previous literature on development gave little reason to expect Central and Eastern Europe's experiment of building capitalism under democratic rules to be successful.

Democracy First

Yet democracy was indelibly stamped upon the revolutions of 1989. The revolutions in Central and Eastern Europe represented a mass rejection of the socialist system, which after all was a developmentalist authoritarian regime that had failed. No one wanted to try that route again. With the rejection of communism came a powerful and sincere affirmation of democratic principles, articulated through the forceful idealism of leaders such as Lech Wałęsa in Poland and Václav Havel in Czechoslovakia. Democratic values were further reinforced by appeals to earlier democratic political experiences in the interwar period (1918–39) or before (1789–1848) that were etched deeply on the political consciousness of most nations in the region. And finally, strict adherence to the principles of procedural democracy was required by the European Union as a condition for membership.

It was not enough for East Central Europe to become capitalist in order to "return to Europe" (the Czechoslovak Civic Forum's rallying cry in 1989). Any serious applicant to the prosperous Western club of nations had to govern itself by democratic means. Just as East Central European countries had mimicked fascism in the 1930s and socialism in the 1950s, in the 1990s they emulated parliamentary democracy under Western eyes. Western supervision became stricter over time, with the European Union eventually formulating democratic political criteria for membership and lambasting Slovakia for not meeting them in 1997 (Smith 1999, 142). Even before then, however, most East Central European political leaders understood they had to act within parliamentary democratic rules of the game or risk being locked out of the West European club. Indeed, most East Central Europeans seemed to understand this, as if it were simply natural. As Timothy Garton Ash wrote in *The Magic Lantern*, a key text on the events of 1989:

> It is not just a Czech phenomenon, for in different ways it is repeated all over East Central Europe. Take a more or less representative sample of politically aware persons. Stir under pressure for two days. And what do you get? The same fundamental Western, European model: parliamentary democracy, the rule of law, market economy. And if you made the same experiment in Warsaw or Budapest I wager you would get the same basic result. This is no Third Way. It is not "socialism with a human face." It is the idea of "normality" that seems to be sweeping triumphantly across the world. (1990, 105)

However, it is important to note that Poland and the Czech Republic (part of Czechoslovakia until 1993) exited communism and arrived at democracy by different routes, creating somewhat different conditions for the pursuit of economic reform. The following sections provide a brief sketch of their experiences of revolution and democratization.

Democratization in Poland

Democracy came to Poland in June 1989, after a nearly ten-year struggle between Solidarity and the communist regime. Solidarity, a broad civic movement that brought together trade unionists, Catholic activists, clergy, and liberal intellectuals under the same banner (Garton Ash 1983), was founded in 1980 during a strike at the Lenin shipyard in Gdansk. A young electrician, Lech Wałęsa, rose swiftly to become the charismatic leader of the movement and won a Nobel Prize for his efforts to gain legal recognition for Solidarity and the right to civic self-organization in communist Poland. The communist regime initially tried to negotiate with Solidarity and adopt some of its demands. However, after a period of compromise, the Polish communist party and military finally cracked down on the Solidarity movement, under pressure from Moscow. The communist regime declared martial law in December 1981, suppressed Solidarity, forced the movement underground, and imprisoned many of its leaders (Michnik 1985). Concurrent with this political repression, the communist regime launched several failed attempts at economic reform during the 1980s (Kamiński 1991), the last of which cul-

April 5, 1989
June

minated in strikes at the end of 1988 in protest over the rising price of food. Solidarity was reborn in this unrest, and in February 1989, the communist government again invited Solidarity leaders to the bargaining table to discuss increasing the sphere of political participation in the country. These so-called roundtable talks ended in an agreement on April 5, 1989, on power sharing between the communists and Solidarity (Gross 1992, 58). As a result of these talks, elections were held in June 1989 for one-third of the seats in the decisive lower house of parliament in Poland, the Sejm, and all of the seats in a newly created Senate. These partially free elections were intended to produce a kind of power-sharing arrangement, in which government would be dominated by communists, but Solidarity would have some voice as well. However, as Timothy Garton Ash (1990) describes, Poles took enormous delight in crossing out the names of the communists who had ruled their country for forty years and subjugated it to the Soviet Union and an economic system that did not work. The outcome of the vote was an overwhelming rebuke to the communists. Solidarity won almost all of the contested seats. With votes from two small parties that had cooperated with the communist regime in the past, Solidarity was able to construct a majority in parliament and found itself in a position to form its own government. Solidarity leaders took power in the summer of 1989 in an atmosphere of absolute shock and euphoria, shaking their heads in disbelief at events that exceeded their imagination (cf. Kuroń 1991). Political events had quickly spiraled out of the control of reform communists and the democratic revolution of 1989 elevated a new set of leaders to power. They began, in this heady atmosphere of world historic change, to consider an economic program that would bring Poland out of the red and stabilize an economy that was threatened by hyperinflation and systemic collapse.

Democratization in Czechoslovakia

In Timothy Garton Ash's (1990, 78) famous phrase, the revolution that took ten years in Poland would take ten weeks in Hungary and ten days in Czechoslovakia. Czechoslovak communism remained stable for longer, but when the edifice began to crack, it fell apart more rapidly. During the 1980s, Czechoslovakia had experienced neither the mass protests against communism, as in Poland, nor the economic reform attempts that Poland's communist leaders hoped would satisfy the population and stave off economic disaster (Adam 1989; 1993b, 629). The communist regime remained conservative and tightly repressive till the end. Czechoslovakia's dissident movement, Charter 77, was limited mainly to intellectuals, although Catholic Church activists and some workers did play a role. As a result, Czechoslovakia was mostly quiescent during the 1980s, while Poland was in turmoil. After the brutal suppression of the Prague Spring in 1968, when Soviet tanks hit the streets of Prague to drive out a reform communist government that Leonid Brezhnev felt had become too democratic, most Czechs and Slovaks preferred to wait quietly until the time was right. Finally, following on the heels of the regime transformation in Poland in 1989, and the exodus of East Germans to the West (Garton Ash 1990), Czech and Slovak citizens burst out against the communist regime in a series of massive public demonstrations in November 1989. The spark that set off the Czechoslovak democratization movement was the police suppression of a student march on November 17, in which hundreds of students were beaten in the center of Prague. Thousands, and then tens of thousands, of Prague citizens turned out on the streets to protest, and within a few days, dissident intellectuals founded a new mass movement, Civic Forum, to give leadership to the demonstrations, keep them going, and use them to force a transition to democracy. The communist regime gave way. Roundtable talks in Czechoslovakia ended in December 1989 with an agreement to transfer power to a government of national unity that would hold office until fully free elections in June 1990. Civic Forum won these elections in a landslide similar to that in Poland one year earlier. Dissident leader and playwright Václav Havel was elected president and planning began for the launch of an economic reform that would bring Czechoslovakia out of communism and return it to Europe.

Reform Later

Democracy, and particularly parliamentary democracy, was an indelible part of the foundation of the new society East Central Europeans wanted to build. Installation of developmentalist authoritarian regimes was not an option. This introduced the theoretical and practical problem that lies at the heart of this book. What strategies could governments use to build capitalism under democratic rules of the game?

This book compares strategies that governments in postcommunist Europe used to reconcile the sometimes competing demands of building capitalism and democracy. It chronicles the central conflict between those who feared that democracy would pose obstacles to radical economic reform and those who feared that radical economic reform would pose dangers to democracy. This debate has played out in academic and policy discourse, but has also had a strong influence on the practice of reform in every country in the postcommunist European region. I have chosen to analyze two countries,

Poland and the Czech Republic, whose initial transition strategies represented opposing theoretical approaches to the problems of simultaneous transition.

Poland's "shock therapy" strategy for transformation is the primary example of the neoliberal economic and strategic program that dominated transition discourse in postcommunist Europe after 1989. It called for rapid and radical economic changes to be pushed through a brief "window of opportunity" opened by the collapse of communism. Taking advantage of this moment would allow for the implementation of tougher economic measures than would be possible under normal democratic politics.

Czech reformers adopted a different path. They supplemented neoliberal economic policies with social measures designed to cushion the costs of reform and thereby win and maintain popular support. Czech strategies of social cohesion and democratic consolidation reflect the views of theorists writing in the social democratic tradition and were implemented on top of otherwise neoliberal economic policies. Therefore, I call the Czech approach a "social liberal" strategy of reform, to indicate its distinctive mix of neoliberal and social democratic elements. It is not purely social democratic or neoliberal, but social liberal, and represents an important alternative strategy for transformation.

Strategies and Alternation

Chapter 1 presents the theories that lay behind these two different strategies for transformation and explores the roots of their difference, while chapters 2 and 3 provide a detailed analysis of the strategies adopted in each country and the impact these have had on democratic politics and economic performance.

Chapter 2 shows that shock therapy resulted in a powerful antireform backlash in Poland, though its effects are far different from what most analysts have suggested. Most analysts expected that antireform backlash would scuttle reform and/or destabilize democratic politics (Dahrendorf 1990; Przeworski 1991; Sachs 1993). And indeed, as Polish citizens experienced the harsh effects of neoliberal economic policies, they reacted by voting out neoliberal reformers, much as analysts expected at the outset of transition. However, the effects of this backlash defied expectations. Reformers changed their behavior. They began to adjust to popular demands for policies that would serve the goals of both economic efficiency and social cohesion. When voters roundly rejected the policies of radical neoliberalism in elections in 1990, 1991, and 1993, center-right governments struggled to find more socially sensitive alternatives to neoliberalism. However, they ultimately lost power to a resurgent left that promised greater attention to the social dimension of transition. Center-left governments from 1993 to 1997 implemented cohesion-oriented policies that significantly modified the policies of shock therapy, but also kept the country on the path to Europe. When neoliberals returned to power in 1997, the second neoliberal reform program, Balcerowicz II, was not as radical as the first and reflected a centrism dictated by democratic coalition politics. Democracy thus caused alternation between the policies of technocratic neoliberalism and social democracy within an increasingly centrist policy range. Democratic policy alternation therefore facilitated both economic efficiency and social cohesion, despite earlier concerns about economic backsliding and political decay.

Chapter 3 investigates the Czech case. I argue that the Czech strategy of social liberalism employed a complex set of ameliorative measures, compensation strategies, innovative structural reforms, and political institution-building to complement neoliberal economic policies of stabilization and liberalization. These strategies worked to dampen the backlash against neoliberalism in the Czech Republic and extended the life of the reform government led by Finance Minister, then Prime Minister, Václav Klaus. While Polish finance minister Balcerowicz stayed in power for little over a year, Klaus dominated the Czech transition for seven years, winning multiple elections in the interim. His reign ground to a halt, however, in 1997, when a dramatic economic crisis showed some of his economic policies to be deeply flawed—particularly his signature mass privatization program and laissez-faire attitude to financial sector regulation. While cohesion-oriented policies had allowed reform to take place in the Czech Republic in an atmosphere of "social peace," lack of democratic policy alternation enabled major reform mistakes to continue unabated. The Czech Republic was ultimately harmed by a lack of alternation, despite the presence of a committed reformer in power. Policy alternation finally began to take shape in the Czech Republic after the fall of the Klaus government in 1997, though it was slowed and stifled by the provisional and minority nature of succeeding governments.

Poland has experienced alternation between governments emphasizing efficiency-oriented and cohesion-oriented policies. The efficiency-oriented strategies produced the predicted backlash, and the cohesion measures improved political stability, creating a better climate for investment and greater acceptance for reform, but at the cost of reform speed in some areas. The Czech Republic implemented both types of measures simultaneously and enhanced government popularity, stability, and opportunity for radical reform. But government stability extended the life of bad policies along with good ones, harming the economy. Neither country has followed purely neoliberal policies in the last decade; and neither has followed purely cohesion-oriented policies. Instead, we have seen a strong democratic policy alternation among these options, marked by entrepreneurial adaptation and convergence, bringing surprisingly positive results. East Central European countries that have succeeded in the transformation to capitalism and democracy have done so not by sticking to a single strategy of reform, but rather by vigorous policy alternation and learning.

Chapter 4 further explores the surprisingly positive effects of policy alternation by focusing on one key area of institutional reform—privatization. While policy stability enhanced the ability of governments to follow through with their reform programs in the Czech Republic, these innovative programs turned out to be flawed. Democratic policy alternation in the Polish case slowed the progress of privatization programs. However, it also slowed the adoption of mistaken policies, and allowed for more substantial interim policy corrections. The result is that Poland is now widely believed to have slower, but higher-quality, privatization, with a substantial positive effect on economic growth and productivity (Kornai 2000; Spicer, McDermott, and Kogut 2000). This seems to suggest that, contrary to most theories of economic transformation, democratic policy alternation can have fruitful economic effects.

The final chapter develops a model of democratic policy alternation in East Central Europe and argues that most previous theorists of transition badly miscalculated the effects of policy alternation on economic reform. I suggest that parliamentary democratic procedures did limit the extent of neoliberal reform, but did not have the negative economic consequences that people expected. Instead, strong domestic and international constraints forced political parties to develop broad-based coalitions around reform strategies that promised to deliver the goods of transition at a price people would support. This spurred a process of policy innovation, as parties tried to find ways to achieve the dual goals of efficiency and cohesion. Democratic competition between political parties supporting alternative strategies of reform also tended to correct mistaken reform strategies adopted by the other side. Parties learned from one another. Since alternation in East Central Europe took place within the context of party systems that were mostly united in their pursuit of European Union membership, and thus simultaneous transition to capitalism and democracy, disputes over transformation strategies revolved mainly around questions of means, rather than ends, about which there was wide, if only general, agreement. Under such circumstances, reform alternation in East Central Europe accelerated a learning process that has everywhere enhanced the success of transition.

East Central Europe is a very particular case of economic reform under democratic conditions. Parliamentary democratic traditions were relatively deeply rooted; the drive to join the West was strong; and the establishment of both democracy and markets was reinforced by the international context. While democracy placed limits on the style of reform, its content, and its stability, special political and economic conditions present in East Central Europe prevented instability from reaching such an extent that it would endanger the progress of reform. Instead, a democratic policy alternation developed that allowed East Central European countries to make more intelligent and suitable choices about the progress of their economies than were possible a priori in neoliberal blueprints. In order to understand why East Central European countries have succeeded in dealing with the economic legacies of communism, it is important to eschew the dogma of both neoliberals and social democrats and instead explore the reasons why a vigorous alternation between opposed policies appears to have been the best way to build both capitalism and democracy. In the context of a transformation where policymakers did not know which policies would work at the outset, and where they needed to achieve multiple goals—enhancing economic efficiency and social cohesion—no single strategy was sufficient. Multiple changes of course were required, and the question was how to develop institutions to manage and counterbalance diverse policy priorities and choices. Democracy has hidden strengths as a mechanism of policy learning. Yet its effects on the style, content, and progress of reform are still widely misunderstood.

Strategies for Transformation

The danger does *not* lie with the *masses,* as is believed by
people who stare as if hypnotised down into the depths of
society. The deepest core of the *socio*-political problem is not
the question of the *economic* situation of the *ruled* but of the
political qualifications of the *ruling and rising* classes. The
aim of our socio-political activity is not to make everybody
happy but the *social unification* of the nation, which has been
split apart by modern economic development, and to prepare it for the strenuous struggles of the future.
   —Max Weber 1994, 26

Poland's goal is to be like the states of the European Community. Although there are many submodels within Western
Europe, with distinct versions of the modern welfare state,
the Western European economies share a common core of
capitalist institutions. It is that common core that should be
the aim of the Eastern European reforms. The finer points of
choosing between different submodels—the Scandinavian
social welfare state, Thatcherism, the German social market—can be put off until later, once the core institutions are
firmly in place.
   —Jeffrey Sachs 1993, 5

Governments that came to power in 1989 in East Central
Europe had to develop "strategies for transformation" that
addressed the central problem they faced of building capitalism under conditions of political democracy. Throughout the postcommunist countries, the
most influential strategy, in both its economic and political dimensions, was
the "neoliberal" strategy, often called "shock therapy." Neoliberal strategy for
transformation emphasized the importance of establishing basic economic
reforms to promote growth and market rationality in the face of democratic
interest group opposition. It proposed to create free markets, free trade, and
a stable monetary environment quickly before such political opposition
could emerge. The neoliberal strategy for transformation was widely debated
in postcommunist Europe and criticized in some circles for posing a threat to
democracy. These critics generally argued that shock therapy's single-minded
pursuit of economic reform endangered support for and development of
democratic institutions. They recommended that governments should

instead pursue more cohesion-oriented strategies that would compensate reform losers and tie the interests of a broader cross-section of the population into the reform effort. This chapter explores both theoretical positions and the conflict between them that unfolded over the period 1989–99. This provides an important background to the study of actual governmental strategies for transformation in Poland and the Czech Republic since 1989, because these theories often deeply influenced practitioners of reform.

Neoliberal Economic Blueprint

In both Poland and the Czech Republic, neoliberal economic blueprints were deeply influential for the project of building capitalism. Neoliberal economic programs proposed for postcommunist Europe drew heavily on previous applications of the so-called Washington consensus on economic policy in countries around the world (Williamson 1990, 1997; Naím 2000). Despite some obvious peculiarities of the postcommunist countries, leading neoliberal economists quickly came around to the view that postsocialist economies would respond favorably to the same basic package of stabilization and liberalization measures normally applied elsewhere in the developing world (Blanchard et al. 1991, 1). According to a short book coauthored by Olivier Blanchard, Rudiger Dornbusch, Paul Krugman, Richard Layard, and Lawrence Summers in 1991 that I take to represent a consensus statement of "the mainstream of modern Western economics" (as claimed on the back jacket), two features distinguished the postcommunist countries from others. First, the distorted price structure of socialism was expected to result in "larger changes in relative prices, income distribution, and firms' financial positions than is typically the case during stabilization" (Blanchard et al. 1991, 2). Second, the different institutional and ownership structure of the former socialist firms was expected to cause them to adjust differently than in traditional market economies. Under socialism, most enterprises were state owned and responded more to administrative decisions of the responsible "line" ministries than to price signals or market demand. For this reason, rapid privatization became a major priority of neoliberal reform, along with macroeconomic stabilization and price and trade liberalization.

Neoliberal economic reform programs consisted of three basic elements: stabilization, liberalization, and privatization. The logic of stabilization and liberalization derives from the equilibrium theory that lies at the heart of neoliberal economics, combined with the monetary theory of inflation. Since inflation is caused mainly by monetary expansion, neoliberals prescribed a stabilization package that would cut fiscal deficits, stem monetary growth, and eliminate price-distorting subsidies to public enterprises (Blanchard et al. 1991, 5). Simultaneous price and trade liberalization would cause prices to quickly adjust to equilibrium levels, under a sustainable macroeconomic regime. Accurate price signals, once attained, would cause economic actors to adjust their behavior spontaneously to market rationality (Johnson and Loveman 1995).

However, recognizing that stabilization and liberalization would at first cause an initial bout of inflation, neoliberal economists counseled reliance on stiff tax-based wage controls, to prevent incomes from catching up with prices (Blanchard et al. 1991, 7). In employing wage controls, neoliberals departed from the free market prescriptions of their orthodox liberal forebears. Their reliance on these so-called heterodox techniques, including state intervention to control the price of labor, is part of what marks them as "neoliberals."

Neoliberal economists expected their reform program to be particularly painful in the postcommunist context, but they felt that there was "no way to avoid this outcome" (Blanchard et al. 1991, xiii). Stabilization and liberalization would sharply reduce average real wages in the economy over the medium term. Unemployment rates would rise as enterprises shed labor in an effort to enhance productivity. But these social costs of adjustment had to be paid, and the quicker the better. The process of transition from communism to capitalism was envisioned as a process of creative destruction, like all innovation (Schumpeter 1942; Havrylyshyn and McGettigan 1999b).

Since they expected state-owned enterprises to adjust less quickly than private firms might to market signals, neoliberal economists strongly recommended rapid privatization (Blanchard et al. 1991, xiv). Neoliberal economists also recognized other institutional changes would have to be made, summed up in the rubric of "restructuring." Within restructuring, Blanchard et al. included transforming the banking and financial system; creating conditions for foreign investment; reforming the legal system, particularly commercial law; creating a market in housing to insure labor mobility; and promoting training in core capitalist professions, such as law, accounting, and finance (Blanchard et al. 1991, xvi–xviii). However, neoliberals tended to underestimate the difficulty of such reforms (Johnson and Loveman 1995, 38) and regarded institutional reforms as distinctly secondary, to be left, perhaps, for a second stage of transition. Some important items were left off the list almost entirely, particularly reform of the social sector, such as health, education, and welfare. Only unemployment insurance was a priority area (cf. Sachs 1993, 46). Furthermore, neoliberals offered few substantive ideas or theories for how to restructure supporting institutions of the capitalist economy, such as banks, courts, and universities. Neoliberal blueprints emphasized spontaneous adjustment to market signals and offered little guidance on restructuring institutions, short of destroying them altogether or "privatizing" them.

Neoliberal Political Strategy

Neoliberal economic blueprints were certainly radical, entailing a wholesale transformation of postcommunist economies and societies. How did neoliberals plan to implement painful, long-term programs of stabilization, liberalization, and privatization under conditions of political democracy?

Neoliberal economists generally took an ambiguous stand on democracy, praising it in principle, but decrying many of its effects. While neoliberal economists appreciated the democratic idealism of East Central Europe, they viewed real democratic politics as a potential obstacle to sustainability of radical reform blueprints. Jeffrey Sachs (1993), a Harvard economist who advised the government of Poland on its radical "shock therapy" program of reform, expressed concern that new democratic institutions could undermine reform as a result of (1) organized opposition from interest groups associated with the old regime; (2) disorganized opposition from new populists hoping to capitalize on economic disappointment; and (3) popular uncertainty about the benefits of reform. Sachs notes that reform winners often take years to feel sure about their economic success, while losers feel the costs immediately (see also Dahrendorf 1990). Given this problem of timing and coordination, "the great political task is to follow the path of reform in the face of inevitable anxieties, vested interests fighting for the status quo, and demagogues ready to seek political power by playing on the public's fears" (Sachs 1993, 3). Providing stable political backing for the reform effort was key. Neoliberals therefore generally viewed the problem of simultaneous transition as one of insuring continuity in the face of democratic political risk. This risk was judged to be higher in new democracies than in consolidated ones, because of weak party systems and inexperience in dealing with democratic institutions (Balcerowicz 1995, 151–52).

Neoliberals' strategic response to the dilemma of democratic instability and risk was twofold: to call for the political insulation of reformers from "normal" democratic politics, and to push reform as quickly as possible through a window of opportunity they saw opening after the political revolution of 1989.

In calling for the political insulation of reformers from normal democratic politics, the neoliberal perspective was deeply technocratic. Neoliberals believed that only a politically insulated team of trained economists could devise and implement a radically efficient set of reforms, while withstanding pressures from well-organized interest groups and guarding the stability of reform. They argued that the strongest opposition to reform would come from interest groups attached to the old regime that would take advantage of weak democratic institutions to serve their own particular interests, at the expense of the public good. This discourse of opposition to "special interests" was evident in Western neoliberalism as well under Thatcher and Reagan. Neoliberals, pointing to "public anxieties" about the transformation in the East, also did not believe that individual postcommunist voters would necessarily understand or act in their best interests in the confusing context of transition. Most former communist citizens would not be able to judge what economic policies were advantageous to them and which were not. Therefore, neoliberals argued for placing extraordinary authority in an apolitical "reform team" to enact changes to serve the public interest, properly understood. Neoliberal economists had unbounded confidence in the ability of the Ministry of Finance to isolate itself from politics and make unerring judgments about optimal economic policies. Furthermore, policy mistakes were never a real concern. Like all modern revolutionaries, neoliberal economists believed that they had discovered the right way forward by scientific means. The political problem of transition was envisioned as one of ensuring that the people followed along.

As part of their technocratic political approach, Sachs and others argued for an increase in executive power to facilitate the transition (Sachs 1993, 113). Sachs advocated a strong presidential system similar to that of France, where the president has wide authority to rule by decree. This would enable the president to enact decisions of the neoliberal reform team by decree. Such a strategy corresponded with neoliberal political tactics in countries around the world, which often relied on a "concentration of decision-making power in coherent reform teams that are insulated from the influence of other bureaucratic groups and from business associations, labor unions, various civil society organizations, and political parties" (Greskovits 1998, 35–36). Neoliberals were skeptical of parliamentary democracy, which they believed could easily be manipulated by special interests, and pinned their hopes instead on strong, insulated executive powers. However, despite calling for limits on parliamentary democracy, neoliberals implicitly argued that their strategy would produce more substantively democratic results. Neoliberals were sincere democrats insofar as they believed that remaining true to a technocratic program of economic change would bring widespread public benefit in the future. Public welfare was their chief concern, and this altruism is what they believed set them apart from the "normal" democratic politics of self-interest (Balcerowicz 1995).

The second element of the neoliberal political strategy was speed. Neoliberal economists argued for the necessity of pushing reform through in a brief window of opportunity and getting as much done as possible before a democratic reaction occurred—to ensure against democratic policy instability. Poland's neoliberal finance minister, Leszek Balcerowicz, provided the most sophisticated theoretical presentation of this view in his article "Understanding Postcommunist Transitions." He wrote, "The key to understanding the interaction between the political and economic dimensions of post-communist transitions is to realize that any great political breakthrough in a country's history is followed by a period of 'extraordinary politics' that soon gives way to 'normal politics'" (1995, 160–61). In other words, a political breakthrough like the one that occurred in 1989 was expected to produce a "special state of mass psychology" in which individuals were more willing to act and think in terms of the common good, eschewing the narrow interest-based perspective of "normal politics." Extraordinary politics, according to Balcerowicz, translates into an exceptionally high readiness to sacrifice for the common good; and therefore to accept neoliberal economic reform. "The brevity of the exceptional period means that a radical economic programme, launched as quickly as possible after the breakthrough, has a much greater chance of being accepted than either a delayed radical programme or a non-radical alternative" (1995, 162). Reformers should therefore seize the window of opportunity provided by extraordinary politics to achieve as much of their reform agenda as possible, before the normal politics of self-interest returns.

While Balcerowicz acknowledges that "time-consuming institutional reforms" cannot be completed during the brief window of extraordinary politics, he does not offer any theory of reform under normal political behavior. Balcerowicz instead offers a theory of revolutionary moments, providing the theoretical justification for the political insulation of a reform team, free from "normal" democratic pressures, pursuing its work as quickly as possible, and implementing reforms, if necessary, by decree, before interest groups mobilize and the public sheds its willingness to sacrifice.

Neoliberal political-economic strategy for dealing with the problems of building capitalism under conditions of democracy therefore consisted of three elements:

1. an emphasis on "getting the prices right" quickly and creating a macroeconomic environment that encourages spontaneous adjustment to economically efficient behavior;

2. political insulation of reformers from interest group pressures; and

3. the use of a window of opportunity to push reform through.

Political Sociological Critiques of Neoliberalism

Neoliberal theory and strategy of reform was deeply influential in postcommunist Europe. However, it was far from uncontested. The most influential alternative to neoliberalism came from the standpoint of institutional political sociology or socioeconomics. This approach is based on the view that the economy is only one among several social subsystems (Offe 1984, 52; Etzioni 1988; Potůček 1999), and that for a society to modernize successfully, it must forge complex linkages between the increasingly diversified arenas of politics, society, and economics, effectively institutionalizing conflicts and organizing participation (cf. Huntington 1968, 8–9). This view has its roots in the political sociology of Max Weber and Emile Durkheim. Therefore, I call this the political-sociological or cohesion-oriented perspective (see quote from Max Weber at the start of this chapter), since it emphasizes the need for mechanisms of social cohesion to counteract the powerful and divisive forces of modern economic development.

Many previous authors have identified "gradualism" as the main alternative to "radical" neoliberal economic thought. However in my view, gradualism has always been somewhat of a straw man, constructed by radical neoliberal theorists to help justify their own approach (see also Kornai 2000 on this point). No one, to my knowledge, ever argued that postcommunist Europe should follow the same policies as the radicals advocated, but only more slowly. There have been institutional economic approaches to the problems of transition that suggested that the spontaneous adjustment expected by neoliberals was unlikely to occur because of institutional factors, and that institutional change would necessarily take a long time (Murrell 1992a, 1992b; Dewatripont and Roland 1996; see also Amsden, Kochanowicz, and Taylor 1994). However, it seems more accurate to label this an institutional critique of neoliberal market economics, rather than gradualism. In fact, almost everyone now agrees that some reforms can be undertaken quickly, and some more slowly, so even if there once was a division between radicals and gradualists, it no longer exists. The division I point to between efficiency-oriented economic theories and cohesion-oriented political-sociological theories has been the relevant divide in debates on the political economy of simultaneous transition to capitalism and democracy. Still, many analysts have couched the debate in terms of radicalism versus gradualism, so it will sometimes be necessary to use these terms, though advisedly and with the above caveats.

The first political-sociological critique of neoliberal transformation strategy came from Adam Przeworski, a political scientist and social democratic theorist with long experience analyzing neoliberal reforms in Latin

America. When the locus of neoliberal revolution shifted from Latin America to his native Poland, Przeworski in 1991 came out with a book, *Democracy and the Market*, that challenged some of the key propositions underlying the neoliberal strategy. Przeworski's critique centered on the "technocratic policy style" of neoliberalism, particularly the insulation of reformers from interest group pressures and the emphasis on speed. Przeworski argued that neoliberal reformers' insulation from the social costs of transition made them likely to implement reforms that were more costly than most people would prefer. This, combined with the inevitably high social costs of reform and uncertainty about its eventual benefits, would cause an antireform backlash to occur. Here Przeworski concurred with the neoliberals, who also expected a backlash. But he went further by hypothesizing that this antireform backlash would foster a start-stop-start cycle of radical and gradualist reforms (represented by lines R and G in figure 1) that would destabilize democratic politics and undermine the progress of market economic reform.

In Przeworski's model, voters would first choose the transformation strategies offered by neoliberal radicals (line R), which promised greater benefits over time, but at the expense of a steeper decline in consumption at first. After experiencing such a sharp decline, voters would lose patience, become disillusioned with the high costs of reform, and vote for parties offering the less costly gradual approach (line G). But gradual reforms would take too long to produce positive results, and voters would again be tempted by the promise of radical solutions. This cycle of democratic policy alternation would prove ineffective. It would slow reform progress and eventually cause one or another organized political group to opt out of democratic politics altogether, choosing an authoritarian path to sustainable reform. As he colorfully put it, neoliberal "technocracy hurls itself against democracy and breeds the inclination to proceed against popular resistance. . . . And, on the other side, as suffering persists, confidence erodes, and the government seems less and less competent, temptations are born to defend one's interests at any cost, even at the cost of democracy" (Przeworski, 1991, 187). Neoliberal reform would imperil democracy, Przeworski argued. Authoritarian temptations from above and below would eventually endanger the progress of simultaneous transition in countries with new, weak, or incomplete democratic institutions.

In order to ensure sustainable and politically stabilizing reform, Przeworski and his collaborators advocated an alternative strategy for transformation that emphasized (1) elaborating a social policy and putting it in place at the same time that neoliberal stabilization is launched; (2) designing reform to minimize social costs and reignite growth, in part by protecting public investment in health and education; (3) processing all economic pro-

Consumption

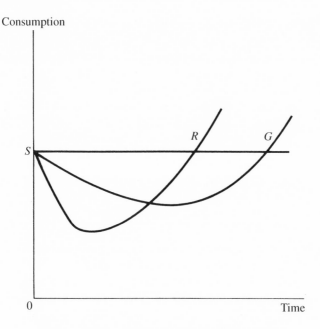

Fig. 1.   Przeworski's model of transition politics

posals and programs through normal democratic institutions and eschewing the use of decrees and emergency measures (Przeworski et al. 1995, 85). Prze- worski argued that grounding economic policies in democratic deliberation would strengthen social cohesion by building linkages between different social groups and democratic politics. Przeworski and his collaborators argued that such social cohesion is an important building block of long-term policy stability (1995, 84). While neoliberals viewed democracy as a potential obstacle to reform, Przeworski viewed radical neoliberalism as a threat to democracy and as a destabilizing force that would cause both political and economic disaster.

Extended Accountability

An important extension and revision of the political-sociological critique of neoliberal policy came in the concept of "extended accountability" developed in David Stark and László Bruszt's *Postsocialist Pathways* (1998). Stark and Bruszt argued against the "unconstrained executive model" that underpins the neoliberal strategy by arguing that, paradoxically, executive capacity to create coherent reform programs can be increased by placing limits on the unilateral prerogatives of executives (188).[1] While neoliberals assumed that internally coherent radical programs of economic reform held the best prospects for growth, Stark and Bruszt argued that policy coherence has to be seen as the product of a dialectical process between policy formulation and implementation.

> Policy coherence is a direct function not of the thoroughness and precision of initial design but rather of the integration of design and implementation. . . . Neither aimless nor rigid, the iterative, deliberative process through which goals are established and their implications recognized facilitates learning from the changing circumstances brought about by reform efforts. Policy coherence is thus the product of reflexive learning. (1998, 198)

Stark and Bruszt doubted the infallibility of reform blueprints and saw the reform process as one of "bricolage," whose performance depended on creating systems of reflexive learning within political-economic institutions and systems of feedback. In making this argument, Stark and Bruszt drew upon the writings of evolutionary economists such as Murrell (1993) and Poznanski (1995), who had been arguing since the start of the transition that it was impossible to construct a new economy from blueprints, but instead that economic transformation was necessarily an evolutionary process that would take place over a long period of time. They argued that it was wrong to expect institutions to spontaneously adjust to market signals. Instead policymakers needed to pay greater attention to feasible ways of reconstructing pre-existing institutions and endowments.

Like Przeworski and the evolutionary economists, Stark and Bruszt argued that adherence to neoliberal "blueprints" would undermine the institutionalization of positive patterns of policy learning. However, in contrast to Przeworski, they had greater faith in the policy effects of democratic institutions. Stark and Bruszt argued that the associative and deliberative properties of democratic institutions would enable not only social cohesion, but also policy cohesion and better reform (1998, 9). Therefore, economic reforms needed to be processed through broadly representative political institutions in order to facilitate sustainability of reform trajectories. Here, Stark and Bruszt directly contradicted both neoliberal economists, with their suspicions about the policy effects of representative democracy, and Przeworski's pessimistic predictions about the outcomes of interaction between neoliberal economic policy and new democratic institutions.

Critique of the Critique

Early debate about simultaneous transition strategies centered on problems of dealing with the inevitable tensions between capitalism and democracy. However, beginning in the late 1990s, a new wave of scholars began to argue that these tensions had been overblown or misidentified by both sides. Joel Hellman, in an influential article in the journal *World Politics* (1998), argued that Przeworski and others had misidentified the threats to reform and the backlash thesis. Hellman argued that the main threat to the continuation of economic reform came not from reform losers, but from winners. Winners who profited from the disequilibrium of partial reforms wanted to suspend further change. This was the greatest threat to reform, not an antireform backlash from below. Béla Greskovits (1998) and Steven Fish (1998), meanwhile, pointed out that the empirical evidence showed that radical reform and democracy were not actually at odds. On the contrary, everywhere in the postcommunist world, the two went together. Greskovits mocked what he labeled the "postcommunist breakdown of democracy literature" for overstating the contradictions between building capitalism and democracy.

The analysts who argued that capitalism and democracy were not incompatible took several approaches to attacking the backlash thesis. The most fundamental attack came from a few economists who argued that the social costs of reform had not been particularly severe, thus muting any backlash. Sachs, for instance, pointed to increased access to consumer durables, unregistered growth in the "gray" economy, overreported unemployment, and understated domestic currency purchasing power to make the case that the much-vaunted costs of transition had not been substantial (Sachs 1993). However, while many analysts were persuaded that government statistics gave an incomplete picture of the postcommunist economic situation, few doubted that a severe output decline and drop in living standards had occurred. The mainstream economic view remains that Central and Eastern European transitions entailed substantial social costs, measured in terms of unemployment, poverty, and health status (cf. Boone, Gomułka, and Layard 1998; Milanovic 1998; UNICEF 1994).

A more persuasive analysis accepted that social costs were severe, but pointed out that for some reasons, they had not caused a destabilizing, antireform backlash. Rather, to the contrary, Fish (1998) used cross-country statistical analysis to show that democratic progress (as measured by Freedom House ratings) and progress on radical economic reform (as measured by the reform indicators of the European Bank for Reconstruction and Development) were actually tightly linked in Central and Eastern Europe. Fish

emphasized the importance of the first postcommunist elections in his explanation, showing that in countries where dissident democratic leaders came to
power in founding elections after 1989, they both strengthened democracy
and set in place radical economic reforms.

Béla Greskovits drew out the implications of this observation in *Political
Economy of Protest and Patience*: "The unexpected and interesting development is that the political 'good times' for market oriented reforms have lasted
much longer than just the brief moments granted by extraordinary politics.
Clearly, the democratic implementation of the neoliberal project has
advanced without much political disturbance well into times of 'normal politics'" (1998, 47–48). In other words, both the neoliberals and their critics
were wrong to worry about the incompatibility of building capitalism and
democracy.

Through a striking review of the literature on simultaneous transition in
Latin America and Eastern Europe, Greskovits argues that what most analysts
of postcommunist transition missed were the critical differences between
Eastern Europe and Latin America that made East European publics much
less likely to respond to neoliberal reform through violence, voice, or popular
protest. In short, "communism left behind certain structural, institutional,
and cultural legacies that put a brake on effective opposition to neoliberal
transformation strategies" (1998, 67). Such legacies as "the lack of extreme
income inequality, the smaller number of marginalized poor, the relatively
lower degree of urbanization of the population, and the absence of recent,
violent experiences with coups and riots may all have contributed a stabilizing influence under postcommunism. It is also important to mention in this
context that reformers in the East have not been in a hurry to eliminate the
'premature welfare states'" (1998, 85). Greskovits also highlights governments' use of what he calls "compensation strategies" to neutralize opposition to reform, such as popular-sector policies targeting lower and lower-
middle income groups; policies enhancing mobility of factors of production;
grace periods and phased implementations of reform; and initiatives to
extend political benefits (1998, 139). However, Greskovits criticizes these
compensation strategies for tending to elevate the interests of a minimum
winning coalition for reform at the expense of less well organized and often
more needy groups. This type of compensation strategy lays the basis for what
he calls "exclusionary democracy" in the East.

Greskovits does not deny tensions between building capitalism and
democracy. Instead, he argues that the organizational weakness of civil society after communism and substantial, widely distributed economic reserves
defused the potential backlash against neoliberal reform. Greskovits con-
cludes that neoliberalism and democracy have proven surprisingly compati-

ble in the East, reaching an enduring "low-level equilibrium" between incomplete democracy and an imperfect market economy (1998, 178). This low-level equilibrium did not force an abandonment of neoliberal economic reforms, but did cause them to advance "more slowly than the radical reformers initially expected." Similarly, democracy has not been imperiled by heavy-handed neoliberal tactics or social unrest, as Przeworski feared, but neoliberal reforms have demobilized East European societies, causing "some important ingredients of fully developed Western-type democracies. . . . . to be in short supply" (1998, 181). Greskovits sees the emergence in Eastern Europe of an exclusionary democracy in which economic elites band together with a selected minority of the opposition to rule by demobilizing the rest of society.

Democratic Policy Alternation

Where does this literature on simultaneous transition to capitalism and democracy leave us? On the one hand, neoliberals and political sociologists have provided us with powerful models of the expected tensions between capitalism and democracy, and two contrasting policy strategies for dealing with these tensions: technocratic and cohesion-oriented. On the other hand, Greskovits, Fish, and other analysts have cast doubt on central tenets of these models, focusing particularly on the backlash thesis. Some have suggested that a backlash against neoliberal reform either never emerged (Greskovits 1998; Aslund, Boone, and Johnson 1996; Sachs 1993) or emerged, but not in the manner expected (Hellman 1998).

More than a decade into the transition, it seems we are still faced with some of the most basic empirical questions: Did a backlash occur against neoliberal reforms? If so, what form did it take? What role did government strategies for transformation play in reducing or eliminating a backlash response? If backlash did occur, did it produce the type of policy alternation that Przeworski predicted? The reflexive learning Stark and Bruszt suggested? Or some other type of response? In short, what have we learned about the influence of democratic institutions on the course of economic reform?

I will make three theoretical points in the course of this comparison of transformation strategies in Poland and the Czech Republic. First, I will defend the proposition that strict adherence to democratic institutions and procedures had a major impact on the political *style* employed by reformers. In my view, a backlash against reform did occur, and this backlash negated the purely technocratic approach of neoliberals. It forced reformers to change their policy style, to engage in normal democratic interest-group politics, and to become what Dominguez (1997) calls "technopols." Technopols are individuals with technocratic training who do not shun politics but instead realize that normal political engagement and pragmatism are the best methods to create a stable basis for long-term structural change. Second, I will show that strict adherence to democratic procedures in East Central Europe had a major impact on the *content* of reforms, forcing reformers to adjust their policies to the demands of democratic politics and coalition governments. Third, I will argue that strict adherence to democratic procedures in East Central Europe caused policy *instability*, as neoliberals and political sociologists predicted. However, contrary to their predictions, the surprising and counterintuitive finding of this study is that this policy instability did not damage the economy or the course of reform. Instead, democratic policy alternation proved to be an important force for correcting reform errors and reaching more desirable and sustainable policies, particularly in contentious areas such as privatization.

CHAPTER 2

Poland's Shock Therapy and Beyond

When Poland's Solidarity movement came to power after partially free elections in 1989, it undertook a neoliberal "shock therapy"[1] strategy for economic reform, also called the "big bang" approach (Gomułka 1998, 20; Sachs 1993, 35). Shock therapy represented a major departure from previous Solidarity economic programs and raised crucial political issues for a movement that was dedicated to building democracy and capitalism simultaneously. The "big bang" combined a radical program of economic stabilization with rapid price and trade liberalization and institutional changes intended to withdraw the state from the economy. In the words of one of its leading strategists, Jeffrey Sachs, shock therapy was designed to address "deep and politically sensitive structural issues . . . at the same time that it battled hyperinflation" (Morales and Sachs 1990, 189).[2] Shock therapy was intended to produce a rapid and painful adjustment to a market economy while dismantling many of the institutions of communism. Central elements of the shock therapy strategy were speed and simultaneity in enacting these changes. As Sachs put it, "you can't cross a chasm in two jumps."

Shock therapy in Poland therefore depended on a political strategy of insulating reformers from interest group pressures and pushing ahead as quickly as possible before civil society groups could mobilize against reform. Critics of shock therapy have argued that this "technocratic" political style leads to "authoritarian temptations" (Przeworski 1991, 187)—in short, that the strategy tends to justify the use of extraordinary powers and suspensions of democratic procedures in order to push through with reform. I will show in the case of Poland that such authoritarian temptations did emerge. However, they were consistently rejected. Poland, unlike Russia and some Latin American countries that have used a shock therapy style of economic reform, adhered to the constraints of parliamentary democratic procedure. Because of this insistence on democratic procedure, instead of forfeiting democracy, Poland forfeited shock therapy. As the reform program became increasingly unpopular in 1990–91, Poland's shock therapists were forced from office and new strategies for transformation came to the fore.

This political backlash caused a fragmentation of the Solidarity alliance and the center-right parties that together constituted Poland's first postcommunist governments. This fragmentation culminated in 1993 when Solidarity trade union representatives initiated a vote of no confidence in the Solidarity government. Subsequent parliamentary elections in 1993 brought an unexpected victory of left parties, a "return of the left" that was later replicated across much of postcommunist Europe. After winning parliamentary elections in 1993, Poland's reformed communist party candidate, Aleksander Kwaśniewski, defeated the incumbent president and hero of the anticommunist movement, Lech Wałęsa, in direct presidential elections in 1995.

The center-left government that ruled Poland from 1993 to 1997 initiated a change in transformation strategy toward policies that emphasized social cohesion and stability. Meanwhile, in opposition, Poland's neoliberal reformers regrouped and also reoriented their strategy for transformation. Poland's neoliberals began to pay more attention to political organization and social issues, rather than insisting on top-down, technocratic conceptions of reform. A brief review of the second phase of neoliberal reform in Poland shows that this strategic reorientation reflected democratic learning.

The neoliberals learned after they were voted out

In sum, the Polish transition has progressed through a succession of transformation strategies (see fig. 2). The willingness to abandon shock therapy when it lost the support of parliament and allow democratic policy alternation proved critical to the development of Poland's democratic institutions and the future course of economic reform. While many policy analysts predicted adverse consequences of policy change, the establishment of democratic procedural rules for the conduct of economic policy started a process of policy learning that proved beneficial to political and economic reform. Policy learning and government alternation forced political parties to adapt their economic policy programs and strategies to the constraints of parliamentary democracy.

Furthermore, such policy alternation has proven remarkably successful in economic terms and belies reformers' insistence that it is necessary to stay the course of reform. Poland's reform strategies have been grounded in a respect for democratic procedures and, contrary to accepted wisdom, a willingness to give up shock therapy when it lost public support, rather than to continue it against the public will. Reformers have been subjected to democratic instability and forced to find policies that combine the objectives of economic efficiency and social responsiveness. Their ability to do so is the true Polish success story.

Choosing Shock Therapy

The initial choice of a technocratic, shock therapy approach to economic reform in 1989 was an odd one for the Solidarity movement. Solidarity was

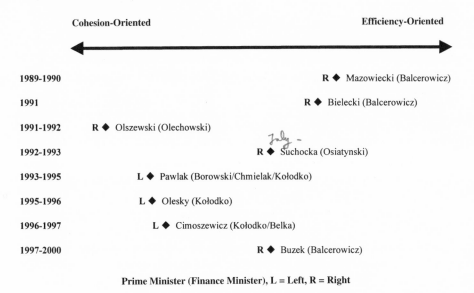

Cohesion-Oriented   **Efficiency-Oriented**

1989-1990	R ◆ Mazowiecki (Balcerowicz)
1991	R ◆ Bielecki (Balcerowicz)
1991-1992	R ◆ Olszewski (Olechowski)
1992-1993	*July –* R ◆ Suchocka (Osiatynski)
1993-1995	L ◆ Pawlak (Borowski/Chmielak/Kołodko)
1995-1996	L ◆ Olesky (Kołodko)
1996-1997	L ◆ Cimoszewicz (Kołodko/Belka)
1997-2000	R ◆ Buzek (Balcerowicz)

Prime Minister (Finance Minister), L = Left, R = Right

Fig. 2.   Strategies for transformation in Poland, 1989–2000

worker self-manage–

grounded in a workers' struggle against communist oppression, low pay, high prices—and for an egalitarian vision of worker self-management. Previous Solidarity programs had a strong syndicalist current, emphasizing worker ownership of the means of production and self-management of state enterprises. Self-management enjoyed a long tradition in Poland, dating back to 1945, when Polish workers liberated their factories from German occupiers and owners. Self-managing workers' councils epitomized the democratic socialism that Solidarity fought for in the face of a communist regime that insisted on central control. In both 1956 and 1981, large demonstrations and strikes by workers forced the state to empower enterprise workers' councils and grant them a measure of autonomy in management. This autonomy typically lasted only until the state managed to reassert itself.[3] But support for self-management remained a prominent and consistent trend in the working-class movement in Poland, and part of the Solidarity heritage.

Employee councils, moreover, were reinvigorated in 1988 and 1989. They formed an essential part of the Solidarity movement and its base of support. Roundtable negotiations between Solidarity and the communist regime in 1989 reaffirmed the rights of worker self-management (Winiecki 1997, 41). This was to have a tremendous impact on the process of enterprise restructuring. Between September 1989 and March 1992, 86 percent of all state-owned enterprises under the Ministry of Industry changed management. In an estimated 76.6 percent of the cases, former managers were recalled at the initiative of trade unions or worker self-management councils (Winiecki 1997, 41). In many cases, worker self-management councils selected new managers, often from within the Solidarity movement.

However, in 1989 Solidarity neoliberals, who were quickly elevated to leadership of the government economic reform team, opposed worker self-management on theoretical and ideological grounds. They perceived the rise of worker power in enterprises to be one of the greatest problems of the Polish economy. For instance, Polish economist and Solidarity adviser Jan Winiecki, appealing to property rights theory, argued even in 1997 that the "very unequal balance of rights and obligations between labor and capital in the Polish economy in favor of the former" is "the basic problem of the labor market" (1997, 41). Neoliberals believed that self-managed enterprises would pay excessively high wages, fail to invest sufficiently, and therefore contribute to continuing inefficiency of Polish industry. Solidarity economists, including Finance Minister Leszek Balcerowicz, who had joined the struggle for self-management in 1980–81 (Balcerowicz 1992, 12; Torańska 1994), now regarded self-management as one of the key institutional obstacles to radical economic change (Winiecki 1997).

Solidarity's neoliberal reformers also opposed the wage indexation that had been Solidarity's major economic demand at the roundtable discussions with the communists in early 1989 (Sachs 1993, 37). At Solidarity's insistence, the roundtable agreement promised wages would be indexed to 80 percent of inflation to offset the effects of price liberalization (Balcerowicz 1995, 292ff.). However, at the end of 1989, Balcerowicz and other neoliberals advocated sharp wage controls that would cause an enormous drop in worker incomes. Neoliberals believed that a onetime spurt of high inflation was a necessary part of price liberalization, and allowing wages to rise in step could create a disastrous inflationary spiral (Sachs 1993, 55). Therefore the Balcerowicz team and the new Solidarity government would consciously turn its back on one of the key constituencies of the Solidarity movement, the workers whose economic fate was tied to the socialist system they had fought to dismantle (Modzelewski 1993; Balcerowicz 1995, 294).

Why did the first Solidarity government choose a neoliberal shock therapy approach to economic reform that departed so fundamentally from its previous programs? Three interrelated factors appear to have played a role: first, the suddenness with which the Solidarity government took power; second, the dramatic economic crisis that Poland faced at the end of 1989; and third, the choice of Leszek Balcerowicz as finance minister, and more broadly the trend toward neoliberal thinking among Polish economists in the 1980s (cf. Szacki 1994).

The suddenness of Solidarity's rise to power and the lack of preparation
of its leaders certainly played a role (Kuroń 1991). Solidarity's dramatic rise to
power in 1989 was miraculous and unexpected. Solidarity had originally organized in 1980–81 around a shipyard strike in Gdansk (Garton Ash 1983). The
strike spread to other factories and was joined by groups of intellectuals,
Catholic clergy, and laypeople, until it finally became a mass movement of
"society" against the communist regime. Solidarity was banned and repressed
following a declaration of martial law in December 1981. However, in late
1988, after a series of uncontrollable strikes, Solidarity was resurrected and its
leaders were invited to negotiate a power sharing agreement with the communist regime (Gross 1992, 58ff.). In April 1989, after long years spent in prison
or in underground political activity, Solidarity leaders negotiated a political
pact that would give Solidarity minority representation in the Polish parliament, the Sejm. Solidarity had planned to reassemble its national organization
during its first four-year term and develop a program for reform. However, in
partially free elections in June 1989, Solidarity won nearly all the contested
seats in parliament. With the help of two minor parties formerly allied with the
communists, Solidarity won the votes to form its own government and suddenly found itself faced with the daunting prospect of governing the country.

Poland was in a deep economic crisis in 1989. The previous communist
government had relaxed price controls and then caved in to higher wage
demands, causing an inflationary spiral. Inflation hit 54 percent per month at
its high point in October 1989 (Sachs 1993, 40). One famous cartoon of the
time depicted the communist leader General Jaruzelski as a pilot, walking to
the back of a plane with engines on fire and diving at a dangerous angle, holding the steering column in his hand. He says to Solidarity leader Lech Wałęsa,
"OK, now you try to fly this thing!" (Sachs 1993, 41–42). Poland in 1989 was
in the grip of hyperinflation; it could not pay its foreign debt; strikes were
breaking out across the country; and the communists were giving up power.
And yet Moscow seemed content to leave Poland alone, under the new "Sina-
tra doctrine" of Soviet foreign policy that let the countries of Central and
Eastern Europe do it "my way."

As a result of these developments, the old Solidarity leadership was ush-
ered into power unprepared, without any comprehensive economic program
(Kuroń 1991; Sachs 1993, 38–39) or trained bureaucratic or parliamentary
cadres. In such a situation, it was natural to search for a man with a plan.
Tadeusz Mazowiecki, the Solidarity adviser who was entrusted with the position of prime minister in the first postcommunist government, reportedly
told future finance minister Leszek Balcerowicz that he was "looking for my
Ludwig Erhardt" (Sachs 1993, 44), the finance minister who stewarded Germany through the construction of a "social-market economy" in the postwar

era. After sounding out a few candidates, Mazowiecki settled on Leszek Balcerowicz and entrusted him with the task of developing a comprehensive program of economic reform. Balcerowicz (1995, 293), "after a short but strong hesitation," accepted the challenge and was appointed finance minister and deputy prime minister for economic affairs on September 8, 1989.

Balcerowicz since the late 1970s had been head of a group of reform economists that extensively debated the type of reforms needed in Poland (Blejer and Coricelli 1995, 33–34).[4] Balcerowicz was a member of the communist party from 1969 to 1982 but had always supported reform of the communist system. His reform group was called upon to advise the Solidarity worker self-management movement in 1980–81 and had developed a program calling for a type of market socialism. Balcerowicz later explained that he thought worker self-management was the only type of reform possible at that time (Torańska 1994). However, after the suppression of Solidarity in 1981, Balcerowicz and his economic group turned away from visions of reform communism and began to support a decisive shift to a capitalist market economy. Reform economists' disillusionment was increased by several failed attempts at incremental reform during the 1970s and 1980s (see Adam 1989; Batt 1988; Kamiński 1991; Slay 1994).

Balcerowicz assembled a small and cohesive team of Polish economists to plan the 1989 reform program, together with foreign advisers. He and his team urged the government to take advantage of popular euphoria to launch a radical overhaul of the economic system in one great jump. When they came to power in 1989, Balcerowicz and his group were determined not to produce just another round in the cycle of halfhearted and unsuccessful attempts that had characterized late socialism. They were committed to radical reform and were able to produce a comprehensive reform program in a matter of weeks (Blejer and Coricelli 1995, 35).

Thus, a combination of factors produced the unexpected shift to neoliberalism in Poland: the sudden and unexpected system change, Solidarity's lack of a comprehensive program for the transition from socialism to capitalism (previous programs were geared toward reforming the socialist system), the severe economic crisis that demanded immediate action, and the willingness of Leszek Balcerowicz to take charge of reform—an economic expert with Solidarity worker self-management credentials, who had made the switch to neoliberalism during the course of the 1980s.

Technocratic Policy Style

The neoliberal reform program in Poland in many ways typified the technocratic policy style associated with similar reforms in other countries around the world (Greskovits 35–36). Technocrats are "individuals with a high level of specialized academic training which serves as a principal criterion on the basis of which they are selected to occupy key decision-making or advisory roles in large complex organizations—both public and private" (Collier 1979, 403, quoted in Dominguez 1997, 5–6). Balcerowicz and his team were appointed as experts, not political leaders. They had not played a leading role in the Solidarity electoral victory in 1989. Indeed, Balcerowicz himself was dedicated to playing a nonpolitical, technocratic role. He often appealed to the prewar Polish tradition of independent finance ministers to explain his decision not to belong to any political party.[5] Balcerowicz wanted his policies to serve the national interest, rather than any specific partisan interest. He shared a suspicion of parties that was prevalent in postcommunist Poland. An apolitical, appointed expert, Balcerowicz was a confirmed and committed technocrat.

The team Balcerowicz assembled at the Finance Ministry and its methods also displayed other typical features of a technocratic policy style, including a high degree of internal coherence, cooperation with foreign advisers, insulation from domestic interest group pressures, and reliance on top political leaders for support (Greskovits 1998, 35–36).

Like many technocratic reform teams, members of the Balcerowicz team drew on a shared opposition intellectual background from their participation in the "Balcerowicz group" reform seminar in the 1970s and 1980s. This shared background enhanced the team's coherence and enabled it to decide quickly on the key principles of a radical economic change program. Many of the basic elements of the reform package had already been developed in the Balcerowicz group seminar.

A like-minded group of foreign advisers reinforced Balcerowicz's radical reform plans. Jeffrey Sachs visited Poland just before Balcerowicz's appointment and impressed Solidarity representatives in the Senate Economic Commission with his program for "a sudden, decisive jump" to the market (Myant 1993, 82). Though Sachs and others played an influential role, Balcerowicz had already decided on a radical approach (Sachs 1993, 44). In assessing the impact of foreign advisers, Balcerowicz stated that "foreign advisers played an important role in strengthening my own beliefs" (quoted in Blejer and Coricelli 1995, 61). Foreign advisers participated in the reform through an Economic Council that Balcerowicz set up in December 1989. But in large part, the Polish program was a homegrown affair (cf. Greskovits 1998, 56–58). After years of discussion in domestic policy circles, Balcerowicz and others had come to the conclusion that radical stabilization and liberalization were the best way forward for Poland. They had reached this conclusion independent of the influence of foreign advisers, although under the influence of the mainstream of Western economic thought (Blejer and Coricelli 1995, 61).

The Balcerowicz team enjoyed almost total insulation from domestic political pressures during the planning and early implementation phase of its program. This extraordinary insulation derived from three factors: the decision of top Solidarity leaders to go ahead with radical reform without seeking a popular mandate for the program; the extraordinary willingness of the Polish parliament to pass reform legislation to deal with the economic crisis at the end of 1989; and the ability of Lech Wałęsa and the Solidarity movement to hold an "umbrella" of political support over the program in its early stages. Despite the fact that the shock therapy program of economic reform had not been part of Solidarity's electoral program in the run-up to the June 1989 elections, the first Solidarity government decided to use its extraordinary popular legitimacy to implement a painful, radical program of economic reform. At the time, the Solidarity government enjoyed support from 75 percent of the population in opinion polls. This allowed Solidarity political leaders to shield a reform that was billed as unpopular, but necessary, like bad-tasting medicine.

Authoritarian Temptations

Since the shock therapy program constituted a complete departure from past Solidarity programs and had not been part of the Solidarity election platform, the methods of its implementation were hotly debated in Solidarity circles. In late 1989, as the architects of Poland's "big bang" were drawing up their strategy for transformation, Solidarity chairman Lech Wałęsa concluded that shock therapy could not be introduced without special powers for the government. The ensuing debate over "special powers" for economic reform deeply divided the Solidarity movement.

On December 12, 1989, Wałęsa suggested that the Mazowiecki government be granted "special powers" of decree by the Sejm in order to facilitate economic transformation. Wałęsa's statement read, "I hereby propose that the government be given special powers to reorganise the economy, amend the property laws, demonopolise the state and cooperative sectors, reform the tax, accounting and banking systems" (quoted in Boyes 1994, 219–20). However, Prime Minister Tadeusz Mazowiecki rejected Wałęsa's suggestion, wishing to adhere to principles of parliamentary democracy and rule of law (RFE/RL, July 19, 1991). This was the beginning of a major split within the Solidarity movement over the political strategy of radical economic reform.

Mazowiecki and other political liberals believed that economic reform should not be implemented in such a heavy-handed manner that it jeopardized the development of democratic institutions. The "Mazowiecki camp" of democratic fundamentalists wanted any reform program to be based in law and passed with the approval of parliament. The Wałęsa camp saw increased presidential powers and extraordinary measures as necessarily to undo the damage of communism (Staniszkis 1991). This issue arose again and again in relation to the shock therapy strategy of transformation. Poland's initial decision to uphold democratic procedures, and its continual reaffirmation of this decision, played a fundamental role in shaping the Polish transformation.

Instead of using decrees, the Mazowiecki government convinced the Sejm to set up a "fast lane" for passing the Balcerowicz plan at the end of 1989. Under normal parliamentary procedure in Poland, a bill is read first by a plenary session of the Sejm, then sent to committee, then read a second time and possibly sent back to committee before a final vote, making passage of complicated legislation a lengthy process (Winczorek and Majchrowski 1993, 43–51). The "fast lane" put the Balcerowicz program directly before a "special commission" that considered amendments before sending the laws to the floor only for a final yes or no vote. The Balcerowicz plan passed through the fast lane in the final days of 1989, and economic reform in Poland passed its first democratic test.

Economics of Shock Therapy

The shock therapy program introduced in Poland on January 1, 1990, was based on the same stabilization, liberalization, and privatization measures (Sachs 1993, 46–47) applied in developing countries around the world under the neoliberal "Washington consensus" of the late 1980s (Williamson 1990, 1997). Although economists recognized that postcommunist countries were distinguished from others by "the revolutionary change . . . required in the institutional infrastructure" (Bruno 1994, 20) and made some efforts to take account of these differences, the cure they prescribed remained more or less the same (Sachs 1993, 2–3).

The emphasis in Poland's shock therapy was on getting the prices right, that is, creating a stable and efficient price structure that would give economic actors appropriate signals and incentives for rational economic behavior. Neoliberal institutional reform was aimed primarily at withdrawing the state from the economy (Elster, Offe, and Preuss 1998, 156) and freeing up markets to adjust spontaneously to the new macroeconomic conditions. The big bang emphasized breaking down distortionary barriers that had built up throughout forty years of socialism. Jeffrey Sachs (1993, 13) noted six main sources of "structural distortion" at the outset of market transition:

1. Poland was overindustrialized compared to other countries at a comparable level of economic development;

2. Poland still had a large peasant agriculture sector;

3. The economy was overwhelmingly state-owned;

4. Poland lacked small- and medium-sized industrial enterprises;

5. Poland's international trade was excessively directed toward the East;

6. Poland had a remarkably egalitarian distribution of wealth and income.

In addition to these structural features, Poland also had several pressing immediate problems at the start of transition.

1. Poland was on the verge of hyperinflation in 1989, with inflation reaching a peak of 640 percent per annum in 1989 (Rostowski 1998, 3).

2. Poland was not able to service its international debt and was in default.

3. The balance of payments was collapsing as imports outpaced exports.

4. The economy was still wracked by shortages, despite partial price liberalization by the last communist government (Sachs 1993, 41).

Given Poland's macroeconomic disequilibrium, the most immediate and essential goal of the big-bang reform package was to stamp out inflation and stabilize prices in the economy (Sachs 1993, 46). This would be achieved through a combination of monetary and fiscal measures "designed to cut decisively the rate of credit expansion from the National Bank of Poland to the government and to the enterprises. By tightening the expansion of domestic credit, it would be possible to stabilize the market exchange rate as well as domestic prices" (Sachs 1993, 46). Liberalization aimed to dismantle central planning, eliminate administrative price setting, free international trade, and generally "get the planners out of the process" (Sachs 1993, 46).

Sachs proposed radical and sudden trade liberalization to force Polish enterprises to adjust rationally to world market prices.

Berg and Blanchard (1994, 52) provide a comprehensive list of the main components of the Polish reform package:

1. *Fiscal consolidation.* Moving the budget from a deficit of about 3 percent of GDP in the last quarter of 1989 to rough balance in 1990, mainly through a decrease in subsidies.

2. *Control of inflation through a domestic credit squeeze.* Creating high refinancing rates for banks, 36 percent at a monthly rate in January 1990.

3. *Tight incomes policy aimed at limiting wage growth.* An excess wages tax was levied on firms that paid wages in excess of a state-regulated total wage-bill growth level. No such restrictions were put on prices, allowing firms to readjust relative prices without strong wage pressure.

4. *Convertibility of the zloty.* Exchange rate was set and pegged low, making the average Polish industrial wage forty cents an hour initially.

5. *Trade liberalization.* Tariff rates were decreased to an average of 10 percent and made more uniform. Pervasive quantitative restrictions and licensing requirements on trade were largely eliminated.

6. *Price liberalization.* Food prices had been freed in August 1989 by the communist government. The proportion of controlled prices was further decreased from 50 percent to 10 percent. Most remaining regulated prices, especially energy prices, were sharply increased.

7. *Curtailing enterprise subsidies.* Firms could no longer expect ad hoc transfers from the budget to make up for losses, as had been the case in the previous regime. Bankruptcy rules were strengthened.

8. *Privatization.* Privatization was planned and debated in 1989–90 but did not form part of the initial package of reforms, being left for a second stage.

Sachs also stressed two additional "pillars" of the reform: "creating a social safety net" and "mobilizing international financial assistance" (1993, 47). However, except for the establishment of a system of unemployment benefits, these were distinctly secondary goals, to be achieved at a later stage in transition.

Impact of Reform

Poland did not adjust to this sudden shock as quickly or as positively as neoliberal economists had hoped. The initial impact of reform was mixed. There were some tremendous achievements. Almost overnight, the shock therapists managed to eliminate the shortage economy that had been one of the worst features of state socialism, with people wasting hours standing in long lines to find and purchase scarce goods. Poland experienced an explosion of commerce as new enterprises sprung up in a liberalized trade regime and offered their goods to market. New kiosks, stores, and open-air markets were the most visible element of this change. And after a great initial surge, prices did begin to stabilize, although double-digit annual rates of inflation persisted for several years.

However, while shock therapy jump-started a process of structural change, an explosion of entrepreneurship (Johnson and Loveman 1995), a massive reorientation of Poland's foreign trade, and a renewal of markets, Poland also plunged into a deep recession. Poland experienced a severe output decline in 1990–91, more severe than economists had predicted (Rosati 1992; Murrell 1993, 114; Nuti and Portes 1993), and deeper than the Great Depression of the 1930s in the West (Gomułka 1998, 13). Poland's officially measured GDP fell by 15 percent (Gomułka 1998, 16) or more (Kołodko 1999), while industrial production declined by 40 percent (Gomułka 1998, 20).

Since 1989, economists have debated the reasons for this unexpected decline (cf. Layard 1998). Rostowski (1998, 10) identifies three basic schools of thought. First, there are those who believe that the fall in output was far smaller than official statistics suggest (Berg and Sachs 1992). A second group suggests a "demand-side" explanation: in order to stabilize prices in the distorted postsocialist economies, the unemployment rate had to rise above its natural level, causing a deeper-than-normal decline in output (Rostowski 1998, 10). A third perspective is a "supply-side" view that says that the transition caused a sudden and enormous change in consumption patterns across the economy. Enterprises (the supply side), on the other hand, were not able to adjust quickly enough to supply this new demand function. Therefore output declined rapidly in areas where old levels of consumption had collapsed and did not increase rapidly enough in new areas of high demand (Gomułka 1998, 24).

Part of what is at issue in these debates is whether shock therapy caused the deep recession of the early 1990s. Gomułka (1998) argues that shock therapy was the main cause, but also points out that radical decline may have been inevitable in postcommunist Europe after the collapse of the Soviet bloc. While shock therapy was undoubtedly the proximate cause of recession in

Poland, the depth of recession was greater in every other postcommunist country, regardless of whether it used a radical or gradual stabilization strategy. Deep recession has been a universal feature of the postcommunist economic transition (Gomułka 1998, 17). Of course, in 1990, economists did not fully understand the causes of the recession and were surprised by its depth, as were most Poles.

Backlash against Reform

While a significant proportion of the population began to benefit immediately from freer consumer markets, greater availability of goods, and new economic opportunities, a majority of the population experienced a drop in its standard of living (Milanovic 1998).

Almost as soon as economic reform began in January 1990, support for the Solidarity government began to fall from the extraordinary level of around 75 percent in January 1990 to around 55 percent by the middle of the year (see fig. 3). Przeworski (1993) argues that increasing unemployment was the main reason Poles began to oppose reform. Certainly, unemployment was one of the most frightening and visible impacts of the market transition. Unemployment increased from 0.1 percent in 1989 to 11.8 percent of the labor force in 1991. Nearly one hundred thousand people were losing their jobs each month (EBRD 1994, 165). However, Przeworski suggests that fear of unemployment extended well beyond those households actually hit by it, causing a general loss of confidence in the government's reform program (Przeworski 1993). Furthermore, while joblessness was a temporary state for some, a large portion of the unemployed found it difficult or impossible to find new work (Góra 1997, 119–21). Unemployment often meant poverty for whole families (Grootaert 1995).

Steep declines in real wages and the collapse of budgetary expenditure also had a negative impact on public support for reform. Worker opposition to reform was already voiced at the Solidarity congress of April 1990, where Balcerowicz was forced to defend his program in an angry hall; in May a railroad strike in Słupsk threatened to paralyze the country; and in June a dairy farmers' strike clogged the roads until the government cleared it by force.

Polish voters quickly lost faith in the way the Solidarity government was managing the transition. A "war at the top" broke out among Solidarity leaders in 1990, displaying damaging differences of opinion on the conduct of transition. These were reflected in the presidential election campaign in 1990, which turned into an early referendum on the progress of transition.

The "war at the top" pitted the Mazowiecki camp and the Wałęsa camp

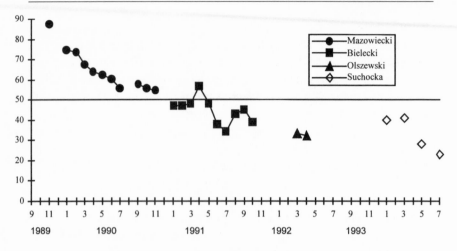

Fig. 3.   Government approval ratings in Poland, 1990–93 (percentage). (Data from CBOS, various reports, 1990–93.)

in a showdown over which leader would be the first directly elected president
of Poland. By far the shrewder campaigner, Solidarity chairman Lech Wałęsa
capitalized on public displeasure with shock therapy by attacking the
Mazowiecki government for mismanagement of economic reform. Wałęsa
promised that as president he would "accelerate" reform and at the same time
reduce its social cost. However, Wałęsa never carefully defined what he meant
by "acceleration." This angered the Mazowiecki camp, which thought that
Wałęsa, as a Solidarity leader, should have supported the government in its
difficult and unpopular reform effort, rather than dredging up public rancor.
Wałęsa, on the other hand, was angry at being pushed out of the main corridors of power by his former intellectual advisers, who were increasingly out
of touch with public opinion.[6] Wałęsa was constantly being called in to contain worker strikes and other symptoms of mass discontent (Boyes 1994,
224), but the Nobel Prize–winning organizer wanted to be treated as more
than a part-time troubleshooter. Mazowiecki's group believed the moment
for charismatic, "strong" leadership had passed, but Wałęsa refused to be
pushed aside.

    In what turned into a highly destructive election campaign, focused on
the painful effects of economic reform, Prime Minister Mazowiecki failed to
advance to the second round of Poland's two-round presidential election system. He came in third, losing to Party X chairman Stanisław Tymiński, an
aspiring émigré demagogue. Mazowiecki was humiliated. Solidarity publicist

Adam Michnik wrote, "Tymiński's success was the rout of reason and has brought shame on us all. If Wałęsa capitalised on his own myth and the frustration of part of the old Solidarity camp, Tymiński exploited the frustration of the people who did not identify with Solidarity. The mixture of these two frustrations produced the defeat of the Mazowiecki government" (quoted in Boyes 1994, 258). Stunned by the public rebuke, Mazowiecki resigned the post of prime minister on the day after the first round of elections on November 25. A few weeks later Wałęsa defeated Tymiński in a runoff, entered the Belweder presidential palace in Warsaw, and began the process of forming a new government.

Wałęsa had won the election by campaigning against the Balcerowicz plan and its unpopular effects, with support from the Catholic right elements of Solidarity. However, once in power, Wałęsa opted to form a government of "continuity and change"—and retained Balcerowicz as finance minister. In doing so, he angered both his own right-wing supporters, who wanted a chance to lead the new government, and the Mazowiecki camp, which was furious that Wałęsa had displaced and humiliated them only to continue with their economic program. Wałęsa seemed to be acting, in part, to assure his own continuing political importance. Wałęsa had consistently opposed the formalization and institutionalization of Solidarity as a political party or a trade union, in order to increase his own importance as the linchpin of the movement. He destroyed Solidarity's plans in 1989 to turn its citizen committees into a permanent electoral organization and fought pitched battles with Solidarity's parliamentary club in 1990 and 1991 (Grabowski 1995). Wałęsa seemed inclined to prove that only he could hold the diverse strands of Solidarity together and keep a political "umbrella" over the technocratic reform program.[7]

Wałęsa nominated Jan Krzysztof Bielecki, an economist from Gdansk and the leader of the small Liberal Democratic Congress, to be prime minister in a "government of experts." Bielecki represented a group of liberal economists close to Wałęsa who believed in the general outlines of the Balcerowicz program but also saw the necessity of making the reforms more socially acceptable. As a condition of his appointment Bielecki agreed to keep Balcerowicz on as finance minister and deputy prime minister for economic affairs. The center-right parties who refused to work in coalition with Balcerowicz were thanklessly excluded from Bielecki's government. Wałęsa instead sidelined them in comfortable but toothless jobs in the office of the president. Wałęsa had decided to protect the economic reformers, singlehandedly extending the Solidarity "umbrella" of political support.[8] In order to do so, he twisted the democratic mandate received in the 1990 elections, translating a popular *rejection* of shock therapy into a mandate for continuing the much-resented Balcerowicz plan. Wałęsa's popularity began to decline almost as soon as he took office, most strongly at first among right-wing supporters, then among workers and peasants, and finally among the intelligentsia and the new middle classes (CBOS; see fig. 4).

More Authoritarian Temptations

From the beginning of his presidency, Wałęsa believed that presidential power would be the best guarantor of a continuation of the shock therapy strategy. This was in line with the views of Jeffrey Sachs (1993, 113) and others, who believed that presidential power was necessary to push through with reform against the will of powerful interest groups and public anxieties. When the Bielecki government failed to win parliamentary support for its programs and could not get either the economy or the reform program moving again, Wałęsa renewed his request for "special powers" that would enable the government to complete economic reform by decree. At first Bielecki was reluctant to request such powers (RFE/RL, July 1991). "Authoritarian temptations" were a large part of what divided Wałęsa from the Mazowiecki camp during the presidential campaign and beyond. Indeed, many former colleagues of Lech Wałęsa were afraid of his authoritarian tendencies. During the 1990 presidential campaign, a prominent group of politicians and economists on the Solidarity left argued,

> Acceleration should be achieved without infringing the law or democratic principles. We must not allow populistic phraseology to lead to the adoption of semidictatorial solutions. There is such a danger and such leanings, but there is no reason to assume that taking that road would result in greater efficiency or effectiveness of the desired changes. Political transformations can be speeded up without resorting to extraordinary measures. (*Życie Gospodarcze* 18, 1990)[9]

A call for special powers would have confirmed these fears. Therefore, Bielecki instead proposed a new "fast lane" for necessary economic legislation, as was used in the first phase of the Balcerowicz plan.

However by mid-June 1991, none of the twenty-seven bills initiated by Bielecki's government since January had passed the Sejm. Bielecki threatened to resign. When he finally offered his resignation, however, the Sejm rejected it by a 211–114 margin. Bielecki then seized this opportunity to propose an act on "special powers" to the Sejm on September 6 (RFE/RL, October 4, 1991). Bielecki suggested that the government be given the power to rule by decree

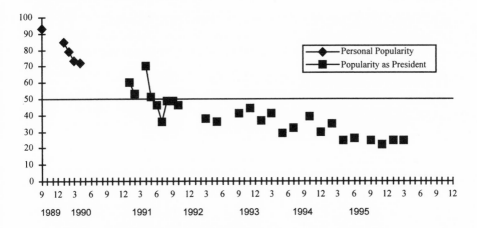

Fig. 4.   The Wałęsa presidency, 1990–95 (pre- and postelection
approval ratings). (Data from CBOS, various reports, 1990–95.)

until two months after the coming parliamentary elections, scheduled for October 1991, leaving enough time for a new government to form. To assuage worries of undemocratic rule, he proposed to exclude certain areas from legislation
by decree. The Sejm considered granting Bielecki decree powers but finally
requested that instead of excluding sensitive areas, the government should suggest specific, carefully conscribed areas where it wished to issue decrees with the
force of law. The government drew up such a list. However, accusations and
suspicions of antidemocratic behavior persisted, with one commentator arguing that "the government seeks to change the political system in a way reminis-
cent of the imposition of martial law" (*Warsaw Voice* 37, 6).

Bielecki emphasized that the emergency measures he was proposing
were only temporary. He simultaneously proposed a long-term solution in
the form of a "constitutional law" to increase the powers of the president, giving him the right to nominate and dismiss the prime minister and members
of his cabinet. Bielecki argued that the law would "prevent democracy from
slipping into chaos and anarchy." However, this concept of a strong presidency was bitterly resisted by parliamentary democrats within the Solidarity
camp and former communists. Although a majority of Sejm deputies voted in
favor, Bielecki failed to get the two-thirds majority required to pass either the
special powers act or the proposed "constitutional law" (*Facts on File,* October 31, 1991).

October 1991 elections put an end to Bielecki's government and the Balcerowicz plan by returning a highly fragmented Sejm. Much had been done in

a year and a half to transform Poland into a free market economy. But a large proportion of the neoliberal reform agenda remained to be accomplished, and the economy was still in the grip of a severe recession. In October 1991, the International Monetary Fund suspended its 1989 standby credit agreement when Poland failed to meet budget deficit and other performance criteria (East and Pontin 1997, 44; *New York Times,* February 21, 1992, 11).

Political backlash against shock therapy had deeply divided the Solidarity camp. Divisions over the Balcerowicz plan and other major issues, particularly church-state relations and settling accounts with the past, caused the former Solidarity camp to go to the polls in fall 1991 elections as at least seven different "unions," "alliances," and "congresses." Many of these ran on platforms opposing the Balcerowicz program. The main Solidarity successor party associated with economic reform, Mazowiecki's Democratic Union, won only 12 percent of the popular vote. Angry, confused, and apathetic voters returned a fragmented Sejm dominated by a post-Solidarity Catholic right that opposed radical economic transformation. Shock therapy had ground to a halt.

End of Technocracy

The previous section showed that there was a public backlash against shock therapy in Poland, expressed mainly through protest votes, but also through strikes and other forms of collective action (Ekiert and Kubick 1999). It arose after less than a year of shock treatment and soon resulted in legislative paralysis on key elements of the reform program. In other words, the backlash against shock therapy was politically effective in Poland, insofar as it stopped or delayed the implementation of additional reform legislation. It was effective largely because this backlash occurred within the Solidarity coalition itself, as elements of the movement turned against its own government's economic program. This caused a fragmentation of the Solidarity movement, and the quick dissipation of parliamentary support for neoliberal economic reform, even before the "return of the left" in 1993. Democracy halted the first phase of technocratic neoliberal reform.

Why did shock therapy lose political support so precipitously? There are both economic and political reasons. The economic reasons are not hard to identify. First, its economic effects were severe—and more severe than expected. As numerous theorists have pointed out, paying the costs of reform is never popular (Dahrendorf 1990; Przeworski 1991). Second, Polish policies allowed unemployment to emerge quickly, which seems to be correlated with decline in support for reform (Przeworski 1993).

The technocratic political organization of shock therapy also contributed to its decline. First, the shock therapy strategy of political insulation of reformers, rather than their political engagement, could not sustain reform for more than a short period of time. Not having his own political party, Leszek Balcerowicz and his team were dependent on the political sponsorship of others, particularly President Lech Wałęsa, who often did more harm than good to public support for reform. Second, the costs of reform fell most severely on key Solidarity constituencies. Forcing the costs of reform onto key Solidarity groups speeded the backlash against reform, since reformers were dependent on Solidarity support for their program.

When parliament ceased to provide the necessary votes for shock therapy to continue, shock therapists, sometimes reluctantly, turned to presidential power. However, parliament never gave the full two-thirds majority to support proposals for conducting economic reform by decree. Authoritarian temptations were thwarted and shock therapy was surrendered after about a year and a half, with only part of its agenda fulfilled. This set in motion a sometimes difficult process of democratic learning or "adaptive adjustment" (Lindblom 1965) that has enabled Poland to build capitalism and democracy simultaneously. Future Polish governments began to seek, of necessity, new strategies for implementing economic reform under conditions of parliamentary democracy. Democratic political pressures forced adjustments in the style and content of economic reform.

Toward New Strategies

Balcerowicz in his theoretical writings contrasts the "extraordinary politics" following the democratic breakthrough of 1989 with a later period of "normal" politics, when economic self-interest starts to guide political behavior, rather than altruistic concern for the common good. However, Polish politics did not suddenly become "normal" after the October 1991 elections, but instead plunged into a profound crisis.

Under the proportional representation electoral law approved by the Sejm in 1991 in the face of multiple presidential vetoes, twenty-nine parties and groups won seats in the legislature. The largest number went to Mazowiecki's Democratic Union (sixty-two) and the postcommunist Alliance of the Democratic Left (sixty), but the center-right Catholic parties collectively made the strongest showing. Voter turnout was only 43.2 percent (Millard 1994, 136). Coalition building was complicated by the refusal of all other parties to ally with the Alliance of the Democratic Left (SLD) (RFE/RL, November 8, 1991). Since only two parties received more than 10 percent of the vote, a coalition of at least five parties was required to form a government. The Solidarity camp was so split over the issues of shock therapy and retribution against former communists that it proved impossible to form a coalition encompassing the entire post-Solidarity camp.

Center-right Solidarity-oriented parties, led by the Center Alliance, attempted to form a government around Jan Olszewski, the staunchly anticommunist former Solidarity lawyer and advocate, as prime minister. But Olszewski had campaigned strongly against the Balcerowicz plan, calling for a "breakthrough" in economic policy, which made it difficult to negotiate an agreement with Bielecki's pro-reform Liberal Democratic Congress. A stalemate ensued.

TABLE 1. Parties Winning Representation in the Polish Sejm, October 1991

Party	%	Seats
Democratic Union[a]	12.31	62
Alliance of the Democratic Left (SLD)[b]	11.98	60
Catholic Election Action (WAK)[a]	8.73	49
Center Alliance (Centrum)[a]	8.71	44
Peasant Party–Programmatic Alliance (PSL)[b]	8.67	48
Confederation for an Independent Poland (KPN)	7.50	46
Liberal Democratic Congress (KLD)[a]	7.48	37
Peasant Accord (PL)	5.46	28
Solidarity[a]	5.05	27
Friends of Beer (PPPP)	3.27	16
German Minority	1.17	7
Christian Democracy	2.36	5
Polish Western Union (PZZ)	0.23	4
Party of Christian Democrats (PCD)	1.11	4
Labour Solidarity[a]	2.05	4
Union of Political Realism (UPR)	2.25	3
Party X	0.47	3
Movement for Silesian Autonomy	0.35	2
Democratic Party (SD)[b]	1.41	1
Democratic-Social Movement (RDS)	0.46	1
Union of Great Poles		1
Peasant Unity (PL plus PSL)		1
"Great Poland and Poland"		1
Solidarity '80[a]		1
Piast Peasant Election Alliance (PL plus PSL)		1
Electoral Committee of Orthodox Believers		1
Kraków Coalition "Solidarity with the President"[a]		1
Union of Podhale		1
Women against Life's Hardships		1

[a]Post-Solidarity party
[b]Postcommunist party
Source: Millard 1994, 137. Reprinted with permission.

President Wałęsa, meanwhile, wanted to step into the breach and provide the necessary political backing to continue the reforms. Wałęsa believed
that he had the constitutional authority to nominate the prime minister, a
power that was not clearly stated in the constitution. Still hoping to provide a
political shield for Balcerowicz's economic reform program, however, Wałęsa   [שׁל]
proposed on October 29 four scenarios for forming a government to master
parliamentary fragmentation. Three of them included Lech Wałęsa as prime
minister. In the first scenario, Wałęsa would lead a government including all
the post-Solidarity parties; in the second he would lead a government formed
from the top seven vote-getters—including the controversial Alliance of the
Democratic Left; and in the third option Wałęsa would lead a "non-partisan
government of political agreement" (RFE/RL, November 8, 1991). The
fourth option was the same as that proposed by Mazowiecki's Democratic
Union: a government of post-Solidarity parties without the president's participation. To many, Wałęsa's proposals recalled Piłsudski's 1926 putsch. As
commentators and legal experts debated whether the same man could be
both president and prime minister under the Polish constitution, the center-
right parties continued their efforts to build a coalition. Wałęsa was suspected
of hampering their efforts by instructing possible ministerial candidates not
to join the government.

On December 5, Wałęsa grudgingly agreed to nominate Olszewski
prime minister after Olszewski assembled a five-party majority, pledging to
radically alter the course of economic transformation and purge communists
from governmental posts. Immediately after his appointment as prime minister, however, Olszewski's coalition unraveled (RFE/RL, January 17, 1992).
Olszewski offered his resignation on December 17, but the parliament
refused to accept it. After surviving a vote of no confidence, Olszewski hastily
assembled a cabinet that met with the Sejm's approval on December 23, 1991,
two months after the elections. With such tenuous support, Olszewski's government began its life crippled, and failed to make good on many of its campaign promises, especially to formulate an alternative to the Balcerowicz plan.
Balcerowicz was excluded from Olszewski's cabinet. But when Olszewski's
initial economic program met with harsh public resistance from the International Monetary Fund (New York Times, March 4, 1992, 8), the Sejm rejected
it by a vote of 171 to 138, with thirty-eight abstentions (New York Times,
March 6, 1992, 6). Eventually, the government had to accept Balcerowicz's
provisional budget for 1992, which contained drastic budget cuts and tax
increases to cope with the vast plunge in government revenue caused by the
recession.

The Olszewski government's failure to overturn the macroeconomic
policies of shock therapy caused a popular upheaval in which Solidarity trade

unions began to openly protest government policy. Price hikes for domestic heating and electricity and an increase in the alcohol excise tax set off a wave of strikes organized by the Solidarity trade union and the postcommunist (All-Poland Alliance of Trade Union Federations) OPZZ in January 1992. Bitter struggles over pension funding and agricultural subsidies followed. Olszewski's government lurched from crisis to crisis. When Olszewski's interior minister, Macierewski, pushed the issue of anticommunist lustration to its limit, accusing Wałęsa himself of being a former secret police agent, the Olszewski government lost its tenuous parliamentary support and was forced to resign in June 1992 (Millard 1994, 93–104). Olszewski continues to accuse many top Solidarity officials of having collaborated with the secret police and with the postcommunist Alliance of the Democratic Left in covering up the records of this time. He believes that the Solidarity revolution was betrayed at the roundtable in 1988–89 and that Poland's problems would be solved by a thorough purge of former communists from public life.

In the wake of Olszewski's government failure, Wałęsa nominated Waldemar Pawlak, the Polish Peasant Party leader, to form a government in June 1992, but after a month of negotiations, Pawlak proved incapable of constructing a majority coalition. In July, Hanna Suchocka of the Democratic Union became the fourth prime minister since 1989, leading a seven-party minority government that encompassed the postcommunist Peasant Party. It was also supported in parliament by the Solidarity trade union, the German Minority Party, and the small Christian Democracy Party (Millard 1994, 106). The Suchocka government was dedicated to restarting the neoliberal reform agenda. According to Balcerowicz, the new government "largely continued the economic strategy launched in 1990, although it made some concessions to various interest groups, especially farmers" (Balcerowicz 1995, 322).

However, some aspects of the neoliberal program had effectively been reversed by mid-1992. The zero budget deficit, which had been one of the main targets of neoliberal reformers in 1990, had expanded to 7 percent of GDP in 1992 (Rostowski 1998, 307). This was mainly a result of successive governments not being able to cut spending quickly enough to keep pace with collapsing tax revenues. Social spending was particularly inelastic. In addition, trade barriers that had been suddenly removed in 1990 were reinstated on some goods, mainly in order to protect politically powerful sectoral interests. Furthermore, the implementation of neoliberal reforms depended on the Polish parliament passing a large quantity of reform legislation, including legislation on privatization, banking reform, and the labor market. But the legislature had been paralyzed during the first six months of 1991 and from October 1991 to July 1992 due to conflicts within Solidarity over economic reform. When the Suchocka government took power in July 1992, substantial parts of the neoliberal reform program had been reversed or delayed.

The Suchocka government attempted to reinstate neoliberal economic policies, particularly passing additional reform legislation and trying to bring the budget deficit below 5 percent of GDP, as agreed with the IMF (*Facts on File*, June 3, 1993). However, to do this, the Suchocka government was forced to develop strategies that were out of keeping with the big-bang style of shock therapy and owed more to traditional clientelism, constituency building, and social pacting. In order to provide more stable political backing for reform, the Suchocka government began to seek solutions to two related problems that had plagued all the post-Solidarity governments, the rising tide of discontent with economic reform (now expressed through mass protest action) and tumultuous relations between president and parliament. Her government was only partially successful in these pursuits, but in emphasizing institutional change and social pacts as a way forward, it added new dimensions to the political strategy for neoliberalism in Poland. And because it began to cater to Solidarity constituencies whose interests had been ignored in the previous parliament, Suchocka's government proved more stable than expected.

Small Constitution

During the government crisis that began in October 1991, a sense grew among political insiders that Polish politics suffered from basic institutional inadequacies. In particular, relations between parliament and the president needed clarification and improvement. In part, the problem arose because the "Stalinist" constitution of 1952 was still in force. This constitution had not been much of a living document in communist times, and it was proving incapable of regulating a democracy. For instance, the controversy over special powers showed that there were only vague rules in the constitution about how, and under what conditions, parliament could grant decree power to the government (Kruk 1994, 11). The 1952 constitution had been drastically revised in three amendments in 1989 and 1990, but since these changes were based on compromises reached in a variety of quickly changing political circumstances, the amended constitution lacked a coherent conception of the division of powers (Garlicki 1992, 67).[10] Work on a new constitution had already begun under the roundtable Sejm, but it was difficult to see how this semilegitimate body could create the founding document of a democratic state (Sokolweicz 1992). Already in September 1991, Wałęsa, through Prime

Minister Bielecki, had proposed a set of constitutional laws that would increase the power of the presidency, among other things giving him the right to dismiss the government or individual ministers at will (RFE/RL, January 17, 1992). After the October 1991 elections, President Wałęsa advocated giving the president greater powers in government formation. During the dispute over Olszewski's nomination in December, Wałęsa suggested that approval of his "small constitution" was the price for nominating Olszewski. In the end, he was forced to name Olszewski without exacting this concession, and the Sejm special commission set up to consider the small constitution discarded most of the president's proposals.

Suchocka's Democratic Union proposed a new "small constitution," passed in September 1992, that increased and clarified the president's powers significantly, giving him the ability to call referenda, to *approve* the prime minister and his government (but not normally to appoint him or her), to dissolve the Sejm in certain circumstances of government failure (for instance the failure to approve a state budget or form a government within six months), and even to form a temporary caretaker government for up to six months (Kruk 1994, 12–14). In essence, the 1991–93 Sejm increased the power of the presidency to supervise political development, but only in periods of government crisis. It did not, however, allow the president or government to rule by decree in the economic arena, except with explicit parliamentary approval. Parliamentary democratic constraints were again reaffirmed and established more clearly in the small constitution. Therefore, what Polish leaders needed was renewed popular support for the transition to capitalism. This reaffirmation of parliamentary democracy caused the Suchocka government to turn to social pacting as a method of implementing further reform.

State Enterprise Pact

By 1992, it was commonly acknowledged that Solidarity had lost public support for its program of economic transformation. Many Solidarity analysts focused on the failure of reformers to communicate the goals of their program to the population (cf. Winiecki 1994), but the deeper problem was that Solidarity reformers had alienated one of its strongest popular bases of support in the trade unions in large state enterprises. Distributional policies in areas such as privatization and employment played a key role in this. In 1989, workers had been willing to accept certain sacrifices, but they also expected visible benefits. The Solidarity trade union's 1990 program statement highlights the complexity and conditionality of its acquiescence in the Solidarity government's policy of building capitalism.

The fundamental statutory aim of the union is the protection of the rights, dignity and interests of employees. The implementation of this aim has only become possible in the new political and economic order. In the present situation the union faces three major challenges. The union will participate in the creation and protection of the democratic system in Poland. It will support efforts to create an effective economic system. The union is aware of the social cost of changes to the system and will strive to minimize them, defending employees' interests. . . . The transformation of the Polish economy should be directed towards a market economy which marries a legally guaranteed freedom of amassing capital, freedom of economic initiative and freedom of employment to the freedom of association of employees into organizations defending their interests and to elements of state intervention designed to correct the deficiencies of the market mechanism. (April 25, 1990)

Such a political program could not be easily joined with the shock therapy strategy for transformation. Solidarity trade unions wanted an empowerment of worker self-management bodies. Instead, "their" government opposed worker control more strenuously and effectively than the communists. Solidarity trade unions wanted guarantees of wage indexation during the transition. Instead, they got the "popiwek" tax on wage increases in state-owned enterprises—a punitive wage tax that imposed fines on enterprises that paid wage increases above a centrally mandated level. Solidarity wanted employment guarantees; instead they got skyrocketing unemployment and refusals from the Ministry of Industry to intervene to save jobs. In short, the state enterprise workers who formed the backbone of the Solidarity movement had their interests opposed by the Solidarity intellectuals in government. The distributional policies of shock therapy left Solidarity trade unionists little choice but to turn against "their" government.

Labor unrest, which erupted periodically throughout the transition period, but was mostly controlled or contained by Solidarity leaders between 1989 and 1991, threatened to plunge the country into economic chaos in the summer of 1992. The Solidarity trade union, which had its own representatives in parliament, was initially reluctant to organize workers against a government it had helped empower. But by 1992 discontent was so great that Solidarity was losing members to the former "official" OPZZ unions that were set up as nominally "independent" trade unions by the communist government in the early 1980s to draw support away from Solidarity. Solidarity was therefore forced to follow its membership into opposition to many aspects of the reforms, especially to punitive tax-based wage regulations. At the annual Solidarity convention in 1991, after Lech Wałęsa's elevation to the presidency, Wałęsa was replaced as chairman by Marian Krzaklewski, who promised to represent the interests of trade unionists against the government.

Pent-up frustration exploded in the summer of 1992 when several large state enterprises failed to pay their wage bills. OPZZ began to encourage unrest to draw members away from the progovernment Solidarity, and the strike wave took on such a momentum that even Wałęsa was unable to stop it. Efforts began to form new interfactory strike committees, a symbol of Solidarity resistance to communism, and in response Solidarity unions were forced to take a more radical stance. At the local level, Solidarity trade unions helped to organize these antigovernment, anti–wage policy strikes.

In response to this uncontrolled wave of labor unrest, Jacek Kuroń, Suchocka's labor minister, began in July 1992 to canvass widely for a compromise with the trade unions in the form of a state enterprise pact. It was an attempt to buy Solidarity support for enterprise restructuring, without which the future of the reforms were doomed. The idea of an enterprise pact had actually been conceived by former prime minister Bielecki, who saw the pact largely as a bargain with the trade unions to speed up privatization (interview with author, November 1993). In return for the quick drafting of privatization proposals by factory works councils and management, the State Enterprise Pact proposed to give workers a significant proportion of free shares and to lift the much-hated *popiwek* wage tax.

Kuroń added new dimensions to the state enterprise pact, in particular articulating a vision of social pacting as a long-term strategy for transformation. Kuroń proposed a system of regular consultation and centralized wage bargaining through a tripartite council composed of representatives of labor, government, and employers' associations. Neoliberal economists from the first Balcerowicz team reacted strongly against Kuroń's notion of social pacting, seeing it as an excessive state intervention that privileged special interests and as a threat to reform.

The state enterprise pact also proved difficult to negotiate because of divisions among the four major Polish trade union associations: Solidarity, OPZZ, Solidarity '80 (a radical splinter group), and the powerful group of branch trade unions in mining, electricity, engineering, railroads, and transport. Solidarity refused to sit at the same table as the postcommunist OPZZ. Solidarity '80 left the negotiations because systemic economic issues were excluded from discussion, and in the end the government had to negotiate three separate state enterprise pacts with each of the three remaining groups (Sobótka 1993, 2). Negotiations were exhausting for government representatives, who had to shuttle between rooms at the labor ministry to speak with different parties in "proximity" talks.

In the end, the state enterprise pacts were signed on February 22, 1993.

But as they awaited parliamentary approval, the Suchocka government fell, brought down by a vote of no confidence initiated by the Solidarity trade union after the cabinet failed to approve pay raises for striking health and education workers (East and Pontin 1997, 46). Unexpectedly, the vote of no confidence succeeded by a margin of one. In one of the great ironies of post-1989 Polish politics, the Solidarity trade union felled the longest-lived Solidarity government and cleared the way for two postcommunist parties, along with the former official trade union federation, OPZZ, to reassert political leadership. Poland's brief experimentation with social pacting to shore up support for neoliberal reform had failed.

In the days after the vote of no confidence on May 28, 1993, Prime Minister Suchocka revived the notion of asking parliament for special powers to push through the enormous unfinished legislative agenda it had left behind. Among other things, her government wanted to pass the legislation implementing the state enterprise pact by decree (PAP, May 29, 1993). However, parliament again refused to oblige,[11] and as a result, reform legislation was put on hold for another five months, until after new elections in September 1993. Democracy had forced a major turn in Poland's economic policy.

Strategies for Cohesion

September 1993 parliamentary elections were conducted under a revised electoral law that set a 5 percent threshold for parties and an 8 percent threshold for coalitions to enter the legislature. Designed to provide more stable government, this formula worked, allowing the two largest vote-getters to form a government: the Alliance of the Democratic Left (SLD) and the Polish Peasant Party (PSL). The resurgence of the SLD and its agrarian former satellite met with considerable surprise and trepidation in Poland and abroad. With 36 percent of the popular vote, the two postcommunist parties won 65 percent of seats in the Sejm (Lewis 1994; Zubek 1994). The Polish Peasant Party seems to have taken votes from some of the Christian democratic parties affiliated with Solidarity and from less successful agrarian parties. The SLD had clearly begun to reap the benefits of its consistent political strategy since its founding in 1990: winning public approval by acting as a responsible, reliable, and trustworthy party fully committed to parliamentary democracy and market reforms, but with more social sensitivity and professionalism than Solidarity leaders. However, the SLD still had problems shaking its image as an alliance of old communists. Although it proposed forming a governing coalition with the Democratic Union, the third largest vote-winner and the leading Solidarity reform party, the Democratic Union refused. It did not want to enter a coalition with the postcommunist "social democrats." This refusal forced the SLD to form a coalition with the Peasant Party, which contributed to a considerable slowing of the pace of reform (Blazyca and Rapacki 1996, 96).

In keeping with its social democratic profile (the SLD was itself a coalition led by the Social Democratic Party of Poland, along with the OPZZ trade union and a number of smaller left-wing parties), the SLD promised to continue on the course of reform charted by the Solidarity economists, but with modifications that would render the program more acceptable to society. A characteristic statement was made by Finance Minister Grzegorz Kołodko in September 1994: "We intend to carry out the three-year dynamic development program, which will bring us closer to a fully developed market economy and at the same time lower the community costs of reform" (Kołodko 1994).

Kołodko's program was outlined in a document entitled "Strategy for Poland." The 1994 strategy for Poland reflected continuity in many areas, recognizing the constraints of Poland's drive for membership in the European Union. The center-left governments of 1993–97 remained committed to continuing the "fundamental processes of transition and stabilization" (Kołodko and Nuti 1997), including fiscal and monetary restraint, trade and price liberalization, fast integration with the European Union, privatization, restitution, and price stability. However, the center-left developed a new set of strategies for achieving many of these goals. According to Finance Minister Kołodko, "These changes are due partly to a different vision of the transformation, as a more participatory and more open-ended process; partly to different government preferences, attaching greater weight both to economic growth and to the social costs of stabilization and transformation; partly simply to learning from previous errors and mistakes" (Kołodko and Nuti 1997).

The new strategy changed the emphasis of economic policy in several key areas. It placed greater emphasis on restarting growth, rather than adhering to strict austerity. It emphasized state participation in building new institutions, rather than state withdrawal or creative destruction of former institutions. It was "more interventionist, less doctrinaire and surprisingly managerial" (Blazyca 1995, 31) compared to previous neoliberal policies. Instead of advocating dramatic spurts of radical change, the "Strategy for Poland" attempted to establish policy credibility through consistency. And instead of seeking political isolation for reformers, the new strategy focused on direct engagement and bargaining between economic policymakers and important interest groups, particularly organized labor (Kołodko and Nuti 1997). These changes were most visible in privatization, the labor market, and social policy.

Strategy for Poland contained ambitious macroeconomic goals, of reducing inflation to single digits by 1997 while achieving fast, export-led growth, high levels of investment, constrained consumer spending, positive real interest rates, and exchange rate depreciation to track inflation (Blazyca 1995, 31). In fiscal policy, the center-left governments of 1993–97 adhered to the Maastricht criteria of a budget deficit not exceeding 3 percent of GDP in a given year (Kołodko and Nuti 1997). In order to set a sustainable basis for conservative fiscal policy, the center-left government initiated a major reform of the social welfare system, and in particular the pension system. Social sector reform had been delayed and mismanaged under previous center-right governments. The "Strategy for Poland" proposed to lower the social cost of reform through more effective pension and welfare benefits, improved conditions for farmers, and a continuation of the policies of the former state enterprise pacts regarding labor relations and wage negotiations in a national tripartite council. After first amending the *popiwek* in 1994, making it more discretionary, the SLD-PSL government replaced the hated tax in 1995 with a system of indicative wage bargaining through a tripartite commission, involving both major trade unions, the government, and employers' associations. This system of bargaining was particularly important as a mechanism of containing public sector wages. Restructuring of state-owned industries, particularly in declining sectors, began to be addressed by more concrete, though controversial, plans, after being ignored for several years by Solidarity (Blazyca and Rapacki 1996, 92). And Kołodko launched an ambitious plan to "commercialize" state enterprises, giving them the legal form of a joint stock company and placing them under the firm authority of a new State Treasury, in preparation for privatization. This represented a significant departure from the fast privatization policies of Solidarity governments, which emphasized privatization before restructuring (Blazyca 1995, 30–31).

While many Polish observers had issued dire warnings about the consequences of handing economic policy over to the center-left (Blazyca 1995, 28; Kołodko and Nuti 1997), the economic performance of 1993–97 allayed these fears. The economy performed far better than expected, with dramatic growth of around 6 percent of GDP per annum during this period. Center-left policies of economic reform with greater attention to cohesion and stability led to a reduction in the level of strikes and protest action and an increase in foreign investor and domestic business confidence in Poland (Blazyca 1995, 31). Foreign direct investment in Poland boomed during the center-left government's period in power. Critics soon began to claim that the center-left had either experienced "dumb luck" by presiding over a recovery (Kołodko and Nuti 1997) or simply continued Solidarity government policies. Another interpretation is that Poland's economic performance resulted from both Solidarity and center-left government policies (Kołodko and Nuti 1997).

In essence, the SLD-PSL government proposed a new strategy for economic transformation that was intended to continue the transformation to capitalism while lowering the social costs of reform, enhancing stability in government and economic policy, and accelerating growth. It led to a slower pace of reform in some areas but also achieved many of its policy objectives. Important structural reforms, including privatization and pension reform, were advanced in an atmosphere of dramatic economic growth and increasing political stability. Two major achievements of the center-left governments were the passage of a new constitution in 1997 that finally resolved and clarified relations between president and parliament (in favor of a mixed parliamentary-presidential system with a weakened president) and an invitation to join NATO in July 1997. These and other important measures were passed with the support of both government and opposition parties, signaling the emergence of a broad centrist alliance on some of the key policies of transition. Most importantly, the postcommunist Alliance of the Democratic Left conducted this moderate, institutionalist program of economic transformation while maintaining electoral support, demonstrating that reform could be pursued without negating one's political base.

However, maintaining electoral support was not enough for the Democratic Left to win elections in 1997. While the Democratic Left maintained its percentage of the vote, the right regrouped. During the four-year parliamentary term of 1993–97, post-Solidarity right-wing parties teamed up with the Solidarity trade union to form Solidarity Electoral Action, a reasonably coherent alliance that swept into power on a wave of renewed optimism about Poland's future. Solidarity Electoral Action (AWS) formed a coalition with the third largest party, Freedom Union, an amalgam of Mazowiecki's original Democratic Union and Bielecki's liberal party. Since 1995, Freedom Union had been led by former finance minister Leszek Balcerowicz.

From Technocrat to Technopol

Leszek Balcerowicz's voyage from technocrat to technopol was an important feature of Poland's democratic transition. Balcerowicz had strongly resisted the idea of joining a political party after 1989. In part, this may have reflected his earlier negative experience with party membership, as a member of the Polish communist party from 1969 to 1982. Many Poles had negative attitudes about political parties, which explains why most Polish political parties after 1989 called themselves movements, alliances, or unions instead of parties. However, Balcerowicz also formulated a principled reason for not joining a political party, rooted in the technocratic ideal. Balcerowicz believed that a good reformer would be a technocrat who stands above narrow interest groups and pursues policies that serve the welfare of society as a whole. Political insulation would facilitate this goal (Balcerowicz 1995).

However, a nonpolitical role for reformers ultimately meant technocrats were dependent on the sponsorship of strong political leaders, such as President Wałęsa. Polish neoliberals were attracted to this type of alliance between a strong charismatic leader and nonaligned technocrats (Filar 1994). However, relying on Wałęsa for support proved problematic. For one thing, he won the elections of 1990 in part by campaigning against neoliberal reform, causing the reform program to lose public legitimacy. For another, his attempts to gain decree power for neoliberal governments ultimately foundered on the parliamentary fundamentalism of some elements of Solidarity. As Poland consistently upheld the values of parliamentary democracy, the efficacy of the technocratic, strong-president strategy diminished.

After several years out of power, Balcerowicz changed his mind about political engagement. In 1994 he joined the liberal Freedom Union, and in 1995 he was elected its leader, replacing former prime minister Tadeusz Mazowiecki (East and Pontin 1997, 37). Balcerowicz had finally entered the normal democratic fray. In the terminology suggested by Dominguez (1997) and others, Balcerowicz had become a technopol.

Dominguez (1997) has argued that the success of economic reform in much of Latin America has depended on "technopols," who combine the virtues of a technocrat (strong academic training and leadership) with the pragmatism of a political operative. Instead of focusing on the coherence of a technical economic program, technopols realize that "a rational policy is not just technically correct but also politically enduring. Rationality thus defined can only be achieved through politics" (Dominguez 1997, 7). This pragmatic approach to politics leads technopols to temper economic dogmatism with a "'sense of proportion' necessary to shift policies in response to practical circumstances, not necessarily from personal virtues, but because the procedures of democracy require such prudence from politicians who seek to be effective" (Dominguez 1997, 11).

Balcerowicz took up the mantle of political engagement and led the Freedom Union to a reasonable showing in parliamentary elections in 1997, winning 13.4 percent of the vote. After difficult coalition negotiations between Solidarity Electoral Action and Freedom Union, the two parties formed a coalition government with Balcerowicz as finance minister. He took power in 1997 backed by a substantial proportion of the popular vote, which made his tenure in office considerably more secure than during the shock therapy period.

Balcerowicz's move from political insulation to political engagement reflected a major change in the political style of neoliberals in Poland. Similar changes were made in the content of reform itself, reflecting pragmatic compromises under democratic constraints. The Solidarity–Freedom Union coalition focused heavily on institutional reforms. It called for implementation of public administration reform, stalled for years; health care reform; pension reform; and education reform. What was striking about this reform agenda is that it focused on institutional and social policy areas that had been neglected in previous neoliberal programs. In addition, the government emphasized greater budgetary austerity, tax reform, and restructuring of troubled sectors such as mining and agriculture. Growth slowed in 1998–99 from the heights achieved under the center-left governments but still continued at a moderate pace.

There was no question this time that the political strategy of reform in Poland had to involve parliament. All reform legislation had to be extensively debated in parliamentary committees, and this meant making substantial compromises, often with the left opposition. Pension reform and local administrative reform legislation, for instance, was passed with substantial involvement at different stages from the postcommunist Alliance of the Democratic Left. The Freedom Union was often obliged to seek opposition support because of the fragility of support for market-oriented reforms within the Solidarity Electoral Action.

It is impossible to give a complete overview of the so-called Balcerowicz II package of economic reforms, since they are ongoing at the time of writing. However, a few trends seem clear at this time. First, Balcerowicz II does represent a substantial acceleration over the pace achieved by the previous center-left government. The center-right government introduced four major reform programs simultaneously, of public administration, health care, education, and pensions, pushing for an ambitious pace of change. Second, the political strategy for this set of reforms is explicitly parliamentary, and therefore more pragmatic. There have been no more authoritarian temptations since the constitution of 1997. Third, this parliamentary pragmatism has required compromises on key issues, such as tax reform, the number of regional administrative units, and so on. Fourth, public support for reform has again degenerated because of the quickened pace of change. This is particularly evident in the area of health reform, which was implemented without sufficient preparation in terms of public information and institution building. At the time of this writing, the Solidarity and Freedom Union parties have lost a substantial proportion of their electoral support. It is not yet clear how this decline in support might influence the future course of reform in Poland, though a return to center-left government in the future seems likely. Thus policy alternation and learning will continue to dominate the dynamics of transition—not stable pursuit of a single reform program.

Conclusions

Poland has experienced a progression of reform strategies since 1989. Poland began the transformation process with a technocratic, shock therapy strategy of reform. However, this strategy undermined the political bases of support for the Solidarity governments that implemented it. Solidarity parliamentarians began to oppose the Balcerowicz plan, and by the end of 1990, reform was stalled because of legislative paralysis. A new government in 1991 tried to restart reform, but none of its legislative proposals were passed by mid-June. Finally, the government was tempted to demand special powers to enact economic reform by decree, a logical outgrowth of the technocratic shock therapy strategy, and a political method advocated by President Lech Wałęsa, who wanted to establish a presidential regime. However, a sufficient proportion of the Solidarity "left" and the former communists remained committed to a largely parliamentary form of democracy. Ultimately, the Sejm did not have a sufficient majority to grant special powers of decree. The big-bang method of economic reform therefore ground to a halt in mid-1991.

Backlash against shock therapy was expressed first in the fragmentation of the Solidarity camp, and then in the appointment of the Olszewski government, which promised a reversal of neoliberal reforms. Olszewski met with substantial resistance from President Wałęsa and an embarrassing public rebuke from the IMF (*New York Times,* March 4, 1992, 8) and ultimately failed to enact a complete reversal of neoliberal policies. His government fell, and after a few months of coalition negotiations, a deteriorating budgetary situation, and no reform legislation, the next Solidarity government of Hanna Suchocka aimed to restart faltering neoliberal reforms. In order to do so, the Suchocka government adopted a different style and strategy of reform, attempting to reach a social pact with trade unions and employers that would enable industrial restructuring and privatization. This shift from technocratic to social pact strategies is similar to what Przeworski (1991) had predicted at the outset of reform. Both strategies met with the expected difficulties: the neoliberal reforms caused a substantial political backlash and encouraged "authoritarian temptations," while the social pacts proved ineffective and difficult to negotiate. Ultimately, the Suchocka government fell before it could enact its state enterprise pact, brought down by a vote of no confidence initiated by the Solidarity trade union. In new elections in September 1993, a coalition of left parties won 65 percent of the seats in the Sejm.

This coalition was able to implement a new strategy for transformation in Poland that emphasized social cohesion and side-payments for a wide variety of interest groups. This policy brought a sustained level of political support for the more reformist senior coalition partner, the Alliance of the Democratic Left, and positive economic results. In particular, political stability contributed to an increase in foreign investment in Poland, while looser fiscal policy contributed to high growth rates between 1993 and 1997. However, the left government also achieved stability by slowing the pace of economic reform legislation.

When a regrouped right won elections in 1997, Leszek Balcerowicz returned to the Finance Ministry and began to implement a new set of reforms. However, this was no longer shock therapy. In place of the earlier technocratic politics of shock therapy, Balcerowicz had become a "technopol." The new government did not request special powers and instead emphasized winning broad support for reform. Most of the reforms had been planned over the course of several years, and several enjoyed the support of a broad cross section of parliament, including both left and right parties. There was no question, this time, of using special powers of decree. Still, the reforms themselves, and the pace of reform, proved controversial. The right government succeeded in accelerating the pace of reform, at the expense of social unrest. Farmers, miners, defense industry workers, and nurses all engaged in protest action against aspects of reform. Popularity of the right parties again plunged.

Poland therefore displays a pattern of policy alternation similar to what Przeworski (1991) predicted: a start-stop-start pattern of reform and reaction between parties that support radical reform and those that support social stability and a more moderate pace of change. However, there are two aspects of the Polish transformation that do not fit well with Przeworski's model. First, Poland was able to attain a high level of economic performance despite repeated policy alternation (see table 2). Second, policy styles and strategies of "radical" and "gradualist" reformers changed over time as learning occurred among both right and left parties.

Rather than the all-or-nothing, mutually undermining and inconsistent type of alternation Przeworski predicted, Poland has experienced policy learning by mutual adaptation. Center-right reformers gave up their earlier technocratic political strategy and engaged in party politics, respecting the boundaries of parliamentary democracy. Center-left reformers have attempted to address the social costs of reform and intervene more in institutional reconstruction, while not abandoning the basic goals of transition and

TABLE 2.   Economic Indicators for Poland and the Czech Republic, 1989–2001

| | 1989 | 1990 | 1991 | 1992 | 1993 | 1994 | 1995 | 1996 | 1997 | 1998 | Estimates and Projections | | |
											1999	2000	2001
GDP growth rate (%)													
Poland	0.2	−11.6	−7.0	2.6	3.8	5.2	7.0	6.0	6.8	4.8	3.5	5.2	5.8
Czech Republic	1.4	−0.4	−11.5	−3.3	0.6	2.6	5.9	3.8	0.3	−2.3	−0.5	1.4	2.3
Inflation rate (CPI) (%)													
Poland	251.1	585.8	70.3	43.3	35.3	32.2	27.8	19.9	14.9	11.6			
Czech Republic	2.3	10.8	56.6	11.1	20.8	10.0	9.1	8.8	8.5	10.7			
Unemployment rate (%)													
Poland	0.1	6.1	11.8	13.6	14.0	14.4	13.3	12.3	11.2	10.6	11.4	10.8	10.3
Czech Republic	0.0	0.8	4.1	2.6	4.3	4.4	4.1	3.9	4.8	6.5	8.9	10.1	11.0
Government expenditures (% GDP)													
Poland	48.8	39.8	49.0	49.5	54.3	49.3	47.2	45.8	44.9	43.4	44.1	42.4	41.4
Czech Republic	64.5	60.1	54.2	52.8	42.2	44.0	43.1	41.7	40.9	40.6	44.7	47.4	
Government fiscal balance (% GDP)													
Poland	−7.4	3.1	−6.7	−6.7	−4.5	−3.5	−2.8	−3.1	−2.9	−2.5	−3.0	−2.4	−2.3
Czech Republic	−2.8	0.1	−1.9	−3.1	0.0	−1.9	−1.6	−1.9	−2.0	−2.4	−5.1	−5.4	−5.5
Current account/GDP (%)													
Poland			−2.6	1.1	−5.2	1.0	0.7	−2.3	−4.0	−5.0	−7.1	−6.7	−6.3
Czech Republic			1.2	−1.0	1.3	−1.9	−2.6	−7.4	−6.1	−1.9	−0.8	−1.2	−1.4
Foreign direct investment (bn USD)													
Poland	0.0	0.0	0.1	0.3	0.6	0.5	1.1	2.8	3.0	6.6	6.5		
Czech Republic	na	na	na	1.0	0.6	0.7	2.5	1.4	1.3	2.5	3.5		

Sources: 1989 and 1990 data from *Economics of Transition* 4, no. 2 (1996). Data on levels from 1993 on, and on changes in levels from 1994 on, are from *OECD Economic Outlook* 66 (December 1999). All other data come from EBRD, 1999.

Note: Data on government expenditures and fiscal balance prior to 1993 are for Czechoslovakia, not the Czech Republic, as are 1989 and 1990 data on GDP growth, unemployment, and inflation.

European accession. Both center-right and center-left reformers have shown a tendency to move toward a centrist position on key economic policy matters, restraining internal constituencies. This is largely because both sides recognize that many economic reforms require substantial support from both government and opposition in a parliamentary democratic system.

The success of democratic policy alternation in Poland is surprising from the point of view of dominant theoretical approaches to simultaneous transition. Neoliberals emphasized the necessity of sticking to a single, internally consistent strategy of reform, and following it through to the end. Poland has not done that, and yet it has met with substantial economic success. Przeworski predicted that policy alternation would produce destabilizing political effects, but this was also wrong. Policy alternation in Poland has produced widespread policy learning and a convergence toward centrist policies that serve the dual goals of cohesion and efficiency. The Polish experience therefore challenges the main models of political-economic transformation, a challenge that is taken up in chapter 5.

CHAPTER 3

Czech Social Liberalism
and Beyond

Reformers in Czechoslovakia, and later the Czech Republic, took a distinctive approach to the politics of economic
reform. Instead of pushing ahead as quickly as possible before opposition
could emerge, Czech reformers developed a political-economic strategy that
was designed to function over the long term within the constraints of parliamentary democracy. They did this in two ways: first, by accompanying radi-
cal stabilization and liberalization with extensive "compensation" measures   *compensation*
(Greskovits 1998) designed to cushion the impact of reform; and second by
engaging in politics, rather than being isolated from it by strong political   *engagement*
patrons. Neoliberals were in the minority in the first postcommunist
Czechoslovak governments and were never elevated to unchallenged control,
as the Balcerowicz team was in Poland. Czech reformer Václav Klaus quickly
learned that he would have to "win political support for myself" (Klaus 1993).
In order to do so, he built out of the ashes of Václav Havel's Civic Forum the
Civic Democratic Party (ODS), a party that provided consistent parliamentary backing for his radical program of economic reform. However, because
Czech reformers were initially in a weaker political position, they were forced
to compromise, adopting ameliorative social policies and a far-reaching
political institution-building strategy. This created what I call a hybrid "social
liberal" strategy for transformation.

The results were striking. Whereas Balcerowicz lost popular support
immediately and fell within a year and a half from the start of Poland's shock
therapy in 1990, Václav Klaus presided over eight years of transition in the
Czech Republic, as Czechoslovak finance minister from 1989 to 1992 and
prime minister of the Czech Republic from 1992 to 1997. Klaus built the
strongest proreform political party in Central and Eastern Europe and won
parliamentary elections in 1992 and 1996 on a platform of radical change. For
a time, Klaus appeared to have solved the fundamental problem of simultaneous transformation: how to conduct a radical program of economic reform
while maintaining popular support. During his victorious 1992 election campaign, Klaus remarked on the political differences between Balcerowicz and
himself:

> When he last visited me . . . I asked him how many times a week he trav-
> eled around Poland and spoke on the town squares, in the cultural cen-

ters, in the sports halls, in order to gain the greatest mass support for his plan. He revealed that he preferred to sit in his study and prepare documents. I have been going to meetings on average about two times a week, and now, before the elections, let's say six times. I think that Poland is paying above all for the inability of certain politicians to gain such marked support of the voters that they have enough power to continue with the reforms. (Klaus 1993)

Václav Klaus was a "technopol" (Dominguez 1997) from the start. Successful political engagement of reformers in the Czech Republic showed that radical reform could be conducted over the long term under conditions of parliamentary democracy, and that a period of "extraordinary politics," extraordinary powers for a president, or temporary suspensions of democracy were not necessary features of postcommunist transformation strategies.

Klaus, however, was often silent about the other part of the Czech strategy for building public support for transition: extensive social protections and guarantees that departed from neoliberal orthodoxy (cf. Tucker et al. 1997). Klaus was a committed neoliberal who often spoke of creating a "market without adjectives" rather than a social-market economy. He consistently railed against any notions of a "third way" and admired British prime minister Margaret Thatcher. However, since Klaus was not in a position of complete power in the early years of reform, he was forced to accept a social liberal compromise that included a larger and more comprehensive set of social programs than he would have liked. These included corporatist-style labor market institutions, low-unemployment policies, a social minimum income, and continued state commitment to a range of universal social benefits. This social liberal compromise was similar to what social democrats like Przeworski (1991, 1995) advocated at the time. And it seemed to have the intended effect, extending popular backing for socioeconomic transformation. Klaus's signature program of rapid voucher privatization also had a mass political component. Under voucher privatization, about one-half the value of state-owned enterprises was distributed through auctions to the millions of citizens who bought a book of privatization vouchers for a small fee. By distributing vouchers to a majority of the adult population, Klaus encouraged substantial participation and support for reform (Earle 1997, 44–45; Večerník and Matějů 1999, 75).

With these social liberal policies and the establishment of an effective electoral machine, the Civic Democratic Party, Václav Klaus was elected prime minister of the Czech Republic in June 1992. At that point, Klaus gained a higher degree of control over the course of economic change. However, his experience of political engagement and his desire to maintain politi-

cal support meant that Klaus could only move gradually away from the policies of social liberalism that guided Czechoslovak governments from 1989 to
1992. The split of Czechoslovakia enabled this shift to neoliberalism, by freeing Klaus from the need to accommodate the economically weaker Slovak
Republic (Rueschemeyer and Wolchik 1999, 114). During 1992–96, Klaus
moved the Czech Republic in a neoliberal direction (Dangerfield 1997), but
social democratic policies were maintained in a number of areas (Tucker et al.
1997). For example, Klaus continued the low-wage, low-unemployment policies of social liberalism, called the undervalued Czech exchange rate and low
wages the "two cushions" of economic transition, and defended rent control
and housing subsidies.

On the other hand, Klaus did mount an assault on the universal welfare
state and corporatist system of labor relations, causing a major falling-out
with trade unions in 1995, labor unrest (Pollert 1997), and a rise in support
for the opposition Czech Social Democratic Party. Most voters, however,
only really began to reevaluate their support for Klaus and the Czech transformation when cracks emerged in the edifice of the Czech economic miracle.

Almost immediately after Klaus won reelection in 1996, a series of financial scandals wracked the country. They seemed to show that Klaus's economic policies and the Czech economy were not as healthy as previously
believed. Until that point, the Czech Republic was seen as one of the star
reformers of Central and Eastern Europe. However, Klaus's voucher privatization produced an enterprise structure that provided very little control over
management and placed bank-led investment funds in an undue position of
power within firms. Combined with Klaus's principled opposition to government regulation, Czech financial markets turned into denizens of corrupt
self-dealing that eventually undermined the economic system at its core (cf.
Economist, May 31, 1997). The Czech economy suffered from a current
account crisis and financial collapse in 1997. Klaus resigned from office in
November 1997 in the wake of a party finance scandal that tied a secret Civic
Democratic Party account in Switzerland to kickbacks from privatization.

The collapse of the Czech miracle is often attributed to the ameliorative
social policies that accompanied radical transition. But the Czech malaise
owed as much to the effects of rapid privatization, a key part of the neoliberal
agenda, as it did to low-unemployment policies (IMF 1999a). It was the
specific combination of radical neoliberalism in some areas (such as the
refusal to regulate financial markets), overprotective social policies (such as
the refusal to countenance enterprise bankruptcy), and economic nationalism (such as the emphasis on creating Czech national champions in finance
and manufacturing) that undermined the Czech miracle.

It turned out that the longevity of the Klaus government not only provided for the endurance of radical reforms, but also the endurance of reform mistakes. The Czech experience thus seems to argue against the necessity of maintaining one group of reformers in power over a long period of time. Instead, policy alternation between strong governments with opposing programs of reform may have more positive effects. However since 1996, the Czech Republic was governed by a series of minority governments that have been hampered in their ability to effect substantial change in economic policy (Saxonberg 1999). Indeed, when the Czech Social Democratic Party won elections in 1998, it was forced to sign an "opposition agreement" with Klaus's Civic Democratic Party that reduced its room for maneuver, although some policy alternation and correction is in progress, for instance in bank privatization.

Through social liberal policies of transformation, Czech reformers extended their time in office far beyond what would have been possible under a purely neoliberal policy regime. But contrary to both neoliberal and social democratic theories of transition, a stable proreform government did not produce better economic results (see table 2, p. 59). The Czech experience thus presents a paradox for the two dominant theories of the politics of economic reform.

The Velvet Revolution

Social liberalism was not the strategy of any single individual or small reform team, as in Poland, but a hybrid strategy for transformation that reflected a compromise among different factions within the first postcommunist Czechoslovak governments. Social liberalism was very much a product of the "velvet revolution" of 1989, a revolution that attempted to produce dramatic political change while at the same time maintaining national unity through policies of inclusion and persuasion.

The Czechoslovak transition began in the wake of a student demonstration on November 17, 1989, held to commemorate the death of a Czech student at the hands of the Nazis in 1939. The demonstration took on anticommunist overtones, lasted longer than expected, and met with suppressive action by the communist state police in the center of Prague. Hundreds of students were beaten in a confrontation on Národní Street near Wenceslas Square. Public reaction to the police brutality was tremendous and spontaneous. Thousands, and then tens of thousands, of Prague citizens turned out to Wenceslas Square to protest the beatings in the following days. They listened to dissident leaders speak from the balcony of the Melantrich publishing house and chanted, "It's already here." The moment many had awaited silently had arrived (cf. Leff 1997, 79–81).

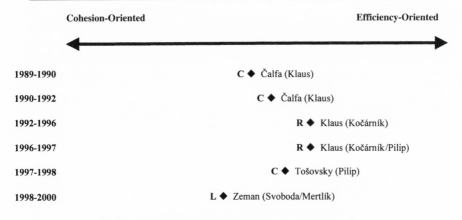

Prime Minister (Finance Minister), L = Left, C = Center, R = Right

Fig. 5.   Strategies for transformation in the Czech Republic, 1989–2000 (Czechoslovak governments from 1989–92)

A group of prominent dissidents formed the new mass organization, Civic Forum, to give leadership to the protests. Václav Havel, a famous dissident playwright, became its informal leader and chief strategist. Civic Forum's main priority was to leverage these mass demonstrations into a change of regime, something that had already occurred in neighboring Poland and Hungary. At first, the communists hoped to quell the protests by reorganizing the government, expelling hard-liners, and opening a dialogue with dissident groups. Rumors circulated that the repression on November 17 had been staged by reformers within the communist government to discredit hard-liners and force them out of power. But the democracy movement could not be contained by a mere reorganization of the government. Civic Forum held firm in its demand for a change of regime. It kept hundreds of thousands of people on the streets and organized a two-hour general strike on November 27 that gained the participation of approximately 60 percent of Czechoslovak workers (East and Pontin 1997, 97). This strike, more than anything else, caused the communist leadership to lose its will to resist. Though brief, it demonstrated mass working-class support for the students, actors, and dissidents in Prague, something the communists had not expected.

Roundtable talks between the communists, their allied "national front" parties, and representatives of the opposition movements, the Czech Civic Forum, and its Slovak sister organization, Public against Violence, produced an agreement on a peaceful transfer of power in the first week of December (Calda 1996). The communist prime minister resigned on December 7, paving the way for the Federal Assembly to appoint a roundtable "government of national understanding" on December 10. This government, composed of reform communists and dissident leaders, would hold power until free elections in June 1990. President Gustav Husák, installed after the suppression of the Prague Spring by Warsaw Pact troops in 1968, resigned the same day. Václav Havel was elected president by the Federal Assembly on December 30. Czechoslovak communism had broken down in less than a month.

Government of National Understanding

The government of national understanding produced by the roundtable agreement between Civic Forum leaders and the communist party played a brief but crucial role in shaping the political and economic transformation. The government initially had a communist majority, but no hard-line communists were included. Two of the communist members, Vladimír Dlouhý and Valtr Komárek, moreover, immediately resigned their party membership. The prime minister was a high-ranking Slovak reform communist, Marian Čalfa, who also joined the democratic opposition. He resigned his communist party membership in 1990, symbolizing the personal and moral transformation that was required of most Czechs and Slovaks who had one way or another been drawn into complicity with the regime. A young and mostly unknown member of the last communist government, Čalfa was nominated for the position by the last communist prime minister, Ladislav Adamec, and was at first rejected by the opposition. However, Čalfa proved himself an able prime minister and an enthusiastic advocate of the new democratic order. He developed an excellent working relationship with Havel and stayed on as prime minister in the first Civic Forum government of 1990–92. Czechoslovak leaders on both sides had agreed to a "velvet" revolution with a smooth, legal transfer of power. Václav Havel was the lead negotiator on the dissident side and the main architect of the strategy of legality and consensus, not allowing power to reside for too long in the street.

Although the Czechoslovak transition is often labeled a "regime breakdown" because of the speed of the demise of the communist regime, the transition was smooth and negotiated in important respects. The communist government and a significant number of parliamentarians agreed to be removed from power in 1989, to make way for anticommunist replacements. Political transition measures were voted through the communist-controlled Federal Assembly, and some reform communists were given an important role in the transitional government of national understanding. Former communists were moreover accepted into the Civic Forum and its successor parties. In the early phases at least, the velvet revolution was dedicated to forgiving the sins of the past, rather than purging communist officials, despite the later passage of a much-touted "lustration" law that banned collaborators of the secret police from holding certain government positions for a period of five years (later extended).

Choosing Social Liberalism

The government of national understanding created in December 1989 was a roundtable government without any electoral basis, founded on negotiations between self-selected elites and intended to last until free parliamentary elections could be held in June 1990. Economic radicals led by the newly appointed finance minister, Václav Klaus, wanted to begin the economic transformation immediately, capitalizing on the revolutionary legitimacy of the new "democratic" government (Batt 1991, 97; Myant 1993, 173). However, the lack of electoral legitimacy for the government of national understanding made its leading members reluctant to launch radical economic reforms. Disagreements over the right of the government to conduct such reforms, reluctance to overstep the bounds of popular democracy, and disputes over the content of reforms caused the government of national understanding to seek to live up to its name by delaying controversial economic programs until after the elections (cf. Dyba and Svejnar 1994, 98). Instead the government engaged in months of talks, both public and private, on the future of the economy.

This decision to delay radical reforms until a democratic electoral mandate was won proved tremendously important in solidifying and organizing political legitimacy for economic reform. Among other things, it allowed time for the government to iron out internal differences in its approach to economic change. When an economic program was finally passed by the parliament in September 1990, almost a year after the Balcerowicz plan was rushed through the Polish Sejm, the program had endured far more discussion and compromise within the government and far more public debate in the media and had won the explicit acceptance of powerful interest groups such as the trade unions and *nomenklatura* business interests. In part, this was because of a bigger "selling" effort by the government. But in part, the Czechoslovak program for radical transformation won support at this stage because its design was altered to satisfy important interest groups and public concerns.

Social Democrats versus Neoliberals

Although the government of national understanding strove to maintain a unified front that Václav Havel thought was important to reassure the population, the Czechoslovak government was in fact deeply internally divided over how to conduct the economic transformation (Klaus 1993, 10). It was clear to everyone that the communist system of ownership and central planning had to be transformed, but there was little agreement on methods. Within the government, a debate developed between "radicals" and "gradualists," although as mentioned earlier, these labels give a misleading impression about the nature of their differences, which did not mainly concern speed, but rather the role of institutions and strategies of transition. Václav Klaus, the Czechoslovak minister of finance from December 1989 until June 1992, emerged as the leading representative of the "radicals," but the majority of the government was initially more sympathetic to a "gradualist" solution, represented by Deputy Prime Minister Valtr Komárek. Komárek was a darling of the crowd in the November days of 1989 and had been Klaus's boss at the Forecasting Institute of the Czechoslovak Academy of Sciences. Komárek's Institute of Forecasting had been an officially tolerated center of reform economists set up in the mid-1980s that allowed a number of leading reform economists to develop their ideas in an atmosphere of relative freedom (Adam 1993a, 262ff.). Many leading reform politicians were shaped by the intellectual discourse, personal relations, and conflicts at this institute in Prague. Komárek's appointment to the position of deputy prime minister for economy signaled the initial dominance of the gradualist camp within the 1989–90 government of national understanding. The deputy prime minister ranked higher than Klaus, the minister of finance, and was charged with overall supervision of economic change. Komárek, a member of the 1968 Prague Spring generation, became the leading spokesman and government advocate of "gradual" economic reform, although his ideas fluctuated between those of reform communism and economic liberalism. Komárek advocated a managerial approach to economic reform and argued for gradualism particularly in the privatization process (Myant 1993, 165–67).

The gradualist camp was initially supported by a majority of Civic Forum representatives and former communists, while Klaus, Central Planning Office chief Vladimír Dlouhý, and their "radical" group were marginalized, not sharing the social democratic values of much of the rest of the government. Former communists within the government of national understanding, including Prime Minister Marian Čalfa, may not have been convinced Marxists, but they did still have certain social democratic sensibilities and a feeling that any economic program should be geared toward facilitating the economic well-being of the majority of Czechoslovak citizens. They felt responsible for the social and political effects of reform and were suspicious of radical solutions (Myant 1993, 170). Besides this group, many Civic Forum ministers and their aides were veterans of the 1968 generation of reform communists. These people had been communist academics or politicians in the 1950s and 1960s and had developed and supported the principles of "socialism with a human face." Their lives had been deeply etched by the drama of those years and the tragedy of 1968. Seeking a more humane socialism, they had introduced a wildly popular economic reform program in 1967, along with increased freedom of political expression. It was a precursor of Mikhail Gorbachev's perestroika and glasnost. Yet the mood in the Soviet Union was not yet ripe for this sort of experiment. After one year of the so-called Prague Spring, Brezhnev sent in the tanks and installed communist hard-liners in power in Czechoslovakia. The new, hard-line Czechoslovak leadership instituted a policy of "normalization," which involved a severe purge of the communist party to eliminate the reformist heresy. Architects of the Prague Spring (henceforth "sixty-eighters") lost their communist party membership and their jobs. In most cases, they were de facto exiled from Prague. The reformed socialist vision of those years lived on, however, in the Czechoslovak dissident community, since many of the sixty-eighters became active dissidents and remained true to the convictions of socialism with a human face until 1989. When they returned to power, they were imbued with the vision and ideals of the Prague Spring—and its social democratic program of economic reform.

Václav Havel, although not a sixty-eighter himself, was close to many of them through the Charter 77 dissident organization and informal contacts. The first president of Czechoslovakia thus had strong sympathies with the gradualist camp and closer personal ties to them than to the radicals. Havel had bad relations with Václav Klaus from the beginning. Klaus was elevated to the inner circle of Civic Forum negotiators in 1989 despite having never been active in dissident circles and was seen as an outsider and an opportunist—part of the "gray zone" of private opposition and public conformity to the communist regime.

As deputy prime minister, Komárek was designated to draft a "gradualist" program of economic transformation. But in what was probably a crucial factor for the decline of gradualism, he failed to do so. Myant (1993, 169) reports that "Komárek was handicapped by an inability to organise his work" and was removed following an intervention by President Havel. In April 1990, just as the government was about to debate the competing "radical" and "gradualist" economic programs, Komárek was replaced as deputy prime minister by Václav Valeš, another veteran of the 1968 movement. It was Valeš who finished work on a "gradualist" program, uninspiringly entitled a "Strategy of Gradual Transition to a Market Economy in the ČSFR (second variant of radical economic reform)." Klaus and Dlouhý's "Radical Strategy" had already become the first variant. Komárek later ran for prime minister on the ticket of the Czechoslovak Social Democratic Party (ČSSD) in 1992, but upon losing he resigned from politics and returned to his study. Gradualists never convinced the government that they had the energy, vision, or personnel to lead the post-1989 transformation.

The sputtering out of the gradualist alternative, combined with increasing public impatience with the slow pace of economic change in 1990, strengthened the radicals' hand. People wanted dramatic changes in the economy, although not necessarily of the type the radicals proposed. However, Klaus still needed to win the support of the more managerial social democratic-minded cabinet members in a vote of approval from the full cabinet, and to do this he was forced to compromise.

Klaus and Dlouhý's proposed "radical" scenario was drafted in cooperation with a team of sixteen cabinet members and their advisers. Klaus simultaneously composed a project for mass privatization with his deputy and former colleague from the Institute of Forecasting, Dušan Tříska. The radical macroeconomic program of rapid price liberalization, currency devaluation, and fiscal stabilization reflected the clear outlines of an IMF-approved "big bang" program for economic reform (Bruno 1994, 27). At the end of 1989, the government had devalued the Czechoslovak koruna against the convertible currencies, revalued it against the ruble, and tightened budgetary policies for 1990. The radical economic transformation, now set for 1991, emphasized a strict anti-inflationary policy (Dyba and Svejnar 1994, 99), aiming at zero growth in the money supply, a government budget surplus, and a positive real interest rate. One of the most striking aspects of this anti-inflationary policy was a tough, tax-based wage policy designed to produce a dramatic drop in real wages. In addition to these firm anti-inflationary policies, the radical program proposed

1. A major tax reform emphasizing the introduction of a value-added tax, a personal income tax, and an "enterprise" tax;

2. Budgetary reform stressing independence of units and ensuring the transparency of budgetary allocations;

3. Privatization and denationalization of property;

4. Liberalization of 85 percent of all prices (more extreme than in Poland, where 50 percent of prices already moved freely in 1989);

5. Internal convertibility of the koruna;

6. Import protection, with a 20 percent initial import surcharge. (Dyba and Svejnar 1994, 99)

The social policy section of the radical program included additional provisions:

7. Reduction in size and retraining of labor force;

8. Legalization of collective bargaining as a mechanism for future regulation of wages, after the ending of state-enforced wage restraint;

9. Restructuring social security and health care systems and gradually separating their funding from the main state budget. (Dyba and Svejnar 1994, 99)

Klaus and Dlouhý did not compromise on most of what they understood to be the key issues of systemic economic change, especially the tight anti-inflationary approach, radical price liberalization, privatization, and currency convertibility. On the other hand, Klaus and Dlouhý adopted the gradualists' scenario for social policy. The social policy sections of both the "radical" and "gradualist" documents are identical and were drafted by the same adviser to labor minister Petr Miller. Klaus was not enthusiastic about the social policy program formulated by Miller and his advisers in the labor ministry, although its aims were modest and geared toward creating a social system compatible with market capitalism. Miller reports many loud arguments between Klaus and himself and states that the reason Klaus was forced to accept his social programs is that "we had a strong minister of labor" (interview with author, May 5, 1994). Other anecdotal evidence from government circles supports the view that Klaus gave in on social policy despite his principled opposition to what he recognized as social democratic policies. Klaus disliked the sixty-eighters intensely and later supported lustration, in part, to marginalize these former communists and force them out of government (Stein 1995). His inclusion of the Miller team's social policy outline in his own "radical" scenario of economic reform represented a strategic compromise. Klaus drafted the sections that were most important to him from the point of view of his position in the Finance Ministry: price liberalization, the introduction of the convertibility of the koruna, reduction of subsidies, macroeconomic policy, and privatization. Not having a strong alternative social policy model in mind and needing the support of a government dominated by social-democratic-minded ministers, Klaus accepted their plan for coping with social tensions arising from radical economic transformation.

As Czech sociologist Jan Hartl (1995, 214) put it, "All actors on our new political scene conformed with the somehow comfortable 'residual' role of social policy. The right, with cheerless silence, conceded the left its traditional issue." Klaus and Dlouhý's scenario for radical reform, then, already reflected a social liberal compromise: it was radically neoliberal in macroeconomic policy and social democratic in its approach to labor relations and the welfare state.

During the long period of intragovernmental debate over the future of reform, the battle was also proceeding in the media and the public sphere. Klaus, who turned out to be a natural on television, won the increasingly restive Czech voters over to his version of economic radicalism. In April–May 1990, Klaus and Dlouhý's program of radical reform won the support of the government and became the official program of economic transformation in Czechoslovakia. Radicalism won in part because of the greater intellectual power and coherence of the program, in part because the Klaus-Dlouhý team showed enormous energy in the drafting of the programs and proved that it had mobilized a competent group of economists for government work, and in part because the "radical" scenario for economic reform already reflected a social liberal compromise.

A Democratic Electoral Mandate

Victory within the government in May 1990 was not, however, the end of the political organizing process for economic reform, as in Poland. During the spring and summer, the social liberal program for radical transformation was subjected to commentary from the trade unions, academic institutes (Myant 1993, 176–83), industry associations, and other bodies. But more importantly, the program was submitted to an electoral test: the June 1990 parliamentary elections that marked the end of the government of national understanding. Václav Havel's Civic Forum won the June 1990 elections on a platform of radical reform, packaged as a "return to Europe." The path of this return was mapped out in the radical program for economic transformation of the government, the broad outlines of which were clear to any citizen who opened a newspaper: stabilization, liberalization, voucher privatization, and social protection. Civic Forum in the Czech lands and its sister party, Public against Violence (VPN), in Slovakia won a landslide victory; the new government reapproved the radical program for economic transformation and submitted it to parliament on September 1, 1990. After much discussion, debate, and some amendments in parliament, the legislature voted to pass the Scenario of Economic Reform and the complementary Scenario of Social

Reform by a vast majority later in the month. Economic transformation was now fortified with democratic legitimation.

Over the course of the ten months since the fall of communist power, the Czechoslovak program for economic transformation was debated intensively within the government; subjected to public commentary and negotiation with various interest groups; given a democratic mandate in the June 1990 elections, where it featured in the Civic Forum electoral program; and finally passed by the new parliament. Civic Forum's electoral victory in 1990 was more a referendum on communism than a vote on programmatic issues of economic reform. Government efforts to discuss the transformation program with the public were mostly symbolic, since the program was already approved in outline. Public debate had only a limited impact, and few real changes were made as a result. Nonetheless, the fact that the economic transformation program went through all these stages and was managed in such a way as to convince the public that the program was fair and acceptable—and something they had voted for—helped maintain public approval of the program even as its harsh effects were later felt. Polish minister of finance Balcerowicz later noted that holding free elections in Czechoslovakia before transforming the economy provided "greater political stability, necessary for founding the economic reforms" (1994, 102). Astute political organization and compromise were key elements of the social liberal strategy of reform pursued in the Czech Republic.

Compensation and Social Protection

The social liberal hybrid character of the Czechoslovak reform package was symbolized by the simultaneous passage of scenarios for economic and social change. While Václav Klaus and his team of neoliberals in the Finance Ministry took responsibility for mass privatization, liberalization of prices, and currency stabilization, actual existing social democrats in the ministry of labor planned and implemented a social dimension of reform.

The social policy program, as grafted into Klaus and Dlouhý's "radical" strategy, attempted both to address transitional social issues in a comprehensive manner and to create the basis for a system of social welfare based on Beveridge-style[1] state-guaranteed minimums supplemented by social insurance programs to emphasize individual responsibility. Transitional social policy was intended especially "to stand up to the risk of extensive unemployment as well as spiraling inflation and a drop in real wages" (Dlouhý and Klaus 1990, 67). This ambitious goal was to be achieved through "structural macroeconomic policies, labor market interventions, and welfare policies designed to preserve a social minimum." The social policy section specifically called for programs to keep large enterprises from failing during the transition to a market economy, since this could have caused mass unemployment. "There must be sufficient time given for adaptation. Otherwise even viable economic potential would be destroyed, creating mass unemployment. Active structural policy must therefore provide temporary protection to viable enterprises, especially through credit, possibly subsidy, and partly also through customs policy" (67). A further transitional measure was the compensation of individual citizens for losses of state consumer subsidies. Under communism, prices of bread, basic food items, heat, gas, electricity, transport, and so on had been subsidized through government payments to producers. Now, while eliminating these subsidies, the "radical" plan enshrined the principle of compensating individuals for this loss of "social" income. These compensations took the form of direct cash payments to all citizens, with special emphasis placed on compensating pensioners and women with young children, who were in the process of being demobilized from the labor force. This approach epitomized Czech social liberalism: individual responsibility was encouraged by a redirection, rather than a withdrawal, of state support.

The social strategy Klaus and Dlouhý were forced to adopt relied heavily on a broad range of labor market interventions. First, the "radical" plan envisioned cutting employment levels and the size of the labor force "above all of women with small children and pensioners" (62). Secondary schooling was also lengthened by one year and an aggressive system of job creation was planned. The Czech employment offices, set up to administer these programs, soon became the most efficient in the region, creating 157,000 jobs in 1991 (Burda 1992; see also Burda 1994, 1995) and a similar number each year from 1990 to 1992, or approximately 2 percent of total employment (Ham, Švejnar and Terrell 1993). Two types of jobs were created: "Socially purposeful jobs" were medium- and long-term positions in existing enterprises. Local employment offices paid employers to create these jobs for the marginal unemployed. Short-term public works jobs were also used, especially in areas with high unemployment. The employment offices were based on Western models and implemented with the assistance of the European Union and the International Labour Organisation. Czech minister of labor Milan Horálek, credited with the efficient creation of the employment office network in the Czech Republic, modestly called it "a Trabant version of the Swedish system" (quoted in Burda 1992, 18), a system that until recently provided near-full employment since the Second World War (Kowalik 1993). The social dimension of Klaus's "radical" strategy also included cash unemployment benefits, although the greater part of government resources were directed toward the "active" labor market policies described above.

While the "radical" social strategy noted that "an integral part of the development of a labor market is freeing space for the development of wages," the program intended to accomplish this gradually, maintaining wage controls during the transition to a system of branch collective bargaining similar to that of Germany. In 1990, wages were still set by the central plan according to a universal system of job classification. In 1991, this system was to be supplanted by wage controls that would limit real growth through an "excess wage tax." With tax-based wage controls, the old job classification system could be scrapped without radical changes in wage levels, since their freedom of movement would be blocked on an economy-wide basis. This was a crucial element in the radical anti-inflationary stance. The radical strategy envisioned an end to wage controls by 1992, but they were actually continued until 1995. The strategy proposed a shift to a system of labor relations based on economy-wide collective bargaining at three levels: national, branch, and enterprise. At the peak of this system would be a national tripartite council, bringing together representatives of the trade unions, employers, and government to agree on general wage levels—both indicative growth rates and agreed-upon minimum wages. The system was designed to control inflation while also allowing trade unions to guard the basic welfare interests of their members once excess wage taxes were phased out. Real wages fell sharply in 1991 but began to grow again in the first quarter of 1992 (Dyba and Svejnar 1994, 109), in contrast to Poland, where real wages fell until 1993. The establishment of a minimum wage, set in relation to the minimum cost of living, was a further fundamental element in the "radical" social strategy.

In summary, it is clear that employment and social policies played a vital role in convincing Czech society, and especially certain vulnerable and politically influential sections of society such as pensioners and heavy-industry employees, that they would survive radical reform without falling into deep poverty. Inequality increased dramatically during the Czech transformation, in a country that previously had one of the most equal income distributions in the world. But living minimums were guaranteed (Průsa 1993; Večerník 1996). This was the bedrock of the Czech transition. The establishment of a state-defined and state-sponsored social minimum, enacted through pensions, minimum wages, and family benefits, and its constant indexation over the transition period provided an important sense of security. Establishment of social minimums assuaged fear of change and provided a psychological basis for public acceptance of radical reform. In 1992, only 3 percent of families were living below the social minimum, according to Czech statistics, compared to an estimated 15 percent living in extreme poverty in Poland (Schwartz 1994).[2] In Greskovits's terminology, Czech reformers adopted compensation strategies geared heavily toward "popular sector policies targeting lower- and lower-middle-income groups," supplemented by "measures granting grace periods to economic actors in the form of phased implementation of individual adjustment policies" (1998, 139).

Neoliberals were clearly dismayed by elements of the social liberal compromise. In 1993, a prominent economic analysis firm complained that Czech policies of wage restraint, even for more qualified employees, and redistributional social policies had created a general, shared impoverishment. "The sooner the Czech government stops its policy of 'equal spreading of poverty among all,' the better" (PlanEcon 1993). Yet this was a key element of Czech social liberalism—spreading costs relatively evenly, with guaranteed minimums. A further result of these social programs was to buy the complacency of the labor unions for the "radical" program, mainly by offering them a future in the new market society, as responsible "partners" in a system of labor relations based on the German model.

The social liberal character of the Czech transformation has mostly escaped international attention because the symbol and leading propagandist of that revolution, Václav Klaus, never believed in social liberalism himself, did not initially approve of its policies, consistently downplayed their importance, and, once they were established, either reluctantly accepted them in the name of "pragmatism" or fought to dislodge them. Klaus's unwillingness even to mention the social democratic side of the Czech approach needs to be understood in the context of Klaus's broader ideological mission, to root out the communist mentality of dependence on the paternalistic state for everything, and to instill in its place a can-do, entrepreneurial, and self-reliant way of thinking (Szacki 1995, 175–81). Despite the continuing strong role of the state in the economy and redistribution in the Czech Republic, Klaus's ideology was oriented toward a hypothetical Thatcherite future. However, under "Thatcherism, Czech Style" (Rutland 1992), "worries concerning a dramatic loss of feeling of social security proved to be unsubstantiated" (Hartl 1995).

Economic Nationalism

Another little-understood aspect of the Czech social liberal strategy was its appeal to historical traditions and its inherent economic nationalism. Jessop (1990) argues that encompassing state projects very often have a national character, and indeed it is hard to think of a politician who does not sell his or her policies as being good for the nation as a whole. However, because the nationalist logic of the Czech economic program has been ignored, it will be helpful to say a few words about it here.

Czech nationalism is an odd subject. Czechs generally believe themselves to be relatively unnationalistic, especially in comparison to other Central and East European nations. The subtlety of Czech nationalism can be accounted for by the fact that it is the nationalism of a small country. This theme was first articulated by František Palacký, the historian who was a central political figure in the Czech uprising of 1848 and the "father of the nation." Dominated by the larger and more powerful imperialist nations of Germany (and more recently Russia), the Czechs always understood that self-determination would involve compromise with more powerful neighbors. Limitations of size have thus induced a certain humility, redirecting Czech national politics toward the art of the possible.

After the humiliating defeat of the 1848 Prague student uprising, the Czechs chose new battlegrounds in their fight for national sovereignty: the Vienna parliament,[3] cultural life, enterprise, and trade. Attempting to wrest the Czech nation free from the hold of German capital, the Czech bourgeoisie, small shopkeepers, tradesmen, and farmers united for self-determination through economic strength. In the countryside, this movement concentrated on developing cooperative sugar beet refineries and other food-processing industries, often with the participation of Czech local self-government bodies tolerated by the enlightened Hapsburg regime. The nationalist agricultural cooperative movement formed an important base for the Agrarian Party that dominated political life in the Czechoslovak First Republic (Teichova 1988, 29).[4] Nationality-based credit unions financed a variety of agricultural development projects (Teichova 1988, 29), while the Czech petty bourgeoisie invested their money in Czech savings banks. The Czech grand bourgeoisie developed new heavy industries, such as Škoda Works in Plzeň, with strong connections to the Czech banks, Živnostenská Banka chief among them. Živnostenská Banka, the mostly purely Czech bank (Teichova 1988, 54), became a powerful national symbol, occupying a fantastic art nouveau mosaicked building in downtown Prague.

Another unusual characteristic of Czech nationalism is the prominent role of banks in the construction of national identity (Rutland 1992). Therefore it is no surprise that the chief hero of the economic transition, Václav Klaus, worked in the Czechoslovak State Bank for sixteen years before rising to the Ministry of Finance (Leff 1997, 85). It should also be no surprise that Klaus is something of an economic nationalist, and while this has been implicitly clear to Czechs from the beginning, this observation has been mostly lost on an international community that expects nationalism to be expressed in the type of loud parades and fireworks that are notably absent in the Czech lands. Czech national holidays are more often the occasion for gardening in the country or acerbic arguments among intellectuals and political radicals, as has lately become the tradition on October 28, Czechoslovak

independence day. Czechs cannot seem to decide whether and how to cele-
brate independence from the Hapsburg monarchy, since it implies approba-
tion for a country that no longer exists. Real Czech nationalism is expressed
in a day-to-day ethic of hard work for the greater glory of national prosperity—and a Schweikian[5] attitude toward powerful foreigners.

The radical reform strategy drafted by Dlouhý and Klaus in April 1990
and approved by the government in May is full of statements and policies that
can be construed as economically nationalist. For example, the strategy document shows clearly that Klaus's famous voucher privatization program (discussed extensively in chapter 4) was partly aimed at preventing foreign
investors from buying up the disorganized and undervalued Czech economy.
Klaus and Dlouhý argued that a gradual denationalization program would
run the risk of encouraging "spontaneous privatization" whereby corrupt
members of the former *nomenklatura* would take control of state assets, often
selling them for foreign currency. The "calamitous consequence" would be "a
clearance sale of the national property abroad" (1990, 13) that was "economically and politically impassable" (26). Instead, quick voucher privatization
was intended to "give a concrete part of the national property to the domestic citizenry" (13). Even in the later phase of selling off remaining state property for money, the strategy set a clear order of preferences: "First to domestic subjects, in a further stage to foreign businessmen" (30). Second, while the
radical strategy aimed at a quick opening to the world economy, this was supposed to happen only "after the acceleration of the reform process," giving
the Czechoslovak economy time to adjust, in contrast to Poland, which
opened its markets drastically and immediately. Czechoslovak reformers initially placed a 20 percent surcharge on imports to protect domestic producers
(Dyba and Svejnar 1994, 99). Foreign trade liberalization was not a central
part of the initial plan.

Klaus continued to follow policies of economic nationalism throughout
his term in office. His dislike for international advisers became legendary. As
the privatization process went on, Klaus consistently took the side of domestic over foreign capital—in what came to be known as the Czech path *(Česká
cesta)* of privatization. In the dispute over the privatization of Czech oil
refineries, for example, Klaus publicly took the side of the *Česká cesta* against
two of his own ministers, Dlouhý and Skalický, members of the Civic Democratic Alliance (ODA), the coalition partner of the Civic Democratic Party
(ODS). While ODA stood up for a foreign sale that would bring needed
investment to the Czech refineries, Klaus argued for the Czech path through
the chemical trading company Chemapol. This was the source of a row
between Klaus and Interior Minister Jan Ruml (an ODS member), who
released information showing that the Chemapol chief had cooperated with

the State Security Service (StB) under the old regime and should have been excluded from his job by the lustration law. That Klaus, who supported the lustration law, would stand up publicly for a suspected agent angered his radical anticommunist allies. It also raised questions of exactly how close Klaus and the ODS had grown to a domestic "capitalist" class that included large parts of the former *nomenklatura.*

The nationalist appeal of the Czech transformation has its contradictions, as in the sale of the Škoda automobile factory to the German Volkswagen conglomerate. However, despite ambivalent attitudes toward the Germans, Czech nationalism is largely economic in content and limited in scope. Klaus's neoliberal critique of the EU notwithstanding, Czech nationalism fits nicely with a program of economic development geared toward integration into Western international structures. In a homage to the Old Czech politician Ladislav Rieger, who led the Czech delegation in the Vienna parliament at the time of the national awakening, Klaus echoed his words: "What we need above all is work—real, sustained work both spiritual and industrial. That will help us most rapidly to adulthood, to manly force, to power and honor" (Klaus 1994, 13).

Neoliberals Constrained

Although in 1989 Klaus wanted to do what Balcerowicz had done in Poland, placing neoliberal visions of efficiency above political concerns, he was restrained by the leaders of the government of national understanding, who insisted on attaining a democratic mandate before launching radical reforms. In contrast to Balcerowicz's cry, "There is no alternative," the yearlong debate that resulted in a democratic mandate for the Czech reforms proved crucial to public acceptance of the economic program. Eventually even Klaus became convinced of its usefulness. It lent a measure of legitimacy to the economic program that only a victorious election campaign can supply. And the compromise on social policy, the central element of Klaus's trade-off with the social democrats, softened the distributional effects of reform for a large number of people and provided the security of knowing that no one would fall below a minimum level of consumption during the transition period. The political and social astuteness of the Czech reforms are reflected in the much smoother trajectory of government popularity during the first six years of postcommunism (see fig. 6). They provided a basis for the continued popularity of the neoliberal reform project, for many years after the painful effects of neoliberal reforms were first felt.

It is important to note that social liberalism was not the preferred strat-

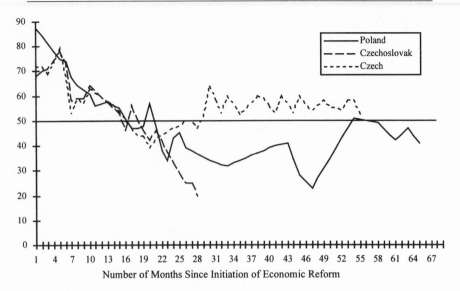

Fig. 6.   Trust in government in Poland and the Czech Republic since the initiation of economic reform (percentage of population expressing trust). (Data from CBOS [Poland] and Institute for Public Opinon Research [Czech Republic].)

egy of any one politician. Czech social liberalism arose fortuitously from political debates within Civic Forum, the government of national understanding, and the dissident community in Czechoslovakia. Whereas in Poland, neoliberals rose to power and were given free range to apply their technocratic program without limits, Czech politicians took a more cautious approach with greater compensation measures and input from social democrats.

Czechoslovakia's Big Bang

On January 1, 1991, Czechoslovakia finally launched its big-bang program of price liberalization, trade liberalization, and stabilization measures. More prices had been administratively controlled in Czechoslovakia than in Poland, so in some ways its liberalization was more radical. However, Czechoslovakia did not have the same level of macroeconomic instability, so the radical stabilization and liberalization was neither as necessary, nor as challenging, as in Poland. The effects of the Czechoslovak big bang were in some ways similar to that of Poland. Prices shot up by 58 percent in 1991 (Svejnar 1995, 7), before stabilizing at 11 percent inflation in 1992. In contrast to Poland, which experienced moderate inflation for several years after the initial shock, inflation in Czechoslovakia was conquered by the end of the year. As in Poland, the Czech Republic experienced a boom in new private economic activity, as a result of property restitution, privatization of small shops, increased entrepreneurial activity, and a rush of new goods to market. Thanks in part to stiff wage controls, real wages fell sharply, by approximately 25 percent in 1991, before recovering slightly in 1992 (Dyba and Svejnar 1995, 36). However, since wage controls had been negotiated with trade union leaders in Czechoslovakia's new tripartite council for economic and social accord, these losses did not result in labor protests, as in Poland. Indeed, a critical feature of the early Czechoslovak transition was the atmosphere of "social peace" that prevailed. Wage reductions were seen as part of a low-wage, low-unemployment bargain struck with organized labor through corporatist bargaining in the new tripartite council. While labor accepted wage reductions without protest, the government upheld its side of the low-unemployment bargain, at least in the Czech Republic.

A major difference in the impact of reform between the Czech Republic and Poland was in the extent of unemployment. While unemployment in Poland skyrocketed in the early months of transition, causing popular disenchantment with reform (Przeworski 1993), in the Czech Republic unemployment affected only a small share of the labor force. This low unemployment rate broadened popular acceptance of reform and may explain differences in support for reform between the Czech Republic and Slovakia, which experienced higher unemployment rates (Svejnar 1995, 5). Although it is harder to establish a clear connection between unemployment rates and government policy (Earle 1997), the Czech Republic had enacted a complex set of antiunemployment measures. Together, Czech social and labor market policy appear to have played a major role in extending the honeymoon period for reformers (see also Pollert 1997, 208). In the Czech Republic, government popularity stabilized after an initial sharp decline and remained above 50 percent for the first years of the transformation (see fig. 6).

Despite its evident success in allowing the implementation of neoliberal reforms to take place in an atmosphere of social peace, the social liberal compromise that dominated the early years of the Czechoslovak transformation was later challenged by two phenomena: the increasing political influence of the leading neoliberal reformer, Václav Klaus, in the Czech Republic (Pollert 1997, 210), and the split of Czechoslovakia at the end of 1992. Both caused a shift toward a more pure form of neoliberalism (Dangerfield 1997).

Václav Klaus, Technopol

Václav Klaus had fought many of the social democratic elements of the reform program while finance minister from 1989 to 1992, but he was forced to accept the social liberal compromise due to his subordinate position in government. In order to gain greater control over economic policy, Klaus built his own political party, the Civic Democratic Party (ODS), which soon became the leading party in the Czech Republic and the vehicle for his increasing personal dominance over the process of transformation in the country.

Klaus's rise to supreme control over the Czech transformation began in October 1990 when he won a surprise victory for the presidency of Civic Forum over Martin Palouš, President Havel's handpicked candidate for succession. Klaus wanted to transform the loose civic "movement" into an organized political party but met resistance from Prague dissidents who still saw Civic Forum as an organic representative of an idealized "civil society." The dissidents refused to realize that their adherence to a disorganized structure served to elevate them into positions of unquestioned power based on historical, rather than democratic, legitimacy (cf. Honajzer 1996, 16). Instead, the dissidents believed a lack of formal organization was a matter of principle and mistrusted party organization and the influence of television. One of the key Civic Forum electoral slogans in 1990 was "Parties are for partisans—Civic Forum is for everyone." The notion that Civic Forum could continue to play a role as an umbrella organization representing society as a whole was still held by many members, including President Havel. However, the *local* election managers and activists of Civic Forum were increasingly frustrated with the disorganized, arrogant intellectual leadership of the Prague dissidents. Palouš's defeat marked the demise of movement politics in the Czech Republic and the end of a number of promising political careers (Honajzer 1996, 32–33).

Election to the leadership of Civic Forum gave Klaus an opportunity to try to turn Civic Forum into a "standard" party organization that would support radical economic reform. These attempts, however, were quickly frustrated. After a short battle, Klaus found that it would be impossible to turn Civic Forum into a real political party because of the resistance of President Havel and his allies, who wanted to maintain a broad civic movement as the leading political force of the transition. After a series of contentious leadership meetings, an agreement was reached in February 1991 to split Civic Forum in two (Honajzer 1996, 41–46). Klaus became the leader of the new Civic Democratic Party (ODS). Pavel Rychetský and a number of left-leaning

Prague intellectuals sought to preserve the movement character of the old Civic Forum by founding a new Civic Movement (OH). Pavel Bratinka's Civic Democratic Alliance (ODA), which existed as a separate movement within Civic Forum from the beginning, was the third significant party to emerge out of the movement that brought down communism. Many individual movement politicians also joined the Czech Social Democratic Party (ČSSD) and the postcommunist Left Bloc. Therefore, unlike the fragmentation of Solidarity in Poland, Civic Forum broke down into a small number of partylike elements, one of which became a successful mass vote-winning party: Klaus's ODS. The ODA was also reasonably successful, although it became mainly a party of intellectuals and technocrats that never won more than 10 percent of the popular vote, mostly in Prague and Brno, and collapsed in 1997. By contrast, the Civic Movement associated with the Havel camp failed to gain representation in parliamentary elections in 1992 and quickly faded from the political scene. Before the 1996 elections, the party changed its name to the Free Democrats and, after considering a merger with the Czech Social Democratic Party, went down to a final defeat in coalition with several other small liberal parties.

Klaus's ODS played an important role in providing mass political backing for radical economic reform. Klaus showed that economic radicals who engaged in politics could win substantial support. Klaus argued publicly that his Civic Democratic Party allowed the continuation and consolidation of neoliberal reforms in the Czech lands, preventing a dramatic turn to the left. In 1994, he stated, "If there were no ODS, we would be in the same situation as Hungary and Poland, and luckily we are not." At that time, after the election of communist successor parties to power in most of the postcommunist states, Klaus called the Czech Republic an "island in a sea of strange returns of an indisputably left-wing type" (*RP*, May 27, 1994). In many ways, Klaus was correct. ODS consolidated public support for reform by winning parliamentary elections in June 1992. This allowed for the construction of a relatively stable and effective coalition government that could continue on the path chosen in 1989, while neighboring countries were moving to the left.

The ODS began operations in a strange and malleable political situation, for although Civic Forum split up just eight months after the June 1990 parliamentary elections, the government it had formed continued to rule Czechoslovakia until the end of 1992. Klaus's party held only two posts in the Civic Forum government. However, it won the allegiance of a majority of former Civic Forum parliamentary deputies, giving Klaus an independent power base in parliament in 1991 and 1992 (Stein 1994). Klaus thus became a parliamentary force that the rest of the government could not ignore. Klaus

mobilized his parliamentary delegation to pass important economic legislation, such as the large privatization act in February 1991, and positioned ODS
as an anticommunist party by voting for a lustration law that prevented
employees and collaborators of the former secret police from holding public
office for five years. Anticommunist measures had the happy side-effect for
Klaus of marginalizing left-leaning former communists and sixty-eighters.
The growing relative strength and coherence of ODS meant that by 1992, the
government appointed in 1990 was a de facto minority grouping, with Klaus
and his ODS holding the balance of power.

ODS faced its first electoral test in the elections of June 1992 and passed
with flying colors. "Standard" party organization paid off, and the fact that
ODS won the support of a vast majority of Civic Forum's election managers
gave it a great edge in the campaign. ODS won 34 percent of the vote and
ODA 6 percent, while the Pragocentric Civic Movement (OH) failed to pass
the 5 percent threshold. As in Poland, dissident elites that did not organize
parties lost elections and were ousted from power. On the contrary, elites that
did organize parties made massive gains. ODS was also extremely successful
in holding on to this mass political support between elections. From June
1992 to June 1996, ODS's electorate held steady at around 26–30 percent.
With only twenty-two thousand members (Reschová and Syllová 1994, 13),
the ODS has played an effective role as a lean avant-garde party for the market revolution in the Czech lands.

The Split of Czechoslovakia

Klaus always believed that only a strong, unified state could provide the basis
for radical economic reform. In November 1991, Václav Klaus felt obliged to
"give a warning that today's maimed federation [is] not capable of guaran-
teeing a continuation of economic reform" (quoted in Žák 1995, 262). Klaus
was worried about the left-wing parties in parliament and constructed the
ODS to counteract them. But Klaus was also concerned with centralization
and decision-making power. For this reason, he opposed all the loose forms
of federation or confederation between the Czech Republic and Slovakia discussed in 1991 and 1992. At the time, some politicians proposed a confederation in which an independent Slovakia would have its own central bank, its
own currency, and its own foreign and trade policies. Klaus wanted a strong
federation or no federation.

While there are a number of explanations for the split of Czechoslovakia,
Klaus's ultimatum of a strong federation or no federation after the June 1992
elections was probably the single greatest cause of the demise of the state. Cer-

tainly the split of Czechoslovakia did not follow from any widespread public distaste for the continuation of a common state. Indeed, there was never a majority in either republic that wanted a split, and "most citizens continued to prefer a common state even as political leaders negotiated the end of the federation" (Wolchik 1995, 232). For this reason, it is not surprising that a constitutionally mandated referendum was never held in either republic (again contrary to the wishes of the majority of the population): it would never have passed. Czechoslovakia's demise was negotiated and dictated from above.

The "velvet divorce" was decided by the top political leaders to emerge in the Czech Republic and Slovakia from the June 1992 parliamentary elections. Václav Klaus's ODS won 34 percent of the vote in the Czech lands, and Vladimír Mečiar's Movement for a Democratic Slovakia (HZDS) won a similar percentage in Slovakia. The two leaders were committed to different visions for their common state. In postelection talks, Klaus presented his ultimatum of a strong federation or no federation. Mečiar, however, was constrained by his preelection program, which included five possible resolutions of the Czech-Slovak dilemma, none of which involved total capitulation to the Czech side. Of course, the widely differing electoral programs of these two parties speak volumes about the differences of understanding and misunderstanding that existed between the two republics. It is often claimed now that these differences had made a split inevitable. Yet the record suggests that political opportunism played a large part. It seems likely that both politicians found it in their own best interest to divide the country. Klaus gained the ability to perform his economic therapy on the Czech Republic, and Mečiar became the father of an independent Slovakia. The split of Czechoslovakia resulted from calculations of political expediency on the part of two politicians and did not reflect the will of the nation or a decision by a state body. Legislatures in both republics were only asked to ratify the split once it had become irreversible (Stein and Orenstein 1995).

The demise of Czechoslovakia left Klaus greater freedom to revolutionize the Czech economy and society with less hindrance from social democrats. Mečiar's victory in Slovakia had raised the possibility that reform in Czechoslovakia would be impeded by a leftist majority in parliament. The new Czech parliament, by contrast, was far more reliably right-wing. Klaus was able to form a solid majority government with the reform-oriented ODA and the Christian Democratic Party–People's Party (KDU-ČSL). Electoral results in the Czech lands thus allowed a distinct turn toward neoliberal economic policies, while those in Slovakia and Czechoslovakia as a whole did not. The loss of Slovakia reduced the pressure for a more gradual, social democratic transformation and elevated Klaus to near-complete control over the course of economic policy.

Neoliberalism in Power

Between 1992 and 1996, Prime Minister Klaus personally dominated Czech economic policy. His coalition government held a sizable majority in parliament. Klaus's Civic Democratic Party held a majority of posts within the government and its all-important economic council, a minicabinet where most important economic decisions were made before being presented to the full cabinet. Thanks to party and coalition discipline, more than 90 percent of government legislative proposals passed parliament (Reschová and Syllová 1994), a level similar to that of many consolidated West European democracies. President Havel rarely used his veto powers on economic policy matters.

During 1992, Klaus was mainly concerned with the split of Czechoslovakia, so he refrained from launching any divisive policy changes. However, starting in 1993, Klaus began chipping away at the social liberal compromise that guided the early years of the Czechoslovak transition and pushed economic policy in a more neoliberal direction (Orenstein 1994; Večerník 1996; Pollert 1997; Dangerfield 1997). The main target was the social welfare system. Here Klaus began a policy of reducing the generosity of social benefits, raising eligibility criteria, and where possible moving away from universal benefits and toward targeting (Večerník 1996, 196–99). In the labor market arena, Klaus let the minimum wage devalue and publicly opposed continued corporatist-style negotiation in the Czech Republic's tripartite council for social and economic accord. Under this more confrontational approach to labor relations, the "social peace" that had characterized the Czechoslovak transition began to break down in 1994 and 1995 with a spate of strikes and strike threats by railway workers, doctors, and teachers (Pollert 1997, 213). Klaus maintained firm budget discipline, making the Czech Republic the only postcommunist state to maintain a balanced budget. Klaus also placed great emphasis on rapid privatization and moved ahead with his flagship voucher privatization, while Slovakia suspended the program. In addition, the Czech Republic maintained an open trade regime, a key element of the neoliberal program (Dangerfield 1997, 446–49). Thanks to these policies, and his strong free-market rhetoric, Klaus became known in the West as one of the most prominent neoliberal reformers in Central and Eastern Europe. In 1997, the Cato Institute published a book of his essays translated into English, as part of an effort to canonize him as one of the great liberal theorists of transition.

On the other hand, Klaus remained partly constrained by the original social liberal compromise. Klaus often faced quite serious resistance when he moved away from previous policies. As a result, he was forced to move gradually, at the cost of public support, or not at all. For instance, Klaus was not able to substantially reduce the level of average retirement pensions or the social minimum during his term in office (Dangerfield 1997, 467). He did, however, manage to increase the retirement age starting in 1995, and to introduce targeting of family benefits in 1996 (Večerník 1996), but only at the expense of increased labor turmoil and a loss of public support. Klaus was also blamed for an unpopular reform of the health insurance system that created a dozen or more private health insurance funds, some of which went bankrupt or failed to pay providers on time. Popularity of the opposition Czech Social Democratic Party grew rapidly in 1995 and 1996, largely by speaking out against Klaus's attacks on the welfare state. In fresh elections in 1996, the Social Democratic Party came close to unseating the Klaus government (Saxonberg 1999).

Klaus always put a premium on maintaining public faith in the transition (Blejer and Coricelli 1995, 105). As a result, Klaus had to walk a narrow line between his neoliberal ideals and social policy necessities. In January 1995, Klaus told the *Denní Telegraf* newspaper that "we surely cannot be a kind of social state that would be putting the social aspect above everything else. That would be totally false. . . . At the same time we do not want to be a state that would underestimate the social dimension. It follows that exactly the maneuvering between these two extremes is the ODS' attitude, and I believe it to be right" (BBC, January 14, 1995). Klaus maneuvered toward neoliberal social policies, but slowly and carefully, in order to maintain political support for reform. He was always careful to explain and justify his policies in public and wrote a weekly newspaper column that was published in one of the main daily papers, in addition to regular TV appearances.

In some areas, Klaus kept the social liberal compromise intact and made no progress at all in implementing neoliberal policy. For instance, Klaus continued the low-wage, low-unemployment policies of the previous government throughout his term in office, despite his occasional public calls for more unemployment and enterprise bankruptcies. Klaus also continued housing subsidies and rent control. There is some question whether these policies represented Klaus's own preferences for a type of gradualism (Tucker et al. 1997), or his perceptions of what was politically feasible at the time. Yet Klaus made significant progress in implementing a neoliberal agenda in the Czech Republic from 1992 to 1996. Privatization of the economy was achieved. Integration with Western markets continued apace. Liberalization was nearly complete, although wage regulations remained in place until 1995.

A large part of what made the Czech transformation so unusual in Central and Eastern Europe was the high level of government approval registered during and after the "big bang" of January 1, 1991. Czech government approval ratings fell from the euphoric heights reached in 1989, but, in contrast to Poland, stabilized at a net positive level after the split of Czechoslovakia in 1993. In Poland, government popularity continued its downward trajectory, with the Suchocka government retaining support from only 30 percent of the population. Moreover, Klaus's government maintained this level of popularity for years by projecting an image of successful and relatively painless transition. Only in 1996 did the glow begin to fade, due to Klaus's attacks on the welfare state, increasingly confrontational labor relations, and an escalating series of financial scandals that began to uncover cracks in the edifice of the Czech miracle.

The End of Neoliberalism

Along with Klaus's attack on the welfare state that began in 1993 and continued in earnest until 1996, two interrelated factors combined to destroy public faith in his stewardship of reform: a string of bank failures, starting in 1995, and a concurrent series of scandals over party finances. The connections between the two were not obvious initially and only became clear after the June 1996 elections, in which Klaus's Civic Democratic Party won a slight plurality but was able to form a minority government only with the help of two renegade deputies elected on the Social Democratic ticket. As problems in the banking sector began to reveal evidence of widespread and massive fraud and public losses, as these losses began to have a detrimental effect on the economy as a whole, as investigations pointed to unsavory connections with the ruling party, and as party finances were progressively thrown into question, the evidence of corruption mounted and eventually poured down on the Civic Democratic Party. This forced a split in the party and led to the resignation of the government and the call for new elections in June 1998. When it finally became clear that the Czech Republic was paying a high price for the mistaken reform policies of the Klaus government and evident corruption, a search for alternatives began to take shape.

Bank failures provided the first clear sign that something was wrong with the Czech economy. A medium-sized, private bank called Banka Bohemia failed in early 1994, with losses of around $350 million, after it was found to have issued nearly $2 billion of fraudulent loan guarantees abroad. The head of another new small private bank, Kreditní a Průmyslová Banka, was jailed in December 1994 for embezzlement and falsifying bank data. A handful of other banks failed, after having been emptied out by their managers and owners, who used the banks to borrow money on the interbank market and then lend it to various "failed" pet projects. Václav Klaus successfully portrayed these early bank failures as "traffic accidents" on the road to a market economy, cases of corruption that were an unfortunate aspect of capitalist development. The Czech National Bank took over the banks, insured deposits, and prevented panic from spreading—at a cost of hundreds of millions of korun of taxpayer money.

Foreign advisers recommended that the Klaus government tighten regulation of the banking and securities markets, but this Klaus was reluctant to do, since it ran counter to his free-market ideology (*Economist,* May 31, 1997). When critics, including the Social Democratic opposition in parliament, argued for stricter control of securities trading, Klaus berated them for attacking privatization as a whole. Despite what now look like clear warning signs, before the June 1996 elections, almost nobody in the Czech Republic saw the deep systemic trouble in the banking system. The full picture only became widely known in 1997.

Two megacrises in 1996 and 1997 finally put the whole country on notice that something was wrong. At the end of 1995, it became public knowledge that an aggressive financial group called Motoinvest was buying up shares in privatization investment funds and then "greenmailing" their management companies into buying back these shares at a premium rate—or risk losing control. Motoinvest used two small private banks, Plzeňská Banka and Kreditní Banka, to borrow money on the interbank market to finance their takeover attempts. In 1995, Motoinvest managed a leveraged buyout of the fifth largest Czech bank, Agrobanka, along with its investment fund portfolio. Motoinvest then used its position in Agrobanka to launch a bold attempt to take over the Czech Savings Bank, which controls 65 percent of deposits in the country. Regulators had previously let Motoinvest alone. But once the center of the Czech banking system was in danger of being taken over by leveraged-buyout specialists, the Czech central bank became worried, and regulators finally began to inspect Motoinvest's predatory practices. Although an investigation was officially launched in 1991, it was not until 1996 that regulators found Kreditní Banka to be in serious trouble, having been hollowed out by Motoinvest in order to finance its acquisitions spree. Agrobanka was in danger of meeting the same fate and becoming an empty shell, with the government left to repay depositors. In August 1996, just after the June elections, regulators closed down Kreditní Banka and revoked its banking license, assuming losses of $450 million. Kreditní Banka officials were charged with various crimes, including false reporting. Agrobanka was placed under special bank administration.

The magnitude of Kreditní Banka's losses shocked the public, but the news kept getting worse and worse. It turned out that Motoinvest had sold Kreditní Banka to the largest Czech insurance company, Česká Pojišťovná, just before its problems were discovered, so that the partially state-owned insurance company was liable for all of Kreditní Banka's losses. Since Česká

Pojišťovná did not have $450 million, the Czech government sold a controlling share in Česká Pojišťovná to another aggressive financial group, First Privatization Fund (FPF), to raise the money. It was later revealed that FPF managers had close personal relationships with Minister of Finance Ivan Kočárník. In short, the Kreditní Banka failure cost the Czech government control over one of the largest financial institutions in the country—Česká Pojišťovná—and appeared to reward one group of politically connected private investors at the expense of another. Czech Social Democrats lobbied angrily to set up a parliamentary commission to investigate the matter. The establishment of such a commission in October 1996 marked the first time parliament had empowered itself to investigate financial corruption in privatization since 1989.

In March 1997, scandal struck again as one of the largest privatization investment funds in the country, C. S. Fond, was "tunneled" out to the tune of $46 million. "Tunneling" entered the Czech vocabulary at this time and came to mean any transaction in which the management of an investment fund emptied out its assets to the detriment of small shareholders. In this case, C. S. Fond had been taken over by Motoinvest, which transformed its voucher privatization funds into unregulated "holdings," transferred all their assets into cash, and then traded this cash to a shell company, UMANA, for some worthless shares of a regional chicken farm. Thousands of small shareholders who had participated in Klaus's voucher privatization program lost the total value of their shares. What particularly enraged the public was that government regulators had explicitly approved of the transaction. C. S. Fond's depository bank, Plzeňská Banka, had been under state administration since the beginning of 1997 and the Ministry of Finance charged with monitoring large transactions. That such an obvious fraud could occur under the noses of regulators in the Ministry of Finance utterly destroyed Czech popular confidence in bank regulation. It pointed to major lapses in oversight, if not outright corrupt practices by representatives of the state. Yet the Ministry of Finance did not fire or even discipline the officials responsible but instead tried to obfuscate the matter by launching yet another inconclusive investigation. This time, however, journalists began to call for the resignation of Deputy Minister of Finance Vladimir Rudlovčák and Minister of Finance Ivan Kočárník, both of whom eventually fell.

Outrage over these scandals was quickly overwhelmed by a serious balance-of-payments and exchange-rate crisis that crashed down upon the Czech Republic in the spring of 1997. While a run on the currency had some independent causes—the Czech Republic had a high current-account deficit, growth had been set back by restrictive monetary policies initiated in 1996, and the government adhered fiercely to a now overvalued nominal exchange rate—foreign investors' confidence in the Czech Republic was deeply hurt by the banking crisis. Not only had the government allowed corrupt practices to continue, but these practices had magnified in scale to the point that they were destroying the state budget and threatening the health of the economy. The financial system had become a cancer on the country, moving rapidly to take over whatever it could and destroying everything in its path. Václav Klaus reacted to the multiple crises afflicting the Czech miracle by issuing two "little packages" *(balíčeks)* of economic measures in rapid succession in April and May. His *balíčeks* reduced budgetary spending, introduced import restrictions, and promised a new effort to regulate the banking sector and financial markets. The central bank, meanwhile, lost a pitched battle to defend the value of the currency, and after spending more than $1 billion, the Czech koruna was allowed to float downward in what amounted to a forced devaluation. In contrast to 1989, when Klaus appeared as a vigorous figure with a proactive strategy for economic transformation, in 1997 he seemed to be reacting to events, unable to stem the tide of bad news.

Decline and Fall

Klaus was increasingly held responsible for the atmosphere of corruption in the country. Václav Havel accused the Klaus government of having no long-term plan and putting the country in a bad mood *(blbou náladu)*. Robert Pergl of Vana, Pergl and Partners, a law firm representing the victims of two prominent "tunneling" cases and one of the first lawyers to call for higher professional standards, pointed to widespread government responsibility for the financial morass, in a December 1, 1997, interview with the Czech journal *Success.* "Legislation is lacking, laws are full of holes or too liberal. When the capital markets were developed here, we had laws that were far more lax than in the West, where people are educated and have morality and ethics. I wish it were otherwise, but here they do not. Moreover, I am convinced that our prime minister [Klaus] underestimated the legal side of things. He had all these beautiful macroeconomic calculations, but things work differently." Klaus's distaste for regulation backfired in the financial sector, and lack of policy alternation perpetuated his mistakes.

Moreover, his ODS was soon buried in an avalanche of party finance scandals. The scandals that became public in 1997 showed the ODS to be profiting from privatization kickbacks. In particular, the party received several large gifts from two fictitious donors (including a dead Hungarian) that proved to come from a businessman, Milan Šrejber, who had won a success-ful bid to gain ownership of one of the major Moravian steelworks under the

ODS government. When it further became known to members of the ODS executive committee that the party had a "black" account in Switzerland with millions of dollars in it from unnamed sources, party leaders began to resign (*HN,* November 25–28, 1997). Executive committee members were enraged to find that party finances were being run behind their backs by Klaus and a few corrupt operatives. Further revelations suggested that under Klaus's supervision, the party ran two ledgers and had misled the public about its finances in annual reports.

These scandals revealed a great deal about how the ODS was run. The Klaus party included not only committed neoliberal revolutionaries led by Václav Klaus and centrist leaders like the so-called Pilip-Ruml faction and Josef Zieleniec, but also shady opportunists out to make a quick buck by peddling government influence. The centrist politicians had called for the party to adopt a more explicit political platform, in part to counter the authoritarian style of Klaus within the party. Klaus demanded complete obedience to his economic and political line, regardless of how it changed over time. One of his greatest political skills had been to talk like a Friedmanite or Thatcherite liberal and yet act like a social democrat when necessary.

Klaus resigned in November 1997. Shortly thereafter, more than half of the ODS parliamentary deputies left to form a new parliamentary party, the Freedom Union, under the leadership of Jan Ruml. Klaus's rump ODS began an ill-starred effort to clean up its finances by appointing a bright young financial manager, Luděk Nezmar, and hiring Deloitte and Touche, one of the major accounting firms in the West, to conduct an audit. But Nezmar was forced to resign in February 1998 when it became known that his personal businesses had repeatedly defaulted on multimillion-koruna debts, including an unpaid forty- to sixty-million-koruna loan from Investiční a Poštovní Banka, a bank partly owned by the state. An ODS press spokesman said the party had known about Nezmar's debts when it appointed him, raising serious questions about the party's capacity to deal with the crisis. Later in February, the head of ODS's former government coalition partner, the Civic Democratic Alliance (ODA), was forced to resign after allegations that the party had been paid substantial contributions from private and semiprivatized Czech companies through a front company registered in the Virgin Islands.

Partial Left Turn

The Czech Republic's economic crisis was undoubtedly prolonged by the decision to wait six months before calling parliamentary elections in June

1998 and by the inconclusive outcome of those elections. Although a policy shift did emerge, toward better regulation of financial markets, greater transparency in bank privatization, new industrial policies, judicial reform, and a controversial "clean hands" campaign, the incomplete shift of power weakened their impact.

The caretaker government set up in January 1998 under former central bank head Josef Tošovský launched a set of much-needed economic reforms that responded to international concerns about excessive corruption and poor corporate governance in the Czech Republic (*HN*, various issues). One of its first acts was to pass a law creating a Securities Commission (Komise pro cenné papiry) to regulate financial markets. It also finalized the privatization of one major bank, Investiční a Poštovní Banka, and initiated the privatization of three others in January and took measures to improve regulation and strengthen the position of smaller private banks. The new government sold troubled Agrobanka to GE Capital in June 1998 (*HN*, June 22, 1998). All of these measures were critical to turning around the troubled situation in Czech financial markets and had been impeded for years by the Klaus government. This provides a clear instance of how essential democratic policy alternation is to correct reform errors and enable crucial reforms to occur.

However, this government was only a caretaker until new elections in June 1998, and its tenuous legitimacy and parliamentary backing weakened its effectiveness during the parliamentary election campaign. Klaus used the opportunity of being out of power to criticize the caretaker government and mobilize discontent with the status quo. While the Czech Social Democratic Party won the elections, the six-month hiatus allowed Klaus's ODS to reorganize in an unexpected comeback, winning 27.7 percent of the vote, to the Social Democrats' 32.3 percent. Freedom Union, made up of politicians who split from the scandal-ridden ODS and the collapse ODA, won only 8.6 percent of the vote. Long and complicated coalition negotiations ensued, with the Social Democrats unable to form a majority without support from Klaus's former partners, the Christian Democratic–People's Party and the Freedom Union. Ironically, Klaus could have formed a majority coalition with his former partners but refused to do so because of mutual animosities (Saxonberg 1999). In the end, the Czech Social Democratic Party decided to found a weak minority government on the basis of an "opposition agreement" with the ODS. Klaus's party offered its tacit support for the government in exchange for leadership positions in parliament and an agreement to seek a joint constitutional reform that would strengthen the hand of large parties in government formation.

The Czech Social Democratic Party initiated a number of significant changes in government economic policy. It launched a controversial "clean hands" campaign against corruption, an EU-approved reform of the justice system, a new industrial policy that involved the renationalization of several large, troubled enterprises, as well as changes to social policy programs and the adoption of the European Charter of Rights and Freedoms. However, much of this agenda was fiercely opposed by the right in parliament and failed to pass. Most significant was the manner in which the "clean hands" campaign was scuttled by opposition from Klaus's ODS (Saxonberg 1999, 110).

By mid-1999, the social democratic government was widely acknowledged to be at an impasse, causing the European Union to criticize Czech progress toward accession for a second year in a row. Lack of a majority in parliament caused weak policy alternation in the Czech Republic and the sputtering out of a left alternative. Weakness of policy alternation also contributed to the depth of the economic recession, through its impact on investor confidence. Partly as a result of these concerns, the Czech parliament in May 2000 passed a new electoral law that would enhance the position of larger parties and spur policy alternation between strong center-left and center-right parties.

Conclusions

Despite the persistence in power of a celebrated neoliberal economic reformer from 1989 to 1997, Czech economic performance has been worse than Poland's since 1993. Furthermore, its reform process stalled and fell into disrepute. What accounts for this striking trend? One explanation is that Klaus failed by adhering to the path of social liberalism and not engaging in radical enough reform (Tucker et al. 1997). But this explanation does not account for the fact that many problems of the Czech Republic arose from excessively rapid voucher privatization, a key element of the neoliberal program, and Klaus's ideologically liberal decision not to regulate financial markets.

An alternative explanation is that the persistence of a single group of reformers, and a single proreform party, allowed for the continuation of critical reform mistakes (Kołodko 1999), as well as the entrenchment of a small group of rent-seeking interests (Hellman 1998). The Czech crisis was clearly caused in large part by policy mistakes made by the Klaus regime, which were fiercely criticized by its opponents and by foreign institutions but were never corrected. Many of these mistakes were made because powerful, rent-seeking interests had infiltrated the leading reform party and caused it to perpetuate them. Persistence of reformers in power therefore does not necessarily offer the benefits suggested by both neoliberal and social democratic theory of transition, with their different visions of an optimal, long-term strategy for balanced growth. Changing mistaken policies normally requires a change of government because of the stickiness of policy commitments (cf. Hellman 1998).

The problems of the Czech transition in 1999 demonstrated the need for policy alternation among strong governments with different proreform visions and strategies, as occurred in Poland. There, right governments pursued efficiency-oriented neoliberal policies, while left governments took a more cohesion-oriented approach. Both have contributed to the achievement of market-oriented reforms in a democratic framework. In the Czech Republic, weak governments since 1996 prevented a change in course that would have corrected some of the most serious mistaken policies of the long-lived Klaus regime and dislodged its rent-seeking networks. Nonetheless, even in the Czech Republic, some policy alternation has occurred and may set the groundwork for an unexpected turnaround thanks to policy learning on both the right and the left.

The following chapter deepens this analysis by looking at the critical policy area of privatization, to show that policy alternation in Poland produced surprisingly positive economic results, while disciplined adherence to early reform blueprints in the Czech Republic did not. Reform errors in the Czech Republic and the perverse positive effects of contentious reform in Poland provide strong evidence for the benefits of democratic policy alternation in a complex socioeconomic transformation.

Privatization

Fast privatization was a key element of neoliberal transition programs in postcommunist Europe. The success of neoliberal economic programs depended on enterprises spontaneously adjusting to market signals. Liberalize markets and stabilize the macroeconomic environment, neoliberals argued, and enterprises will suddenly adopt market rational behavior—but not if they remain state-owned. Only private enterprises could be trusted to respond rationally to market signals, organize production efficiently, and generate profits. Privatization was "an indispensable condition of an efficient control of management performance" (Frydman and Rapaczynski 1994, 13). Therefore, most neoliberal economists put a major stress on fast privatization (Johnson and Loveman 1995, 32).

However, fast privatization in postcommunist Europe presented several technical challenges that quickly became the subject of a vast literature in economics and political science. First, the extent of privatization far exceeded any previous experience and rendered most preexisting models obsolete (Błaszczyk and Dąbrowski 1994, 92; Frydman and Rapaczynski 1994, 156; Klaus 1997, 71). Postcommunist countries were privatizing 70, 80, or 90 percent of their economies, not a few isolated enterprises, as in previous experiences in the West. Second, postcommunist countries lacked capital; there was simply not enough domestic capital available to purchase all the companies on offer, and foreign investors were in short supply. It therefore would be impossible to sell all enterprises for cash. Third, privatization was expected to face strong political obstacles from entrenched "insider" interests in state-owned enterprises and a sense of entitlement on the part of the "people," who had been told that state property belonged to them (Lieberman 1997, 1). This too was seen as a reason to speed privatization (Blanchard et al. 1991, xiv). As the prominent public choice theorist Mancur Olson put it, "The dangers of the conflicts of interest inherent in privatization argue that a society will be better off if it can get through this process as quickly as possible" (1992, 74). Innovative methods of privatization were needed to overcome the challenges of fast privatization in lands without capital.

Neoliberal economists quickly developed a technical solution to the dilemmas of postcommunist privatization, called "mass" or "voucher" privatization, that incorporated some elements of social equity. Under voucher privatization, governments would give away shares in enterprises to all participating adult citizens in exchange for vouchers that could be purchased at a nominal price. Voucher privatization quickly received the endorsement of international organizations and the mainstream of the Western economic profession (Lipton and Sachs 1990; Blanchard et al. 1991). Many international organizations, including the World Bank and Organisation for Economic Cooperation and Development, sponsored seminars extolling the virtues of voucher privatization (Simoneti and Tříska 1994, 5–6; Tuveri and Linn 1997, vii). Groups of prominent economists and lawyers drew up rival plans for the best voucher scheme, considering all its technical aspects in detail (Lipton and Sachs 1990; Blanchard et al. 1991; Frydman and Rapaczynski 1994, 2–3). What was particularly attractive about voucher privatization was the way it seemed to solve the problem of quick privatization, while at the same time achieving fairness and popular support (Blanchard et al. 1991; Coffee 1996, 119). It served neoliberal goals of efficiency by combining them with those of social cohesion. As Lieberman (1994, 172) put it:

> A [mass privatization program] is a highly political process, which under favorable circumstances, such as in the Czech Republic, has served its intended purpose. It has created 8.5 million voucher holders, most of whom have become new shareholders. It has created solid political support for the reform government led by Prime Minister Klaus and it has served as the focal point in the transition to a market economy.

The Czech Republic embraced the voucher method and quickly privatized a majority of its state-owned enterprises (Desai and Plocková 1997, 191; Coffee 1996). By the end of 1995, the Czech Republic had approved privatization plans for 3,552 of the 4,800 state-owned enterprises existing at the outset of transition (Kotrba et al. 1999, 12–15). Approximately half of these, 1,849 to be exact, were privatized by the controversial voucher method that formed the centerpiece of the Czech mass privatization effort (Desai and Plocková 1997, 191). The program distributed an equal number of vouchers to all citizens who paid a nominal participation fee of approximately thirty-five dollars (Kotrba et al. 1999, 19). Individuals then used these vouchers to bid for company shares, educating millions of people about the workings of a capitalist economy and enabling widespread share ownership. The idea was that this would enhance people's perception of the fairness of economic transition and distribute state-owned enterprises quickly into private hands.

Popularity of the voucher program was intended to shore up support for market reform, and thus enable a reform government to stay in office long enough to implement privatization. To a large extent, Czech voucher privatization was successful in this regard. According to Czech sociologists Večerník and Matějů, "Voucher privatization was indeed not only an economic operation but to a certain extent also a political act. Vouchers were a kind of election ballot for the chosen transformation strategy and a symbol of its economic returns in the future" (1999, 75). Public opinion evidence shows that participation in the voucher program correlates with overall support for economic transformation. In 1996, 79 percent of those who participated in both waves of voucher privatization in the Czech Republic declared themselves satisfied with the process of reform (Frydman, Murphy, and Rapaczynski 1998, 35). Furthermore, "Satisfaction with privatization progressively increases from the left side of the political spectrum to the right" (Večerník and Matějů 1999, 75), and support for Klaus's coalition government was higher among people who believed they had benefited from voucher privatization. The perceived success of the voucher program clearly contributed to political stability and government longevity in the Czech Republic, which in turn allowed the Klaus government to stay in power long enough to implement its privatization plans. Klaus's victory in the Czech Republic in 1992 enabled him to pursue a second wave of voucher privatization, virtually finishing the process by the time of the next elections in June 1996. By that time, 74 percent of the Czech economy was in private hands, up from 12 percent in 1990 (Kotrba et al. 1999, 7).

Meanwhile in Poland, government instability, parliamentary fragmentation, and policy alternation went hand in hand. Lieberman (1994, 172) writes that "in Poland, the [mass privatization program] has become a bone of contention in the highly fragmented Sejm (lower house of the Polish parliament) which has blocked the program during the last three years." As governments came and went, Poland repeatedly delayed its voucher privatization program, shrank it in size (Frydman, Murphy, and Rapaczynski 1998, 29–30), went through a series of competing privatization initiatives, and managed to privatize a much smaller share of state-owned enterprises during the early years of transition (Johnson and Loveman 1995).

Poland's free market fundamentalists split between those who wanted to adopt traditional cash sale methods of privatization and those who wanted a faster method of transfer (Błaszczyk and Dąbrowski 1994, 93–94; Gomułka and Jasiński 1994, 224). Poland's powerful worker self-management lobby, moreover, wanted direct worker participation in company ownership and control. The result of battles between these disparate privatization blueprints was the adoption of a hodgepodge 1990 privatization law that allowed for multiple methods of privatization (Gomułka and Jasiński 1994, 222–23). With frequent government turnover, no decisive single strategy of privatization emerged from the long political debates in Poland. Instead, conflict emerged around most major privatization programs, and progress was slowed. "The best time from the political point of view . . . was lost" (Błaszczyk and Dąbrowski 1994, 113). Privatization gained negative connotations for most voters, and no method achieved widespread popularity, except for employee buyouts (Kolarska-Bobinska 1994, 111). Observers argued that Poland's lack of progress on privatization undermined its reputation abroad and the progress of reform (Kowalik 1994, 141).

Fast privatization for a time was seen as the greatest achievement of the Czech transformation, while Poland was widely regarded as a laggard in this area. Government stability and the reelection of reformers allowed privatization to proceed without a hitch in the Czech Republic between 1991 and 1995. Democratic policy instability in Poland, meanwhile, hampered reform. For a while, the Czech Republic was held up as a model of privatization success, but soon the tables began to turn. After a few years, performance of voucher-privatized firms began to disappoint most analysts and observers. Czech enterprises were widely accused of being inefficient and lacking restructuring, partly as a result of the voucher program. Meanwhile, economic growth in Poland took off, despite a relative lack of large-scale privatization. Instead, private business in Poland expanded rapidly from the creation of small, new private enterprises, which often leased or bought assets from old state firms (Johnson and Loveman 1995). Lack of state enterprise privatization did not hinder this process. At the time of this writing, voucher privatization is widely considered to have been a costly error in every country where it was tried, including Russia, Kazakhstan, Slovenia, and the Czech Republic. It did not promote enterprise efficiency as effectively as other methods of privatization and caused a number of related problems, such as financial market distress. The failure of this widely touted transformation project, voucher privatization, should give pause to those who argue that "holding the course of reform" is the best method. In the case of Poland, democratic policy alternation produced better results than consistent reform in the Czech Republic. And even in the Czech Republic, evidence shows that important privatization policy corrections were finally enabled in 1997–98, when the reform government of Václav Klaus fell from power and a new government was able to enact changes that began to fix some of the major problems caused by voucher privatization. The case of privatization shows that democratic policy alternation can be a powerful tool for avoiding and correcting major reform mistakes.

The Czech Model

Czech mass privatization was a model of economic policy design in postcommunist Europe. It was implemented early and decisively in the process of transition. It was a stable policy, kept in place with only minor revisions over the course of four years (1991–95), and it fully achieved its goals (Desai and Plocková 1997, 190). It was responsible for the quickest and most extensive privatization process in the region (Lieberman 1997, 5), placing nearly the entire economy in private hands. It also garnered extraordinary public support for such an inherently controversial program, due to its evident fairness—all citizens could receive an equal number of privatization vouchers, used to bid for company shares. This perceived fairness underpinned the stability of this policy and the political success of its primary author, finance minister and later prime minister Václav Klaus. Czech privatization won the admiration of the international financial community and became a model for other countries in the region (Estrin and Stone 1997, 173; Young 1997, 43). Yet ultimately, despite its medium-term political success and achievement of its programmatic goals, Czech voucher privatization was widely judged a failure—and one that has deeply harmed Czech economic performance (IMF 1999b, Kornai 2000, 4). Czech privatization exemplifies the reasons why policy stability may not always be desirable, particularly in transition environments. Policy stability may allow particular reform programs to continue, but it also perpetuates reform errors, enables corrupt practices to develop, and prevents policy corrections that foster reform learning.

Planning for Reform

Planning for privatization in Czechoslovakia began in 1990, immediately after the "velvet revolution" that chased Czechoslovakia's communist leaders from power and installed a government of national unity that was charged with planning economic reforms and preparing for free elections in June 1990. Václav Klaus, finance minister in the new government, assembled a team of economic advisers to grapple with one of the fundamental problems of transformation—how to turn over nearly the entire stock of state-owned enterprises into private hands, and to do so in a manner that was widely viewed as fair—and in keeping with the principle that this was formally the people's property, under socialist law. The answer to this problem was a dramatic voucher privatization that would place a majority of shares in the hands of the people (Lieberman 1997; Coffee 1996, 119).

The initial stages of debate within the government of national unity were dominated by controversy between "radicals" and "gradualists." Klaus wanted to quickly transfer state property into private hands. Gradualists thought that the state should more carefully manage the process of enterprise transition, spreading it out over a longer period of time. The chief gradualist, Deputy Prime Minister Valtr Komárek, wanted "professional management with long-term interests and the gradual selling of shares" in state-owned firms with a 51 percent stake in leading enterprises remaining in state ownership (Komárek 1993, 97). Komárek thought that this formula would enhance enterprise performance more quickly and cheaply than wholesale privatization.

Though radicals and gradualists held opposing views about the objectives and methods of privatization, they agreed on one thing: enhancing central government's power to dispose of state-owned enterprises through a process of "commercialization" or transformation of socialist enterprises with their multiple stakeholders into joint-stock companies owned by a single state agency. This was achieved in the Law on State Enterprises that was passed in April 1990 (Frydman et al. 1993, 52–53). Komárek spoke for both sides when he argued that commercialization would facilitate "stripping [enterprises] of state control without endless debates, discussions, the limits of which have not been defined beforehand," even though this "means to increase temporarily the role of the state" (BBC, April 25, 1990).

Soon after presenting the Law on State Enterprises to parliament in April 1990, however, Komárek fell from power, and Klaus's radical strategy of economic transformation won the approval of the government. In order to enact Klaus's privatization program, the government needed to introduce a "large privatization" act, pass it through parliament, create enabling institutions, and win and maintain public support, all difficult tasks requiring a great deal of political work. Yet "insider" interests were no longer able to block privatization at the enterprise level, as they did in Poland.

When Klaus won his battle with the gradualists in April 1990, he set about planning for privatization and the rest of his economic reform program. Although he would have liked to have moved sooner, the launching of reforms had to be delayed until after free parliamentary elections in June 1990, and until the new parliament could pass key economic reform laws. The first priority was passing the overall Scenario of Economic Reform in September 1990. This experience forced Klaus into parliament and convinced him of the need to organize his own political party to support reform. Klaus was elected head of Civic Forum in October 1990, and he began working the corridors of parliament and the national press in favor of voucher privatization, along with his policy teammates Tomáš Ježek and Dušan Tříska. Journalist Jiří Leschtina characterized the division of labor in an article in *Mlada Fronta Dnes* (June 2, 1994): "While Václav Klaus gave voucher privatization a certain political 'sex-appeal' and imposed it on the public and Dušan Tříska pulled through on technical matters, Tomáš Ježek played the role of bulldozer of the political corridors." Due largely to their combined effort, a so-called Large Privatization Act passed into law in February 1991.

Privatization Methods

Retail shops and smaller enterprises were privatized in a separate process of so-called small privatization that distributed property through auctions and direct sales starting in 1991. A major restitution process was also launched in 1990 to return real estate and some smaller productive assets to owners who had had their property confiscated by the communist government in February 1948 (Frydman et al. 1993, 76–78; Coffee 1996, 118–19; Ježek 1997, 481–83).

Most medium and large enterprises—everything from the monopolistic state chocolate company, Čokoladovny, to the major breweries, textile factories, lumberyards, electronics producers, tram manufacturers, department stores, and porcelain plants—were included in the process of "large-scale" privatization under the privatization act of February 1991. The Large Privatization Act set the general ground rules for an aggressive policy of mass privatization in the Czech Republic, centered around the voucher method. It was highly centralized, thanks to the commercialization of state enterprises in 1990. First, all enterprises slated for large-scale privatization were asked to submit privatization plans to the newly created Ministry of Privatization. These plans would specify what proportion of enterprise shares would be exchanged for vouchers, sold directly to cash investors, transferred free of charge to municipalities, auctioned in the future, used to pay off restitution claims, or left in government hands. Although the enterprise itself was required to submit a plan, other domestic parties could also submit rival privatization plans, and enterprises were supposed to provide these rival bidders with information to help them prepare their plans (Kotrba et al. 1999, 11; Frydman et al. 1993, 80). Bidders were free to choose among privatization methods, but the government announced in advance that it would give preference to plans that called for a large number of shares to be distributed by the voucher method (cf. Appel and Gould 2000, 113–14). In the end, approximately 50 percent of shares were issued in exchange for vouchers (Desai and Plocková 1997, 191). A special committee of the Ministry of Privatization was established to evaluate these privatization plans. The committee approved 988 privatization plans for Czech companies in the first wave (1992–93) and 861 in the second wave (1994–95) (Coffee 1996, 123).[1] A total of 1,849 enterprises were distributed partially by the voucher method, or 56 percent of the 3,278 Czech companies selected for joint-stock conversion (Desai and Plocková 1997, 191). Once the Ministry of Privatization approved a privatization project, it turned the project over to the National Property Fund for implementation.

Voucher Privatization

Shares earmarked for vouchers were distributed in an experiment in capitalism that was notable for its ambitious scope. All Czech adult citizens were eligible to purchase for approximately thirty-five dollars a coupon booklet of one thousand points (Ježek 1997, 484) that could be used in one of two ways. First, individuals could turn the coupon booklet over to a "privatization investment fund" that would aggregate individuals' points and invest them in a manner similar to a U.S. mutual fund. 71 percent of Czechs and Slovaks took this option in the first wave of Czechoslovak privatization, and 64 percent of Czechs did so in the second wave (Desai and Plocková 1997, 191). Alternatively, voucher investors could choose to participate directly in the multiround voucher auction, using their points to bid for shares in privatizing Czech (and Slovak in the first wave) companies. Millions of Czechs got an education in stock market functioning in this way (Lieberman 1997, 7). The government required all privatizing enterprises to disclose some minimal information about themselves and set initial bidding prices, which Czech and Slovak citizens could read in supplements to their daily paper (Kotrba et al. 1999, 19, 43ff.). People formed long lines to submit their bids at their local privatization office. In each round of bidding, when supply and demand cleared for a particular enterprise, shares would be issued at the clearing price. If not, bidding went to a further round (see Young 1997 for more details on the auction process). While many Czechs and Slovaks got a first taste of stock market operations in this way, the real story was the success of the privatization investment funds.

Initially, few citizens understood the complicated voucher program—and few enrolled. It wasn't until one small, upstart company called Harvard Capital and Consulting (HCC) began advertising on television that it would pay 10,000 korun in one year for each coupon book invested (bought for 1,035 korun) that the majority of the population got interested (Coffee 1996, 127). Eventually 80 percent of Czech citizens participated, and HCC became the third-largest fund in the first wave. Later, it also led the way in disillusioning its clientele—first by not coming through on its promise of 10,000 korun after one year and later by brazenly stealing its clients' money. But HCC was not the only, or even the most successful, privatization investment company. Major Czech banks and insurance companies were the greatest beneficiaries of the voucher scheme, developing privatization investment companies that would come to dominate ownership of the Czech economy (Brom and Orenstein 1994; Desai and Plocková 1997; Kotrba et al. 1999).

A second wave of privatization was completed in 1995, basically along the same lines as the first. By this time, however, Slovakia had seceded from Czechoslovakia. As a result, Slovak firms were not included. There were other differences, in the type of companies represented, the share of voucher distribution, and the amount that went to other forms of ownership. The list of privatization investment company winners also changed, as voucher investment and marketing strategies were adapted to the lessons of the first round. One of the lessons learned was that postprivatization regulation of the investment funds was loose, enabling management companies to "tunnel" out the assets of their funds for private gain, at the expense of small voucher investors. They did this in a variety of creative ways, for instance using the fund resources to purchase worthless enterprises for exorbitant prices that they or their colleagues would then pocket. Kotrba et al. point out that a larger number of investment privatization funds participating in the second wave were later put under forced state administration, "suggesting fraud of a much more pervasive nature than in the first wave" (Kotrba et al. 1999, 30). The share of investment company ownership overall was similar, though, among the waves. Overall, approximately two-thirds of Czech citizens gave their shares to privatization investment companies to be invested (Desai and Plocková 1997, 191), and large privatization investment companies tied to banks, insurance companies, and other large state-owned enterprises, themselves being privatized, won a sizable proportion of these shares (Kotrba 1999, 17). Indeed, many of the fiercest struggles that emerged later were over shares of companies that owned large privatization investment companies (Desai and Plocková 1997, 193–94). Webs of cross-ownership were established that often defied external observation and harmed corporate governance (Coffee 1996).

Corporate Governance Issues

At the time, a great deal of concern was raised over the governance of newly privatized companies (Coffee 1996; Pistor and Spicer 1997, 98). Some argued that voucher privatization had duplicated a German-style ownership structure, whereby banks owned a large part of the economy. These analysts worried that banks would care less about industrial transformation and returning a profit, and more about making profitable loans. This might cause them to enforce loan profitability at the expense of shareholder profit and industrial efficiency (Berg and Berg 1997, 382; Coffee 1996, 113). Others were concerned about the ability of privatization investment companies to ignore the interests of small shareholders and enrich themselves and their managers through self-dealing, at the expense of voucher investment clients (Brom and

Orenstein 1994; Berg and Berg 1997, 382). Many remarked on the lack of transparency in Czech capital markets and urged the Czech government to take transparency and oversight more seriously (Desai and Plocková 1997, 196), but these warnings went unheeded. Prime Minister Václav Klaus, whose name was at the bottom of every voucher, and whose political fate was closely associated with the outcome of the voucher program, was philosophically opposed to overregulation of markets (Klaus 1997, 56–57). The voucher program was designed to put market mechanisms to work—and let the outcomes fall as they may. Klaus did not believe it was possible "to introduce the invisible hand of the market by means of the visible and omnipotent hand of a government bureaucrat" (Klaus 1997, 82). Klaus opposed the creation of an American-style securities and exchange commission on the grounds that it would represent excessive state intervention. He argued that "we have to liberalize, deregulate, and privatize at a very early stage of reform, even if we will be confronted with rather weak and, therefore, not fully efficient markets" (1997, 82). He entrusted important regulatory functions in privatization to the commercial banks—the same banks that owned large investment privatization companies in many cases and were themselves the subject of intense takeover battles. Klaus's Finance Ministry did not seem capable of regulating even the most basic provisions of the 1991 voucher law, and early warning signs of corruption in the National Property Fund and elsewhere were ignored within the government. A great part of the initial public enthusiasm for voucher privatization was generated by the marketing campaigns of the investment privatization companies and also by the tight media and political control exerted by Klaus until 1994, when public perceptions started to shift. Only then did a policy correction become possible.

Spin Control

Prime Minister Klaus rightly believed that reports of corruption would undermine public support for the voucher program. Therefore he took care to strongly counter rumors of corruption and often directly or indirectly accused opponents of being communists or leftist opponents of reform. This media strategy worked for several years, by dampening public scrutiny of early privatization scandals and thereby preventing policy alternation. Klaus's tough stance toward journalists also extended to the Western media. In 1994, Klaus told *Forbes* magazine that journalists were "the greatest enemy of the people" and later asserted that *Forbes*'s decision to print this statement was an example of "bad journalism," since Klaus thought the microphone was switched off after an interview (*RP*, September 19, 1994, 2). While *Forbes* reporters were clearly not cowed, Klaus's attacks kept most respectable Czech journalists from muckraking in the privatization area until 1994, when the second wave of voucher privatization was already under way.

Until then, privatization was never endangered by corruption scandals. One large scandal broke in 1992, involving the sale of the state enterprise Book Wholesaler to a company founded by Klaus's deputy prime minister, Miroslav Macek. Macek's company bought the book distributor contrary to the approved privatization project. Macek, backed by Klaus, tried to write this off as an administrative error, a standard tactic, but eventually Macek was forced out of government, although he retained a leadership post in Klaus's Civic Democratic Party. Macek also kept the book company. This affair became the subject of long investigations by the Supreme Control Office (NKU) (*Lidové Demokracie,* January 8, 1993) and the courts but faded from the headlines. Stories of possible conflicts of interest were relatively common, often dredged up by *Rudé Právo,* a former communist newspaper that was the mouthpiece of the left opposition. In another scandal involving another ODS leader, *Rudé Právo* alleged a potential conflict of interest in the approval of a privatization project of the wife of Civic Democratic Party executive vice president Petr Čermák for a farm in Rynoltice. Although Čermák admitted to the "psychological support of my wife" in her business activities, he said his involvement had never gone beyond that. "I never participated, never wanted to profit from it; I don't even understand it." Without proof of conflicts of interest, such stories never made more than a small splash in the opposition press. Two years into the voucher privatization process, National Property Fund supervisory board member Karel Ledvinka could reasonably state that, despite "daily complaints," the courts had yet to prove even one case of corruption (*LN,* January 22, 1993).

Privatization Scandals

All that began to change in 1994, during the second wave of voucher privatization, when a scandal broke that forced National Property Fund chairman Tomáš Ježek to resign. Ježek, along with Tříska and Klaus, had authored the voucher privatization program. He became the first minister of privatization and presided over the approval of privatization projects for the first wave of privatization in 1990–92. Klaus replaced Ježek in 1992, moving him to the National Property Fund, a quasi-state institution whose chief is a member of the Council of Ministers. Questions had been raised about Ježek's administrative ability, and these whispered rumors turned into public accusations when peculiarities arose around the sale of the state chocolate monopoly to the Swiss giant Nestlé, the French BSN, and the European Bank for Recon-

struction and Development (EBRD). According to the approved privatization project proclaimed by government resolution on January 8, 1992, Čokoladovny Praha was meant to be sold 46 percent to Nestlé and BSN and 15 percent to the EBRD, with 35 percent exchanged for citizen vouchers and the
remainder used to cover restitution claims. Yet the Supreme Control Office
(NKU) found that somehow the Czech Investiční Banka had managed to
purchase eighty thousand shares in Čokoladovny from the National Property
Fund at a price 30 percent lower than that paid by the three foreign investors
(*RP*, April 27, 1994, 1). At the time that the scandal went public, the shares
had a market value of over $20 million. Assuredly, this share capital should
have belonged to someone else.

With the Supreme Control Office charging illegal behavior by Ježek's
National Property Fund, pressure for his resignation and for cleaning up corruption in the agency soon became intense. Ježek, however, refused to resign,
claiming that the erroneous sale of chocolate factory shares had been an
"administrative error." But a $20 million error proved too much to paper
over, and a June 10, 1994, meeting of the executive board of the National
Property Fund asked for and received Ježek's resignation. Ježek was replaced
by a "young and ambitious deputy," Roman Češka, formerly deputy minister
of privatization (*RP*, June 11, 1994). The government leadership had clearly
decided to oust Ježek to prevent further embarrassment. But *Rudé Právo* had
finally tasted blood, bringing down a member of the Council of Ministers,
and, emboldened, kept on probing, as did the NKU and the police.

Then, in November 1994, the Czech police caught Jaroslav Lízner, head
of the central share registry for voucher privatization, coming out of a Chinese
restaurant with eight million korun (three hundred thousand dollars) stuffed
in a briefcase after a business meeting. Although no one initially knew what
Lízner had done, the prima facie evidence of corruption was overwhelming.
Klaus said it was like "a lightning bolt out of clear skies" (*MFD*, November 3,
1994). The government tried to portray the Lízner affair as the moral failings
of one man that "do not threaten voucher privatization," but this one spun out
of control, implicating an ever-widening circle of present and former government officials and corrupt businessmen trying to influence the privatization
process. The man alleged to have bribed Lízner said that manipulation of
voucher share prices was a "normal practice" of Lízner and a group of people
from the National Property Fund (*RP*, November 10, 1994, 1).

In the wake of the Lízner affair, even Klaus found himself under suspicion from *Rudé Právo*. On the basis of a letter that Klaus sent to Minister of
Privatization Jiří Skalický on August 27, 1993, *Rudé Právo* alleged that Klaus
had improperly intervened in a privatization decision on behalf of an old
schoolmate, who now represented a German-Austrian company, Hebel-

Hoeg. Skalický had apparently protested to Klaus against the manner in which the government set the price for the privatizing Czech company, a Brno construction materials firm (*RP*, November 5, 1994, 2). Needless to say, this scandal did not move beyond the pages of *Rudé Právo*, although the newspaper said the police had requested a copy of the letter. Around the same time, the national chief of police was dismissed.

In December 1994, a further privatization affair involving Klaus attracted the attention of the usually progovernment paper *Lidové Noviny* (People's News). The newspaper obtained a letter from Klaus's adviser Martin Koucourek to Minister of Privatization Skalický, asking the minister to change a privatization decision. The ministry had approved the privatization project of the Petrof family, the prewar owner of the piano factory in question. Klaus intervened on behalf of a competing project submitted by IFM Piana, a company that had contributed to Klaus's ODS and whose board reportedly included ranking former communists from Petrof, including the heads of the plant's People's Militia unit and its factory organization (ZO) of the Communist Party. *Lidové Noviny* was more disturbed by the former-communist connections than by Klaus's intervention per se. It was not clear that Klaus acted improperly in this case, since the cabinet has the right to overturn decisions of the Ministry of Privatization, and although Skalický and Klaus were both members of the cabinet, Klaus's ODS held a majority within that body. Klaus seems to have hoped that by writing to Skalický, he would force the minister of privatization to comply without actually taking a vote of the cabinet. This informal use of power over the privatization process underlines the extent to which Klaus's party may have exercised control over privatization, sometimes to help its own donors (*LN*, December 29, 1994, 1).

Klaus's effectiveness until 1994 in limiting reports of corruption and political influence-peddling surrounding privatization was assisted by the fact that a state agency, the Supreme Control Office, was responsible for monitoring the privatization process. Czech privatization institutions were not accountable to parliament, and judicial control of the privatization process was "virtually non-existent" (Drabek 1993, 115). The only control body was the NKU, but it was not independent of the government. Instead, its head was a political appointee of the prime minister. The NKU did investigate the two largest privatization scandals, involving Book Wholesaler and Prague Chocolate Works. And NKU reports were treated by the press as valid independent verification of allegations of corruption, worthy of publication, although still not court proof. Yet it seems that the NKU investigated only a few highly visible cases and ignored a vast number of allegations of wrongdoing that emerged in the opposition press. Calls by the left opposition for parliamentary oversight of the privatization process were constantly rejected by the government (*MFD*, August 19, 1993, 2). Nonopposition and progovernment media would not report or probe into unsubstantiated allegations. Weak journalism and a weak parliament, therefore, helped keep Czech privatization on track, allowing reform mistakes and corruption to continue unchecked.

Diminishing Public Support

After the scandals of 1994, public opinion polls revealed for the first time that a majority of Czechs had become critical of privatization: 72 percent agreed with the statement, "The average guy is not gaining anything"; 78 percent agreed that "privatization lacks control"; 69 percent agreed that "firms bribe officials and get property cheaply"; 69 percent disagreed that "journalists are thinking up problems, privatization is basically in order." However, 40 percent still believed that privatization was run "without problems" or with "small problems," indicating that many people thought corruption was not a major problem. And most tellingly, only 32 percent disagreed with the statement, "No one has proven able to do privatization better than in the Czech Republic"; 26 percent agreed, and 42 percent said they did not know (IVVM 1994). Even after the unfairness and inequity of privatization was laid bare, most Czechs remained ambivalent about a process that has been variously called the greatest success—by Václav Klaus—and the greatest swindle of the century—by opposition leader Miloš Zeman (Večerník 1996, 166).

As described in chapter 3, Czech attitudes toward economic transformation shifted firmly in a negative direction in 1996, due to three interrelated factors: (1) large bank failures and the emergence of an economic crisis that showed that the Czech economy was in worse shape than most people had anticipated; (2) failure of the Klaus government to address this crisis through

TABLE 3. Perception of Gain from Voucher Privatization in the Czech Republic (in percentages)

	1996	1997	1998
Certainly yes	21.6	15.0	12.2
Rather yes	37.6	31.2	32.7
Rather no	21.1	22.5	21.8
Certainly no	19.8	31.3	33.3
Total	100.0	100.0	100.0

Source: Večerník and Matějů 1999.
Note: Note the large increase in those answering "certainly no" in 1997.

two "little packages" of economic reform measures in 1997; (3) revelations that Klaus's Civic Democratic Party had profited from kickbacks from privatization that were allegedly channeled to a secret bank account kept in Switzerland. This scandal, in particular, showed that the Klaus government had fixed privatization deals in exchange for political donations and undermined confidence in the program.

When a new government of experts was appointed at the end of 1997 to hold power until new elections in June 1998, it began a much-needed process of policy correction. Important measures included the establishment of a Securities Commission to regulate the deeply corrupt Czech securities markets and improved regulation of the banking sector. These were commonsense measures that had long been advocated by the international financial community but had never been implemented by the Klaus government.

Costs of Policy Stability

Ironically, Czech privatization was ultimately undermined by the same thing that made it a successful program in the first place: its longevity. The longevity of its political leadership made the Czech voucher privatization one of the most successful privatization programs in postcommunist Europe, with a majority of Czech industry privatized in just a few years. But it also prevented accountability for corruption and bad policy decisions that ultimately undermined the program. Opposition members in parliament had been clamoring for years about the lack of parliamentary oversight of the privatization process. The February 1991 law had not allowed for such oversight, and the opposition did not have the votes to change the law. The Supreme Control Office (NKU) made only halfhearted attempts to investigate allegations of corruption, and with virtual impunity, the Klaus administration continued on its path, nodding at instances of corruption within its own electoral alliance. It ignored efforts to establish a national securities council and other measures that would have enhanced the transparency of Czech capital markets. This neglect caught up to the Czechs in 1997, when widespread instances of "tunneling," related to voucher privatization, caught public attention and wiped out several large financial institutions. A pattern of corrupt party finance in privatization deals caused the fall of the Klaus government at the end of 1997, leaving his signature voucher program in shambles.

The appointment of a "government of experts" in December 1997 began a process of correcting some of the most extreme mistakes of the Klaus regime. Particularly important was the founding of a new Securities Commission to regulate financial markets, taking responsibility out of the hands of the politically controlled Finance Ministry. The new government reemphasized banking supervision and initiated long-overdue bank privatizations. Finally, the Czech Republic began to get the policy correction it needed.

After elections in June 1998, a minority Social Democratic government came to power and continued some of the policies of the interim government, but its effectiveness was lessened by lack of a working majority in parliament, by its "opposition agreement" with Klaus's Civic Democratic Party, and by ministerial incompetence and corruption. In addition, negotiations on EU accession heated up, and the Czech Republic came under substantial pressure to make its financial market regulation compatible with EU norms. These have had an enormous impact on the regulatory environment in the Czech Republic, making it more difficult for outright corruption to persist. Change in government and international pressures have ultimately combined to force a policy correction in the Czech Republic. Such change was necessary after years of economic policy domination by Klaus's Civic Democratic Party. It provides a clear example of how democratic policy alternation can promote capitalist development—even when overturning a politician widely recognized as a hero of capitalism.

Insider Control in Poland

Privatization in Poland unfolded in a much less organized and centralized fashion. Many neoliberals saw the slow pace of privatization as one of the negative features of the Polish reform. As Polish economist Jan Winiecki put it in a comparative essay on the mistakes of privatization (1992, 276), "When it comes to avoiding the most damaging mistakes, Czechoslovakia is clearly in the lead, with Hungary next, Poland coming in a poor third, and Yugoslavia bringing up the rear." In Poland, no single overarching privatization program ever got off the ground, and many more interest groups were able to exert influence over the design of reform. There was an abundance of contentious democratic deliberation over privatization, and this slowed the progress of many reform projects. It also slowed the privatization of state-owned enterprises overall, compared to the Czech Republic and other fast privatizers. In 1995, when the Czech Republic was completing the second wave of voucher privatization, bringing the total number of companies privatized by this method to 1,849, Poland was still approving the first 400 companies meant to participate in its analogous mass privatization program. In total, the Czech Republic privatized or transformed nearly 3,278 of approximately 4,800 large and medium state-owned enterprises (SOEs) by the end of 1994, while Poland privatized just 1,225 of its 8,441 SOEs—and most of these were small and medium-sized enterprises privatized through management-employee buyouts. In 1995, of the 100 largest Polish enterprises, 71 remained wholly or predominantly in state hands (Nuti 1999, 82).

Evaluating privatization solely on quantity measures, such as the percentage of enterprises privatized, Poland's privatization would be judged a relative laggard (Błaszczyk 1999). But in terms of quality, Poland is now believed to have had better success with its more gradual methods than the Czech Republic did with its radical voucher privatization (Spicer, McDermott, and Kogut 2000).[2] While the Polish economy grew dramatically in the second half of the 1990s, the Czech economy contracted. And substantial evidence suggests that voucher privatization "impeded efficient corporate governance and restructuring" in the Czech Republic (Nellis 1999).

Slowing the adoption of privatization programs and subjecting them to rigorous democratic tests forced them to meet tough performance criteria and prevented large-scale reform mistakes in Poland. Democratic deliberation and compromise also facilitated the progress of privatization methods that had strong grassroots support, particularly management-employee buyouts. "The last thing that the new post-communist leaders everywhere—from Balcerowicz to Gaidar—wished to promote was precisely the emergence of significant forms of employee ownership" (Nuti 1999, 85), and yet this was one of the main results of Poland's privatization. And in another unexpected result, enterprise restructuring in Poland ultimately was facilitated more by the rapid development of new private enterprises than by privatization of existing state-owned enterprises (Johnson and Loveman 1995).

Privatization in Poland did not proceed according to plan. Intense conflict over privatization in Poland and democratic policy alternation slowed the progress of particular neoliberal programs, but accelerated the learning process of reformers, increased public scrutiny and control of reform programs, allowed for pragmatic experimentation, and prevented large-scale errors. Poland's privatization provides a clear case for the benefits of democratic policy alternation. It therefore demands careful attention in both the analysis and practice of economic reform.

Legacy of Decentralization

The more contentious nature of privatization in Poland derived largely from different historical trajectories of reform that empowered enterprise insiders in the 1980s—both workers and managers—and the unwillingness of neoliberal reformers to support preferential privatization to these inside groups associated with the communist regime. "Insiders" refers to groups on the inside of an enterprises, particularly workers and managers, with privileged access to information about the enterprise and means of control. Neoliberal privatization programs often sought to privilege enterprise "outsiders," including investment banks, funds, and foreign business people, to restrain the self-serving behavior of the insiders who effectively controlled most state property. However, the gradual "withdrawal" of the state from the economy during the 1980s under reform communism in Poland left firm insiders in charge (Kamiński 1991, 162–93). This history of decentralizing reform in Poland made it more difficult for central state actors later to impose privatization programs from above (Frydman and Rapaczynski 1994, 155). As opposed to the Czech Republic, which maintained a very centralized ownership and control structure until the very end of the communist period, Poland, like Hungary, experimented with liberalizing reforms. The result was that while Czech reformers were able to seize complete control of the privatization process through the Large Enterprise Act of 1990, Poland either could not, or did not, revoke insider rights granted during the 1980s. Such a move was discussed in 1989 and 1990, but not taken (Frydman and Rapaczynski 1994, 13, 108–9). Polish governments were forced to negotiate privatization plans with insider interests at the enterprise level and were also subject to far greater parliamentary scrutiny and control. While such parliamentary and insider control was the bane of neoliberal policy advocates in Poland in the early 1990s, it appears to have had fewer negative effects than initially feared and to have facilitated higher-quality methods of enterprise transformation.

Enterprise insiders were originally empowered by the late communist regime in response to demands made by the Solidarity movement in 1980–81. Enterprise self-management was a key element of the Solidarity platform, and in 1981 and 1982, the communist government introduced a number of economic reform measures aimed at "the transfer of some powers from the government to society and economic actors," making enterprises "self-dependent, self-managed, and self-financed" (Kamiński 1991, 52). This was part of a broader effort by the communist regime to pacify the Solidarity movement by acceding to some of its demands.

One landmark piece of legislation passed in September 1981 made elected employee councils the main strategic decision-making body in many Polish enterprises (Federowicz and Levitas 1995). Employee councils brought together representatives of management and organized labor and thus provided Solidarity with some level of representation. Enterprises in a number of sectors, however, were exempted from self-management reform and remained under direct state control (Kamiński 1991, 54). Nonetheless by 1985, sixty-four hundred of Poland's approximately nine thousand state enterprises had employee councils (Federowicz and Levitas 1995). Employee councils were supposed to be elected every two years by a general vote of employees and had the power to hire and fire the enterprise manager. All major enterprise decisions required the approval of the employee council, and the council also had the right to review all enterprise documents and contracts, making this institution tantamount to a United States corporation's board of directors. When the communist government reversed its strategy of concessions and declared martial law in December 1981, employee councils continued to function. However, with the Solidarity movement that had energized them being suppressed under martial law, the councils generally came to be dominated by management.

Besides instituting employee councils, the 1981–82 reforms decentralized the Polish economy by reducing the number of economic branch ministries from nine to four and eliminating the intermediate layer of industrial administration. Enterprises were allowed to set "free" prices on one-third to two-thirds of all products, subject to contractual negotiations. However, "administrative constraints on the choice of customers, obligatory sales to a central wholesaler, traditional ties enhanced by multiyear sales agreements, as well as likely pressures from the central authorities to keep price increases at a minimum" prevented "free" prices from following market principles. The government also experimented with tax reform in an effort to become a neutral actor in enterprise finance, but backed off from "universality" in taxation rather quickly (Kamiński 1991, 55–57). In all, while the 1981–82 reforms attempted to reorient the state's role in the economy, they were only partially effective. Many of the boldest changes were never implemented or were abandoned midstream. In 1986, the government introduced a package of eleven laws that would have reimposed direct state control, but they failed to pass the Sejm, demonstrating the disintegration of state will and decision-making capacity under late communism in Poland.

In April 1987, when reformers had regained dominance within the communist party, the government announced its plan for a "second stage of economic reform." The second stage was not much different from the first stage, but represented a renewed commitment to reform and was subjected to a popular referendum (Kamiński 1991, 58–59). However, price increases under the program set off a wave of strikes and worker protests that ultimately led the communist government to relegalize Solidarity and call for roundtable talks in 1988.

Increasing labor activism in 1988 and 1989 revived the employee councils that were at the heart of the communist decentralization process. Sensing an opening, employee councils began to assert control of their enterprises. In some cases, workers allied with management; in other cases worker-dominated councils fired inefficient or corrupt managers and hired new ones. Some of these new managers were representatives of the worker self-management movement and associated with Solidarity. As one Polish economist involved in the privatization debates within the government remarked, "In practical terms, the whole legal and social-psychological impact of developments from 1980 to 1990 has led to the implicit adoption of a system of group ownership. This has meant that coalitions of self-management council members and managers have attained ownership rights for their state enterprises virtually free of charge. The weakness of the state . . . has contributed to this tendency" (Szomburg 1991, 41). Thus began the privatization process in Poland, with heightened insider control and ineffective state supervision.

Empowerment of employee councils in 1988–89 should have represented a major victory for the Solidarity movement. However, in one of the greatest paradoxes of the Polish revolution, the movement's economic experts had mostly changed their minds about worker empowerment. While the worker self-management lobby within Solidarity was busy asserting employee rights, leading Solidarity economists, such as Leszek Balcerowicz, Stefan Kawalec, Janusz Lewandowski, Tomasz Stankiewicz, and Jan Szomburg, who had previously supported self-management, changed their position 180 degrees and became doctrinaire liberals fully opposed to any sort of worker control. In line with neoliberal economic doctrine, they now believed that an efficient enterprise required a capitalist owner. They argued that worker codetermination and share ownership would only damage firms, causing them to bankrupt themselves by paying excessively high wages and not investing enough. The hardening of this division between neoliberal economists and self-management advocates within the Solidarity camp stymied the privatization process and future Solidarity governments.

Nomenklatura Privatization

While employee councils and worker representatives gained the upper hand in some enterprises, in others, managers began to steal or otherwise privatize state assets in a process called spontaneous, or *nomenklatura*,[3] privatization. This process began under the last communist government of Mieczyslaw Rakowski in 1988. Rakowski, among other innovations, appointed two prominent *nomenklatura* businessmen to his cabinet (Kamiński 1991, 233), giving some indication of his closeness to the dynamic "new" entrepreneurial class arising from within the communist party. The legislative basis of *nomenklatura* privatization was the 1988 Law on Economic Activity and the Law on Joint Ventures that gave SOEs the ability to create joint ventures with or sell or lease assets to private companies (Frydman et al. 1993, 183). Although passed under the pretext of making the economy more flexible, the legal reforms of 1988 are often seen as a means of allowing members of the communist elite to turn themselves into capitalists through a process of "political capitalism"—the transformation of political capital into financial capital (Staniszkis 1991). One of the stranger aspects of *nomenklatura* privatization in Poland is the strong indication that the Solidarity leadership at least tacitly approved of the process, turning a blind eye in exchange for political reforms. This, along with Solidarity's initial reluctance to pass a decommunization law, fuels the fires of those who claim that Poland's transformation was driven by a conspiracy between communist and Solidarity elites (Zubek 1994, 1995).

The Solidarity leadership might have considered *nomenklatura* privatization a reasonable price to pay in 1988 for legalization and political pluralism. Later, however, it handicapped the Solidarity government in its privatization efforts, partly because much valuable state property was already in private hands, and partly because *nomenklatura* privatization infuriated the voting population and made people view privatization as a corrupt process. Public anger over *nomenklatura* privatization forced the Mazowiecki government to put a stop to it in late 1989, despite the support of some Solidarity figures for the process.

Failed Commercialization

To reassert state control over the enterprise sector, the Solidarity government led by Tadeusz Mazowiecki contemplated a "commercialization" of state property that would eliminate employee councils and reassert the dominance of the state in state-owned enterprises. Commercialization would have replaced state-owned enterprises' employee councils with shareholder-elected boards, but initially the sole shareholder would be the state. After considering this option, Mazowiecki's government demurred, not wanting to antagonize the self-management lobby that constituted a significant part of the government's political base (Gomułka and Jasiński 1994, 224). Heavy-handed tactics toward the enterprises might not have worked, considering the strength of Solidarity support for worker control. Furthermore, workers and the general population preferred self-management and worker-management buyouts. From 1990 to 1993, public opinion polling demonstrated that Poles consistently "preferred to work in state-owned enterprises, or alternatively enterprises in which employees had a significant capital share" (Kolarska-Bobinska 1994, 111–12). In the opinion of experts and strategists within the World Bank and IMF, the failure to commercialize was a crucial mistake. In these circles, the belief was widely held that opposition to commercialization "would have been minimal at the beginning of the reform process" (Schipke 1994, 183). Whether mass commercialization would have passed with a little grumbling or would have fueled a massive strike wave among already restless workers is unknown, for Mazowiecki's government took the prudent course and decided against it, thereby preventing the state from asserting total control over the privatization process.

The Capital Track

Without much state control over individual enterprises, and with employee councils holding veto power over privatization decisions, the Polish government depended on the agreement of firm insiders to facilitate privatization. Yet Solidarity neoliberals wanted to found pure capitalism, not a "third way by default." Therefore, they emphasized privatization to outsiders, at first by direct sale. The first director of the Agency of Ownership Transformation, Krzysztof Lis, was dedicated to an orthodox liberal view of privatization. He believed not only that firms should be transformed into "real" joint stock companies without employee councils, but that worker share ownership should be kept to a maximum of 20 percent. Lis wanted to sell enterprises individually through public share offerings for real money, even if it took ten to fifteen years (quoted in *Gazeta International*, March 22, 1990). This corresponded with the advice of Harvard economist János Kornai (1990), who believed that the priority in privatization was not speed, but finding "real" capitalist owners. Lis introduced his "capital privatization" program in January 1990 and early that year his agency selected twenty firms whose employee councils agreed to commercialization and public sale. Delays and the difficulty of placing a reasonable value even on these flagship firms meant that only five firms were actually privatized by this method in 1990. An additional six were sold in public offerings in 1991. At this rate, it would not take ten to fifteen years, but a millennium or two to privatize the Polish economy.

War of Privatization Blueprints

Lis's methods were already called into question within the government in early 1990 in "the big privatization debate," also known as the "war of privatization blueprints" (Błaszczyk and Dąbrowski 1993; Gomułka and Jasiński 1994, 222–24). Although a variety of methods were proposed and discussed in 1989–90, including Lis's "capital path," employee ownership, mass voucher privatization, and privatization through financial intermediaries, in the end none won the decisive support of the government. Instead the Mazowiecki government decided for a "pluralism" of privatization methods. The principle of pluralism, which fit so well rhetorically with the democratic nature of the transformation, thinly veiled an incapacity for making decisions on the part of the government that was visible throughout the privatization process in Poland.

Following the principle of pluralism, the July 1990 Act on the Privatization of State-Owned Enterprises allowed for three modes of privatization: the "capital track," mass privatization, and employee-management buyouts or leases (article 37). The bulk of the law concentrates on the first method, which corresponded with the privatization agency director's agenda. Mass voucher privatization is enabled in the law in two short, extremely general articles (Bohm and Kreacic 1991, 151–60). No concrete steps toward mass privatization had been taken by the government up to this time, so the law seems to have merely allowed the possibility of mass privatization, rather than actually committing the government to carry out such a program. In the case of mass privatization, the law explicitly requires additional legislation, a factor that caused continuous delays over the next five years. The law also enabled continued parliamentary oversight over the privatization process through several channels and provided for parliament to "determine annually the general directions of privatization" (Filipowicz 1993, 145; see also Thieme 1994). While the Czech Republic's February 1991 law on privatization settled the matter definitively, Poland's earlier law left most major issues open to continuing debate.

Worker-Management Buyouts

Provisions for employee buyouts through asset liquidations in companies represented a last-minute compromise with advocates of employee stock ownership (ESOP) in parliament. This opened the door for what became, quietly, the most successful privatization method in Poland, despite the embarrassed silence of liberal reformers. Poland's employee buyout program allowed "workers and managers—often with the help of outside investors . . . to negotiate the value of their enterprises with the state and to lease or buy all or part of their firms" (Levitas 1994). By the end of 1995, 788 enterprises had been privatized by this method (Nuti 1999, 84).

While worker-management buyouts moved along swiftly in enterprises with fewer than five hundred workers, privatization of the large state enterprises that produce about one-half of Polish GDP stalled for five years, producing all sorts of economic and political complications. At the end of 1994, 390 of the 500 largest industrial companies in Poland were still state owned. Of the state-owned companies in this group, 156 had been commercialized in preparation for privatization. Thirty-nine of the top 500 were foreign-owned private companies. Only 64 were private, Polish-owned enterprises (E. Balcerowicz 1995).

Mass Privatization

The fall of the Mazowiecki government at the end of 1990 brought an end to Lis's reign over the privatization process. Prime Minister Bielecki promoted his colleague from Gdansk, Janusz Lewandowski, to the Ministry of Ownership Transformation. Lewandowski had a more sophisticated appreciation of the politics of privatization and was the leading advocate of mass voucher privatization. Lewandowski's conception was to give state enterprises to specially created mutual funds and then to distribute shares in these funds free of charge to all Polish citizens. In an earlier version, the state pension fund and state-owned commercial banks would also receive shares as a sort of endowment to strengthen their shaky balance sheets. After consultation with international advisers and within the government, the final version presented to the Council of Ministers in June 1991 proposed 60 percent of shares for citizen-owned "National Investment Funds" (NIFs), 10 percent for employees, and 30 percent for the Treasury for eventual sale to private investors or transfer to the state pension fund (Ministry of Ownership Transformation 1991). The program underwent further modifications in subsequent years. The National Investment Funds would be operated under an incentive system by experienced Western and Polish investment banks and consulting firms.

During Bielecki's one year in office, the Mass Privatization Program (MPP) never developed the momentum necessary to carry the project to realization. For one, the program required new legislation, although the Sejm had just passed a privatization law six months before Lewandowski came to office. Second, the government remained dependent on the approval of enterprise employee councils for participation. The government had to send "state" enterprises letters of invitation to participate in the MPP. For every three enterprises responding "yes," one had responded "no" by the beginning of September 1993 (*Polityka*, September 4, 1993).

Several elements in the design of the program also created significant impediments to its implementation. Although Lewandowski estimated that the program would cost $50 million (Slay 1991, 14), the Ministry of Ownership Transformation had not included a method of financing in its program. In the Czech Republic, mass privatization was financed by a registration fee of approximately thirty-five dollars,[4] but because Lewandowski aimed to distribute NIF shares free of charge to all citizens, mass privatization placed a burden on the state budget that the Ministry of Finance was unwilling to

accept. Having foreign investment banks run NIFs created a powerful emo-
tional barrier to popular acceptance of the mass privatization program. In a
public opinion poll conducted in September 1992, approximately 50 percent
of Poles objected to the sale of state enterprises to foreigners. Opposition varied according to nationality: 66 percent were against sale to Russians, 59 percent against sale to Jews, 54 percent against sale to Germans, 44 percent
against sale to English and Japanese, and 40 percent against sale to Americans
(*Polityka*, November 7, 1992, 20). In March 1993, the Christian National
Union (ZChN), the nationalist Christian right party within Lewandowski's
own coalition, voted against the MPP out of opposition to foreign ownership,
forcing another three-month delay while Lewandowski negotiated the support of the opposition, postcommunist Alliance of the Democratic Left
(SLD). In addition, the MPP did not go far enough to satisfy the worker ownership lobby, although it did give 10 percent of shares to workers free of
charge.

The MPP was also plagued by technical criticisms of the role of institutional investors in the program. Many economists expressed suspicions that
the NIFs would not do much to help restructure Polish firms, simply selling
off good companies or playing a very passive role (Slay 1991, 15). This, plus
Bielecki's sinking popularity, the failure of his effort to attain decree power,
the fragmented results of October 1991 elections, and subsequent repeated
changes of government, caused delays. Though mass privatization was fully
elaborated by the government in mid-1991, in the absence of "strong political will" (Lewandowski and Szyszko 1999) it was not implemented in Poland
until 1995–96.

Efforts at Acceleration

The failure of Lis's capital track or Lewandowski's MPP to launch a speedy
privatization of Polish state enterprises proved crucial. After an initial period
of "extraordinary politics," public goodwill toward the economic reformers
ran out in 1991. By May 1992, only 18 percent of respondents in a public
opinion poll believed that privatization would benefit themselves (Gadomski
1993). During the summer of 1992, a serious strike wave swept the country.
Elections in 1991 had returned a divided parliament, with Solidarity split in
six and at odds with itself over privatization. Trade unions opposed Solidarity government policies on wages, social policy, and privatization and
demanded a greater say in policies toward state enterprises.

Jacek Kuroń, twice minister of labor under Mazowiecki and then
Suchocka, proposed a new initiative to win back worker support for the
reforms in the summer of 1992. Kuroń was one of the few Solidarity politi-

cians who held the trust of the people. He could talk to workers face-to-face and had long experience both organizing strikes (1980–81) and stopping them (1989–90). Kuroń reentered government with Hanna Suchocka in 1992, promising to negotiate and implement a state enterprise pact. The state enterprise pact had two basic components, dealing with privatization and collective bargaining. The privatization section essentially consisted of a deal between the government and the trade unions to speed up privatization. Enterprise managers and employee councils would draw up their *own* privatization plans, instead of having the state propose solutions, and get a larger proportion of shares for free. However, the state would impose a six-month deadline. After six months, the enterprises would have to decide on a privatization method, or the state would take control. In this way, employee councils were encouraged to plan the privatization of their enterprises, but within a specific time limit, under threat of having their decision rights revoked.

Trade unions eventually agreed to the proposed compromise on privatization after months of difficult negotiations. Talks were complicated by competition and disagreements among the four major trade union federations in Poland, one of which left the talks altogether, and another of which (Solidarity) refused to sit at the same table as the former official OPZZ, the largest federation. In the end, the government and employer associations concluded three different state enterprise pacts with each of the trade union federations that remained at the table. Pact implementing legislation was presented to parliament for its approval in early 1993 but was delayed throughout the year, until finally the Suchocka government fell. With it fell hopes of reaching any overarching deal between the government and employee councils on speeding up privatization.

Mass Privatization Revisited

At the same time that the state enterprise pact legislation languished, parliament was making progress on a limited mass privatization program. Parliament rejected the mass privatization program in March 1993 mainly because right-wing elements of the government coalition believed that the MPP would allow excessive foreign influence in the Polish economy (Gadomski 1993). The government therefore had to turn for help to the left opposition, which demanded and got certain design features changed. One major amendment was the setting aside of a proportion of voucher shares for state employees and certain categories of pensioners. The MPP law finally was passed by the Sejm in April 1993 and signed into law by the president.

New elections in September 1993 again slowed the progress of Poland's MPP. Prime Minister Pawlak of the Polish Peasant Party (PSL) dragged his feet and refused to sign onto a list of companies that had agreed to participate in the program until international pressure upon him caused him to change his mind. A scaled-down and much amended mass voucher privatization was finally implemented for 512 Polish companies in 1995 and 1996. But as in the Czech Republic, its results were disappointing. According to one former proponent of the program, "The performance of the enterprises following this privatization track has systematically worsened," with rates of investment one-tenth those of other privatized firms (Błaszczyk 1999).

State Enterprises in Limbo

As the process of privatization dragged out due to democratic policy instability, many large state enterprises in Poland remained in limbo for years. Several oddities deserve special mention. For one, many companies were "commercialized" without being privatized, a situation that no one had foreseen. Commercialization meant that enterprises were transformed from their state-owned, employee council–dominated form, into joint-stock companies with shares that were initially held 100 percent by the State Treasury in preparation for privatization. The State Treasury, however, did not exist until October 1996. Instituting a State Treasury was discussed in 1990, but ultimately delayed for six years again because of intense political disagreements and government changes (Błaszczyk and Dąbrowski 1993, 8–9). While commercialized companies waited for privatization, for a foreign investor, or for the state to start subsidizing them again, workers began to demand the 20 percent of shares they were due to receive after two years of commercialization. Several court cases were thus fought to force a nonexistent State Treasury to hand over dematerialized shares in very real "commercialized" firms (Levitas 1994).

In the absence of a State Treasury institution, some other government body had to appoint supervisory and executive boards to the commercialized companies. These board seats immediately became a nice source of patronage for government ministers, who could supplement their own incomes or the incomes of their staff. This practice, which directly contradicted Poland's conflict-of-interest law that bars government employees from serving on corporate boards, led to the "clean hands" furor that caused the resignation of popular minister of foreign affairs Andrzej Olechowski in January 1995. Minister of justice Wlodzimierz Cimoszewicz, an SLD member, published a list of state officials who had violated the conflict-of-interest law by serving on the boards of "commercialized" enterprises while holding state jobs, including Minister Olechowski. This was clearly a political gambit, and Olechowski countered it well, but when the episode refused to die, he resigned during the

1994–95 Christmas vacation. Olechowski's departure, which caused negative reactions in the West, underlined the government's chaotic handling of commercialized enterprises.

Given the disorganization of Polish state institutions involved in privatization, it should come as no surprise that public opinion polls show that people believed "bad legal regulations" and "incompetent government administration" were two of the top four obstacles to privatization in Poland. Perception of government incompetence seems to have peaked in mid- to late 1992, with the political crises of that year. Although it subsided somewhat by May 1994, after six months of the "postcommunist" government, the sense that privatization was a deeply troubled process remained strong.

Privatization under the Postcommunist Left

Privatization policy of the postcommunist left government that held office from 1993 to 1997 was substantially different from that of previous Solidarity governments. The left governments finished implementation of the much-delayed Polish mass privatization program in 1995–96, with 512 enterprises finally included. However, they emphasized direct sale of enterprises to investors and also began a policy of developing state-owned conglomerates or national champions in strategic sectors, such as chemicals, refining, and banking. International organizations looked askance at such efforts, and critics accused the government of slowing down privatization. However, privatization continued at a moderate pace under the left government, though with different policy emphases and designs.

TABLE 4. **What Are the Greatest Obstacles to the Privatization of the Polish Economy (responses in percentages)**

	November '92	May '94
Bad legal regulations	57	44
Lack of financial resources of potential Polish buyers	37	47
Incompetent government administration	36	22
Bad economic situation of enterprises	36	41
Unwillingness of state enterprise employees	19	21
Passivity of enterprise directors	18	12
Lack of interest of potential foreign buyers	18	15
Opposition on the part of trade unions	9	13
Lack of interest in privatization by the government		12
No obstacles		5
Hard to say		15

Note: Respondents were asked to list up to three obstacles.
Source: Społéczeństwo o Prywatyzacji po Pierwszym Półroczu Rządów Lewicy. Warsaw: Centrum Badania Opinii. Społecznej (CBOS), May 1994, p. 8. Reprinted with permission.

Perhaps the most significant privatization initiatives of the postcommunist left governments were a "commercialization" process started in 1996 and the establishment, at long last, of a State Treasury to manage commercialized enterprises as part of a major public administration reform. After three years of "tempestuous discussions and negations (including a presidential veto of an earlier draft in mid-1995, over-ruled by parliament, and followed by recourse to the Constitutional Tribunal), a Law on the Commercialization and Privatization of state-owned enterprises was promulgated" in September 1996 (OECD 1996, 68). This new law enabled the state to commercialize state-owned enterprises without the consent of insiders—a major shift. It partially compensated insiders by providing for 15 percent of shares to be transferred to employees free of charge, rather than allowing them to buy 20 percent at half price, as under the 1990 privatization act. The law also allowed the state to commercialize enterprises without privatization and put more privatizations decisions under the authority of the cabinet as a whole, rather than the Ministry of Ownership Transformation alone (OECD 1996, 68–69).

With this law, the postcommunist left contributed significantly to the privatization process in Poland, in ways that previous Solidarity governments either could not, or did not wish to. Policy alternation in Poland had an important impact by focusing attention on previously unresolved issues, shifting policy priorities, and opening up new possibilities for the future. Where previous Solidarity governments had tried and failed, the law on commercialization passed by the postcommunist left smoothed the way for privatization to proceed without obstruction from insiders. The law also aimed to improve management of the many state enterprises awaiting privatization, or remaining under state control, an important fact considering that approximately three thousand enterprises remained under state ownership at the end of 1998, employing 25 percent of all workers in nonfinancial enterprises, but producing only 2 percent of gross profit (IMF 2000, 56). While the pace of privatization slowed somewhat between 1993 and 1997, the postcommunist left made a distinctive contribution to the process of privatization that would not have been possible under conditions of policy stability.

Reevaluation of Fast Privatization

In the end, Poland's slower privatization process did nothing to impede its economic performance (see table 2). In fact, as time progressed, there was increasing reason to believe that slower privatization actually contributed to Poland's rapid growth (Spicer, McDermott, and Kogut 2000). Poland's economy grew at a rate of 6–7 percent between 1995 and 1997, while the Czech economy stagnated. Most analysts came to believe that differences in privatization methods had something to do with this.

Analysts began to connect the Czech Republic's economic decline in the late 1990s with the effects of rapid voucher privatization. The central claim of this literature is that investment privatization companies that held most voucher shares were bad corporate owners. They knew and cared little about the governance of firms in their portfolios and instead tried to make quick profits from the lack of transparency on Czech capital markets. Nellis (1999) concluded, on the basis of extensive data from privatized and state-owned enterprises, that "mass and rapid privatization turned over mediocre assets to large numbers of people who had neither the skills nor the financial resources to use them well." It empowered investment funds without establishing sufficient market regulatory environments, thus encouraging widespread fraud and corruption. Poor market regulation in turn harmed economic growth by discouraging foreign investment, among other things.

By the late 1990s, a revisionist consensus had emerged within the international development community that mass privatization had produced disappointing results (Havrylyshyn and McGettigan 1999b).[5] In a comprehensive literature review of studies on privatization and enterprise performance in the 1990s, Havrylyshyn and McGettigan (1999a, 26) report that the "empirical evidence does not find rapid and mass privatization is clearly better." Instead, rapid voucher privatization produced mixed results and was often criticized for "creating a system of ownership without adequate governance." One IMF team was more straightforwardly critical in its 1999 evaluation of the Czech economy.

> Weak corporate governance has been the result of the ownership structure arising from the voucher privatization program, with strategic investors established in only about one-third of the enterprises, incentive problems surrounding the investment privatization funds, and the ownership of these funds by the major commercial banks. (IMF 1999b, 3)

Although only a few in the international development community said it outright and publicly, advocacy of rapid voucher privatization had been a major policy mistake. Importantly, this mistake was committed not only by the Czech Republic and other Central and East European countries, but by many of the most prominent economic advisers and institutions in the West. According to Nellis (1999):

> International financial institutions must bear some of the responsibility for these poor outcomes, because they requested and required transition governments to privatize rapidly and extensively, assuming that private ownership would, by itself, provide sufficient incentives to shareholders

to monitor managerial behavior and encourage firms' good performance.

Part of this reassessment of the performance of different privatization
methods in the first decade of reform involved a realization that there is "no
one method of privatization that comes out as unambiguously superior to the
others" (Havrylyshyn and McGettigan 1999a, 26). Analysts therefore began
to take a more positive view of Poland's slower, multitrack privatization
effort (Havrylyshyn and McGettigan 1999a, 34).

Conclusions

The Czech Republic, once seen as the shining star of rapid privatization in
Central and Eastern Europe, and a model for the rest of the world, came to be
viewed as one of the primary victims of a major policy mistake in the late
1990s. Voucher privatization, which appeared to reconcile neoliberal reform
agendas with social objectives of fairness and equity in distribution, turned
out to be a costly error. This long-lasting social-liberal reform program produced disappointing results in restructuring and seemed to be partially
responsible for a prolonged downturn in economic growth (IMF 1999b). On
the other hand, contentious democratic politics resulting in slow privatization, political instability, and rapid policy alternation in Poland appears to
have worked better. It facilitated a more varied range of policy alternatives
and a trial-and-error approach that has resulted in more rapid economic
growth.

This conclusion generates several challenges to the current literature on
the relations between democracy and economic reform. First, it suggests the
important and often unacknowledged role that errors have played in the
transformation process (Kołodko 1999). In Central and Eastern Europe after
1989, information about the likely impact of policies was scarce. No one knew
how to transform a socialist economy into a capitalist one overnight. Economic theory provided some possible answers. But it should have been
expected that policy errors would be more frequent and severe than in more
stable economies. After all, even in advanced industrial countries, policy
errors are common and sometimes very severe. Second, the experiences of
Poland and the Czech Republic suggest that policy learning is essential. No
group of reformers was capable of designing a blueprint for reform success at
the outset of the transformation. Knowledge about the most appropriate
methods of privatization was not available at the start of the transformation
process, but only revealed by experience. Though many designs were initially

proposed, research now suggests that no privatization method has proven clearly superior to the others. Policymakers are still learning about the most appropriate privatization strategies (Havrylysyn and McGettigan 1999a). Third, democratic political instability, policy alternation, and enhanced mechanisms of accountability played a major role in facilitating reform learning. Instability and alternation helped to prevent major reform errors in Poland and began correcting them in the Czech Republic starting in 1998.

The story of mass privatization in these two countries suggests that democracy can play a more positive role in processes of economic policymaking than previously envisaged, at least in some countries and under certain conditions. The next chapter presents a general model of how democratic policy alternation facilitated reform in East Central Europe after 1989 and discusses the limits of this model.

CHAPTER 5

Democratic Policy Alternation

Neither Poland nor the Czech Republic emerged out of the red by following a single strategy of reform. Poland adopted a radical efficiency-oriented neoliberal strategy in 1989 but quickly changed course after the effects of a popular antireform backlash were felt. First, reform ground to a halt in 1991, and the IMF suspended its standby agreement with Poland. Then, in 1991–92, the Olszewski government sought, but failed, to overturn neoliberal policies entirely. After this all-or-nothing struggle, compromise solutions began to appear. The Suchocka government tried to move forward with neoliberal reform on the basis of a state enterprise pact negotiated with managers and workers. Following new elections in 1993, left governments opted for a more moderate pace of change, with an emphasis on social-cohesion–oriented policies and better administration. Finally, when neoliberal reformer Leszek Balcerowicz returned to the Ministry of Finance in 1997, he too was forced to moderate his stance and compromise on key issues, thanks to the logic of democratic coalition politics, though some of the fast pace and top-down flavor of shock therapy was restored. As a result, Poland's reforms have oscillated between efficiency- and cohesion-oriented policies, but within an increasingly narrow range over time, constrained by the desire of all major parties to qualify for EU membership. Particularly striking was that Poland progressed through numerous changes of course and leadership without the negative impacts expected by neoliberal and social democratic analysts at the outset of reform (Dahrendorf 1990; Przeworski 1991; Sachs 1993). Indeed, democratic policy alternation in Poland has been accompanied by dynamic economic growth.

In contrast to the vigorous democratic policy alternation in Poland, the Czech Republic enjoyed remarkable policy stability during the first eight years of economic transformation, from 1989 to 1997. Václav Klaus, a reformer celebrated in the West and a major proponent of neoliberal ideas, guided the transition with a high degree of political support. Initially, this support was grounded in the amalgam of neoliberal and social democratic policies that I have called Czech social liberalism, a policy mix that arose from compromises forged during Czechoslovakia's velvet revolution. Social liberalism provided the political stability and backing both social democrats and neoliberals thought was important for the progress of reform. However, the promise of reform stability proved false. Rather than drive economic progress, governmental stability proved to hamper it over the long run, allowing for the continuation of mistaken policies, such as mass voucher privatization, and enabling special interests to become entrenched around erroneous or partial reforms (Hellman 1998; EBRD 1999, 112ff.). Only with the collapse of the Klaus government in late 1997 and the establishment of new centrist and then left governments in 1998 did the Czech Republic begin to correct some of the mistaken policies that had harmed its economic performance, privatizing major banks and cleaning up corrupt securities markets. These policies began to repair the Czech Republic's reputation in the West and encourage renewed flows of foreign direct investment.

By contrasting the positive outcomes of policy change in Poland with the relatively poor results of policy stability in the Czech Republic, this study suggests that democratic policy alternation has been surprisingly effective at facilitating transition progress in postcommunist Central Europe. Both neoliberals and social democrats worried about the consequences of an antireform backlash in postcommunist Europe. Neoliberals believed that countries needed to "stay the course" of reform in order to attain its benefits. Social democrats developed their own balanced-growth strategy that would complement neoliberal policies with social democratic ones designed to avoid antireform backlash. But we have seen in the case of Poland and, after the fall of the Klaus government, in the Czech Republic as well that backlash did not have the expected negative consequences. Instead, policy change and alternation between distinct policy portfolios proved to foster the process of economic reform.

These are only two cases. However, their implications about the effects of democratic policy alternation in Poland and the Czech Republic are strongly corroborated by a cross-national study of twenty-four postcommunist countries conducted by the EBRD in its 1999 *Transition Report* (EBRD 1999, 104–5). The EBRD studied the relations between indicators of executive power, government stability, and transition success. The study found that of twenty-four postcommunist countries, those with the lowest degree of formal executive powers had the highest level of economic reform, exactly the opposite of what neoliberal analysts expected (Sachs 1993, 113). Postcommunist countries where executives had fewer powers to push through a single strategy of reform did better. Likewise, large-coalition governments produced more reform than small-coalition governments. These findings confirm the arguments of those who have suggested that more accountable executives conduct greater reform (Stark and Bruszt 1998). Finally, backlash against reform, the main concern of both neoliberal and social democratic theorists in 1989–90, has not disabled the transition. Instead, "countries in which the incumbent government lost the second postcommunist election have sustained substantially greater reform than countries in which the government won re-election. Therefore, political backlashes and electoral reversals have not prevented progress in market-oriented reforms" (1999, 105).

Unexpectedly, economic reform has been initiated and sustained by both leaders who campaigned as market reformers and those who did not, across a wide range of ideologies and perspectives (EBRD 1999, 104–5). The EBRD study shows that the idea that economic reform had to be pursued by committed free-marketeers bolstered by strong executive powers—and that democratic turnover constituted a major threat—was wrong. The most surprising lesson of a decade of transition in East Central Europe is that government turnover, causing alternation between parties and politicians espousing a variety of different economic views, seems to have been the best way forward for the postcommunist transition countries.

Why has democratic policy alternation facilitated the process of building capitalism in East Central Europe? And why has policy stability, even under reformers, proven so damaging?

This chapter presents a model that seeks to explain these unexpected results. The model is based on three main factors, discussed in the following sections: international and domestic policy *constraints* that were specific to East Central Europe, transition *uncertainty* that has been a major feature of the reform effort in all postcommunist countries, and democratic *learning* processes that are common to democracies around the world.

Constraints

The East Central European countries, comprising Poland, Hungary, the Czech Republic and Slovakia, were subject to very different policy constraints from many of their neighbors in the former Soviet bloc. These countries were historically identified as part of Central Europe rather than Eastern Europe and shared a good part of their history and culture with the West. They were mostly part of the Austro-Hungarian Empire, and before that the Holy Roman Empire and Catholic Europe. Architecturally, culturally, and politically, they shared a common European home that was recognized by leaders and peoples on both sides of the former iron curtain. However, association with the West did not render their transition directions culturally predetermined. As Garton Ash (1999) argued, the boundaries of Central Europe are defined to some extent by culture, and to some extent by "voluntarism," that is, the voluntary choice of Central European states to uphold certain values and ideals. This has been matched by the voluntary actions of the European Union and NATO to recognize these choices by offers of membership.

Analysts have often remarked on the existence of a pro-Europe consensus in East Central Europe (Sachs 1993). Like any consensus, this one is difficult to pin down, but in East Central European political systems, this pro-Europe consensus appears to be rooted in three observable behaviors: First, in public opinion that is broadly favorable toward joining Western institutions, though declining in some countries in recent years (Eurobarometer 1995). Second, in a broad consensus within the party systems on the desirability of membership in the European Union. Third, in the tangible commitment of national governments to seek membership in the European Union, indicated in the Europe agreements that the EU has concluded with a number of Central European countries.

In those countries whose politicians and parties are choosing to be a part of Western institutions, particularly the EU, this choice creates a set of very specific international and domestic policy constraints. These constraints are international, in the sense that the EU, an international organization, has carefully defined the range of acceptable policies in its *acquis communautaire* and various documents drafted specifically to guide East Central European countries to accession. However, these constraints are also domestic, in the sense that the pro-EU aspirations of East Central European populations and leaders cause them to prefer policies that facilitate the goal of EU membership. Once in office, parties come under extreme pressure from international organizations and voters to adhere to policies that keep them on the path to Europe. Ineluctable pressures for EU membership, rooted in cultural identity, international politics, and popular aspirations, present one enormous set of constraints on the range of policies available to prospective member countries, promoting policy convergence around a broad center range. These pressures differentiate the politics of prospective EU members from those of other postcommunist countries.

A second set of constraints is constituted by the economic ideologies of domestic actors. These ideologies may reflect international trends, but often have specific local features. Ideologies are systems of ideas that policymakers use to generate and communicate about policy programs. As explained by Hinich and Munger (1994, 5):

> Ideological messages contain coherent statements of how to choose and what to do. Citizens can, on average, agree with the content and meaning of these statements, though their evaluation of the worth of the statements may differ. As a result, ideologies are the basis for choice in group decisions, and provide a language in which groups debate and disagree.

Ideologies help actors generate policy ideas by providing basic answers to questions of "what is ethically good . . . how society's resources should be distributed, and where power appropriately resides" (1994, 11). Since they provide ready answers to these fundamental questions, coherent ideologies are necessary to the production of policy ideas. But while enabling policy development, they also constrain policy choice within certain bounds. Policies lying within the bounds of a given ideological frame are subject to internal party debate, but those lying outside are clearly inconsistent with the underlying ideology and are therefore unlikely to be chosen by those committed to this viewpoint.

Figure 7 illustrates the ideological range of two hypothetical postcommunist parties, a center-left party (L) and a center-right party (R). Most Central and East European countries have multiparty systems. However, Poland and the Czech Republic show signs of developing two-party dominant systems grouped around large center-right and center-left forces. A two-party model is adopted here for simplicity, but this chart could, and should, be redrawn to map any particular country's party political space. I have mapped the two parties' policy frames on a two-dimensional policy space that consists of a left-right axis of preferred distributional outcomes and a market-state axis of preferred methods of economic organization. However, one could equally well map these policy frames along a number of other dimensions in two- or multidimensional space. The range of EU-acceptable policies discussed above is represented by set (E). Both L and R contain a relatively wide array of policy ideas and perspectives, but L's ideological range is more leftist in preferred distributional outcomes, and more statist in methods. R's ideological range is more rightist distributionally and market-oriented in methods. R's set of preferred policies is more likely to overlap with those policies that form part of the Washington consensus (W) of neoliberal development measures (Williamson 1990, 1997; Naím 2000). Because Washington consensus policymakers are not directly accountable to any broadly representative political body, their policy range (W) is more market-oriented and rightist, but also more narrow and coherent than those of L, R, or E, which must cater to numerous constituencies.

This brings us to a third set of constraints: voter preferences. Parties cannot be guided by the economic ideology of their leaders or the goals of EU integration alone. In a parliamentary democracy, they must also be guided by pragmatism in identifying, developing, and catering to the economic views of a substantial proportion of the electorate. This tends to expand the size of their policy ranges. Domestic policymakers are rational partisans, in the sense that they "want to win in order to implement their desired policies" (Alesina and Roubini 1997, 45). The nature of political institutions will determine

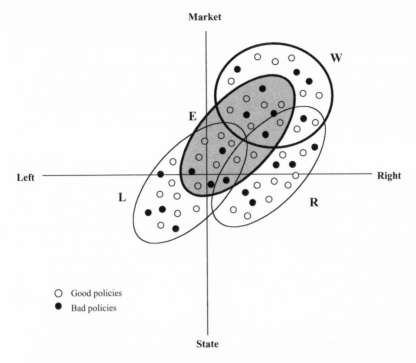

Fig. 7.   Policy constraints and uncertainty in East Central European transitions

how, and how much, ruling parties must conform to voter interests in order to win. As a rule of thumb, in a parliamentary democracy in East Central Europe, a party must win at least 10 percent of the vote to win a substantial role in a coalition government and have a chance to implement its policies. A senior coalition partner often must win 30 percent or more. And since most East Central European countries have vote thresholds to enter parliament, parties must win approximately 5 percent of the vote simply to remain relevant in parliament.

The imperatives of winning elections mean that successful parties must tailor their policy ranges to correspond with the interests of a sizable proportion of voters. Voters choose parties based on a calculation of their current and prospective interests, discounting the future on grounds of risk (Przeworski 1991). Voters evaluate the performance of political parties along two dimensions: *(a)* the extent to which the party's ideological self-definition fits voters' perceptions of their own self-interest; and *(b)* the technical effectiveness of the party in choosing and pursuing good policies. Disillusionment on either grounds will cause some voters to choose an alternative party in the next election. Parties must therefore strive to represent voter interests, and to represent them efficaciously.

Governing parties in postcommunist East Central Europe therefore face triple constraints in economic policymaking. They must find policies that lie at the intersection of EU acceptability, party ideological self-definition, and voter interests.

Uncertainty

Postcommunist policymakers would be relieved if this were their only problem. But there are further complications, arising from the nature of transition uncertainty. This uncertainty is a feature of all postcommunist transformations, in East Central Europe and throughout the region, regardless of the nature of transition constraints. Even though it is theoretically possible for policymakers to determine which policies lie at the intersection of EU acceptability, party ideology, and voter interests, the nature of postcommunist transition makes it impossible for reformers to choose all the good policies within this set.

Neoliberals initially conceived of transition as a simple journey from communism to capitalism. They claimed that the destination—capitalism— was well known (see the epigraph from Sachs in chapter 1), and that the only problem was figuring out how to get from here to there. As time passed, most analysts began to agree that the nature of postcommunist transition was rather different. Instead of constituting a simple journey, postcommunist transition involved a multitude of transformations across a variety of different spheres, whose ultimate endpoint was not predetermined (Stark and Bruszt 1998, 83). This view underpinned the various institutional approaches to transition (Poznanski 1995; Stark and Bruszt 1998; Elster, Offe, and Preuss 1998), but it is an increasingly common viewpoint among neoliberals as well (Winiecki 1997, 2). While institutionalists argue that economic transformation policies must take into account specific features of the institutional environment (Murrell 1995, 81; Stark and Bruszt 1998), or that the state should play a larger part in guiding the process of institutional design (Kołodko 1999, 17), neoliberals argue that radical macroeconomic policies and the withdrawal of the state create the right incentives for individual actors to find the best ways to conduct institutional transformation (Winiecki 1997, 3). However, despite these differences, everyone now agrees that the full range of desirable transition policies is, in principle, unknowable. Therefore, the choice of policies by which to achieve them is by definition uncertain.

Although East Central European countries do have a general end point for their transitions, defined by membership in the European Union, the scope of EU-acceptable policies still leaves a relatively wide range of choice and indeterminacy. As Sachs (1993, 5) pointed out, there are major differences between British liberalism, the German social-market economy, and Swedish socialism. East Central European countries face a wide array of policy choices within the EU-acceptable range.

Uncertainty about what policies to implement across a broad range of transformations in many socioeconomic spheres has made it impossible for any single reformer, consultant, or group of reformers to identify all the good transition policies, even within a given ideological range. Polish finance minister Leszek Balcerowicz developed the concept of a "reform possibility frontier" to characterize this problem. In his view, one of the basic problems of reform was that reformers did not have sufficient time or resources to identify and develop all the good policies they might wish to implement. This was because the postcommunist transformations were enormously complex, defying limits of human understanding and creativity. He argued that "ultimately the inherent human limitations of information processing and learning" establish a reform possibility frontier that determines the maximum possible speed of reform (1995, 240). In short, even the best reformers could not identify all the good policies, even within the constraints of their own ideological range.

Related to this problem of information processing is the phenomenon of reform mistakes. Not only were reformers unable to quickly identify and develop all the best policies within their ideological range, but they made numerous mistakes. There is good reason to think that during the postcommunist transformations, the natural propensity for mistakes was higher than in many other situations. As has been pointed out many times, postcommunist transition was a new phenomenon; no one had experience in dealing with it; and there was no road map for reform. Policies being tried were often new, and information about their effects was therefore scarce. Transition policymaking also often took place in a significant information void, including for instance a lack of high-quality statistics about what was taking place in the economy at large. Therefore, governments were likely to make an unusually high proportion of policy mistakes. Mistaken or bad policies, defined as those with negative unanticipated consequences for economic performance, are represented by the black circles in figure 7. Good policies are those that achieve and further transformation goals without major negative unintended consequences. These are represented by white circles in figure 7.

Policy mistakes have been pervasive in postcommunist transitions. As Przeworski (1995, 68), Stark and Bruszt (1998, 190) and Kołodko (1999) point out, the neoliberal model overlooked the possibility of reform mistakes—that an insulated reform team might chose erroneous policies. Yet the history of postcommunist economic transition is already littered with examples of such reform mistakes. Probably the greatest was mass privatization, advocated by major Western advisers, international financial institutions and governments, and adopted in numerous postcommunist countries with dubious effectiveness. And yet many other mistakes, large and small, were made.

Asked what his major mistakes were, and whether they could have been avoided, Czech reformer Václav Klaus replied, "We have inevitably made hundreds of mistakes, but in my opinion none of them was of strategic importance." Polish reformer Leszek Balcerowicz noted three major mistakes or omissions in 1990 and 1991, whose consequences had not been foreseen at the time (Blejer and Coricelli 1995, 128–30). The phenomenon of policy mistakes clearly needs to be addressed in models of postcommunist policymaking.

While figure 7 shows similar proportions of good and bad policies within each ideological range, it cannot be assumed that all policy actors are equally prone to error. Actors may be more or less technically adept at identifying, elaborating, and implementing the good and bad policies within their range (Balcerowicz 1995, 240). In transition countries, there is no reason to assume a priori that one group of reformers is more technically competent than another, or that an international organization with limited local knowledge will make fewer mistakes. Indeed, the experience of privatization shows that international organizations made significant mistakes. It is safer to assume that no policy actors are perfect, and all are likely to make mistakes.

Finally, it is important to note that some good transition policies always lie outside a given actor's ideological range. This means that even if policy actors were able to identify all the good policies within their range and avoid policy mistakes entirely, they would still not have access to the full range of good transition policies, since some lie outside their ideological range. This causes actors to ignore potentially good policies and increases the chances of committing reform mistakes. As Grzegorz Kołodko, Poland's minister of finance from 1994 to 1997, noted, "Of course, it does happen that policy mistakes occur due to a lack of experience and proper knowledge, but more often this confusion stems from obedience to a particular group of interests, or to 'theoretical schools,' that happen to be ideological and political lobbies too. This is why there are no leftist or rightist doctors or engineers, but there are leftist and rightist economists and policymakers" (Kołodko 1999, 14). Economic ideologies, which are necessary for the formulation of coherent policy positions, tend to blind actors to good policies that lie outside their ideological frame.

As a result of the existence of a reform possibility frontier, the likelihood of reform mistakes, and the inability of a single ideology to encompass all good policies, actors never identify or implement all the good transition policies under conditions of high uncertainty. They implement some bad policies with the good, fail to implement all the good ones that are available to them, and leave some good policies out of consideration entirely. Postcommunist transformations are characterized by a large set of socioeconomic problems searching for solutions (Cohen, March, and Olsen 1972). Under conditions of uncertainty, no single actor has the vision or ability to resolve them all, and any single policy actor is likely to do some harm, as well as good. Given the unprecedented scale and nature of transition (Nelson 1993), this holds true throughout the postcommunist region.

Learning

Parties might be expected to learn from their mistakes. But the evidence of ten years of transition suggests that it is difficult for a government to undo its own policy mistakes. Parties and policymakers are partly pragmatic, in that they recognize errors and often seek to correct them (see Balcerowicz quoted in Blejer and Coricelli 1995, 128). They can sometimes abandon bad policies within their range and adopt good ones outside their range. But parties also tend to become committed to both good and bad policies within their range, despite "warnings, criticisms and intellectual and political opposition" (Kołodko 1999, 15).

Commitment to bad policies may be perpetuated for several reasons: First, since criticism often comes from the opposition, governments may discount accurate criticism and early warnings about the ill effects of their policies as normal partisan attacks (Przeworski 1995, 81). Second, mistaken policies may generate gains for interest groups within the government coalition, which then lobby to prevent correction, as in the "politics of partial reform" (Hellman 1998). Hellman argued that postcommunist countries have been subject to reform hijacking from above by powerful elites, who develop strong interests in sustaining partial reforms, and progressing no further. These elites profit from particular features of partial reform, leveraging discontinuities between markets and continued state controls. The longer a government stays in power, and the more unconstrained the executive, the more vulnerable it is to this type of reform hijacking. Third, governments may feel that an admission of policy errors will reduce government credibility. Reformers in particular may not want to do this, because evident vacillation weakens their ability to command popular support for reform in the future (Przeworski 1991, 169). Fourth, it may undermine a governing party's identity to distance itself from previous policies that played a large role in its earlier platform. A party that is strongly identified with a certain policy may risk losing core constituencies or ideological coherence if it reverses its stance. For all these reasons, policy learning is sticky.

Given the propensity for reform mistakes and the difficulty of reversing them while the same government remains in power, alternation tends to speed up policy learning and institutionalize it within the party system. After losing power, parties often generate internal learning processes and reorganization. They have the opportunity to observe the behavior of other parties in power and assess their own mistakes. In the future, these rational partisans must compete with other parties to provide good policies that the public is willing to support, giving them strong incentives to change. Rather than slowing down reform, the pressures of democratic competition and policy alternation therefore accelerate the process by which political entrepreneurs (Schumpeter 1942) reformulate policy positions and engage in policy learning. It forces the party system to institutionalize the mechanisms of "reflexive learning" that Stark and Bruszt (1998, 197–98) argue are so important to transformation success.

Learning through democratic policy alternation, however, is a nonlinear process. Different parties with different competencies and emphases in economic policy may produce progress along some dimensions, while ignoring or even impeding others. This results in an uneven pattern of policy development, similar to Hirschman's model of antagonistic growth (fig. 8). Hirschman (1988) developed this model to explain why countries often do not take a smooth, linear path to development, and later extended the model to address other issues and problems. Hirschman suggested that development is often characterized by antagonism between two (or more) development goals that cannot be pursued at the same time. Indeed, the pursuit of one goal sets back the pursuit of the other. Under such conditions, both can be achieved through a process of policy alternation, if the rate of damage is less than the rate of advancement. This is what he describes as "sailing against the wind" (1988, 240).

Hirschman argues that this model approximates the way that economic policymaking takes place in a democracy.

> If, in such a system, each of the two parties retains a characteristic physiognomy or ideological consistency of its own, then each party will give very distinct priorities to such social objectives as growth, equity and stability; with the parties alternating in power, society is likely to move, in the best of circumstances, as though it were sailing against the wind. . . .
> At any one point in time, there is always not only strife and clash and

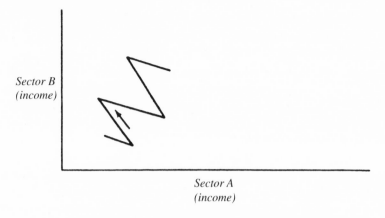

Sector B
(income)

Sector A
(income)

Fig. 8.   Hirschman's antagonistic growth model

conflict, but also loss of some valuable terrain previously gained. Yet it is possible that all-around progress is being achieved behind the back, so to speak, of the parties and groups in conflict. Democracy is consolidated when, after a few alternations of the parties in power, the various groups come to realize that, strangely enough, they have all gained. (Hirschman 1988, 240)

It would be optimal if policy learning could unfold in a more linear way. But under conditions of policy uncertainty and constraint, this may not be possible. Democracy has often been accused of adding constraints, and so it does. Yet democracy also provides a powerful mechanism for accelerating policy learning, by harnessing the forces of competition between rival political entrepreneurs.

Democratic Learning through Policy Alternation

Policy alternation is a natural feature of democratic policy processes. In this model of postcommunist East Central European policymaking, parties L and R choose transition policies from among those available within their ideological range. They may be more or less technically adept at choosing and implementing effective policies within their range. However, they are likely to make policy mistakes and implement policies that turn out to be ill advised.

Alternation occurs because voters tend to abandon an incumbent party, or support an alternative party, on either party-definitional or party-performance grounds. Studies have found that party system volatility is extraordinarily high in Central and Eastern Europe (Kitschelt et al. 1999, 401). On ideological grounds, voters may choose to defect from the incumbent party because it implements policies that do not coincide with voter interests, either current or prospective. On pragmatic grounds, voters may chose to defect because the incumbent party does not implement a sufficiently large number of good transition policies, the party in power implements too many mistaken policies, or the incumbent party fails to implement good policies that lie outside its ideological range.

Given these democratic pressures, centrist competition exists among political parties to provide reform policies that will produce the goods of transition and eventual qualification for EU membership in a way that is consistent with voter ideologies and interests. Parties attempt to maintain their ideological agendas, but they also compete to provide technically effective policies that lie within the intersection of their party's strategic ideological frame and area (E in fig. 9). Voters are ambivalent about EU integration. They want it in the future, and expect that their interests will be served by it in the future, but possibly not at present. At present, their interests may be better served by policies that lie outside of (E). Therefore, parties campaign on policies that serve current voter interests, even if these fall outside of (E). But while in office they seek policies that lie within the intersection of their ideological frame and the (E) set. Because of this voter behavior, because countries are committed to progress toward EU membership, and because an effective consensus exists within the party system on the desirability of this direction of change, democratic policy alternation has produced a centrist convergence in East Central European economic policy choices.

Such competition between parties to provide good transition policies accelerates a societal process of policy learning. One party tries to implement its conception of transition policy. It partly succeeds and partly fails. Meanwhile, an opposition party uses its time out of power to develop an alternative set of transition policies that it believes will work better and garner sufficient popular support. When it wins election, the new party will often maintain the successful transition policies of its predecessors. However, it will try to reverse the most glaring policy mistakes and dislodge reform hijackers. It will seek to implement a further set of transition policies, some of which will work and some of which will fail. Finally, it will be disciplined by criticism and competition from its rival party, while the rival party uses its time out of power to reformulate its policy agenda to win more popular support and achieve more transition goals.

When both parties are competing to provide good policies with the same general goal, such as EU membership, democratic policy alternation causes a cumulative process of policy learning to unfold. Entrepreneurial competition

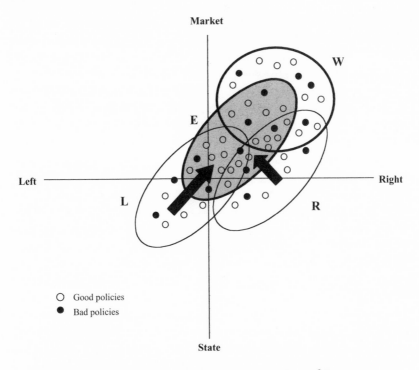

Fig. 9.   Policy convergence and learning in East Central European transitions

between parties with different strategies for reconciling the goals of transformation with citizen interests accelerates reform learning and reduces the dangers of elite hijacking and entrenched mistakes. Over time, it causes an accumulation of good policies within the (E) range. In this context, vigorous party competition and frequent electoral turnover is both good for democracy (Rueschemeyer 1999) and good for economic reform. Democratic policy alternation can work better than adherence to any single path or blueprint of reform, in the presence of sufficient constraints.

Conditions for Learning

However, it is important to keep in mind that democratic policy alternation does not always result in a process of cumulative learning or reform progress. What are the conditions under which democratic policy alternation may play a positive role in economic development?

This model suggests that these conditions may be very restrictive. In the case of East Central Europe, international factors played a large role in keeping democratic policy alternation within certain bounds. Outright defiance of core IMF or EU policy preferences carried high costs for democratically elected East Central European policymakers. For instance, the IMF's strong public criticism of the Olszewski government in Poland caused it to back down from radical antineoliberal policies and contributed to the government's rapid demise in 1992 (cf. *New York Times,* March 6, 1992, 6). And since the late 1990s, governments that implement policies outside the EU's *acquis communautaire* are subject to yearly public evaluations by the EU that can be highly embarrassing. Governments perceived as anti-Western had difficulty surviving in East Central Europe in the decade after 1989, because policymaker and public opinion so strongly supported EU membership. International pressures and domestic support for a "return to Europe" therefore enforced an extraordinary set of limits around policy entrepreneurship in East Central Europe that focused party competition and turned policy alternation into a cumulative learning process, rather than one characterized by radical swings that might negate previous policy efforts and lessons. Yet it is extremely unusual for developing countries to have a neighboring, highly developed economic community that is politically and economically committed to working toward making them full members. However, a high level of international commitment may be a necessary condition to keep democratic policy alternation on track.

More generally, a high degree of social consensus on economic system choices and policy objectives may be required in order to turn democratic policy alternation into an effective mechanism of policy learning. Democratic institutions are probably not very good at sorting out basic questions of economic system design in polarized societies. Democratic policy alternation may simply work better when these issues are taken off the table (Schumpeter 1942; Jessop 1990) and there is relatively widespread agreement on both the nature and purpose of the economic system and the ultimate ends of policy, such as a "return to Europe." Then, policymaking becomes more nearly a game of reaching appropriate decisions about the means to these ends, and the type of policy learning described above becomes more likely. Full reversals of the policies of the previous government are not undertaken, but instead only of those policies perceived to be mistaken or ineffective. This allows a corrective, but cumulative, learning process to emerge.

In countries without such a consensus on the economy, however, policy swings can be expected to be greater because there are fewer perceived limits to policy entrepreneurship. Then the negative effects of alternation predicted by Przeworski (1991) might arise. Pure antagonism between policy options, leading to policy standoffs and total reversals, might occur, rather than the more positive model of policy learning suggested here.

In circumstances where major social forces have no areas of policy overlap, where society is polarized, where there are extreme differences of opinion about the overall direction of a country in the international system, democracy may not function well—and policy learning of the cumulative type may not emerge. Policymakers working under such conditions may select, and historically have selected, other paths to economic development. In some countries, authoritarian regimes may effectively promote development, as in contemporary China or Korea and Taiwan in the 1970s and 1980s. However, authoritarian regimes depend on sage leaders, and the record of authoritarian sagacity is not great. Studies have shown that for every Pinochet, there are two or three Papa Doc Duvaliers, Mobutus, and Brezhnevs (Geddes 1995). Even sage leaders who have an extraordinary record of policy development do not last forever. Policy correction is needed eventually even in successful authoritarian cases. And there is evidence to suggest that authoritarian regimes do better when mechanisms of policy alternation exist within the authoritarian regime, for instance the PRI's revolving presidency in Mexico or the leadership changes in the Chinese Communist Party that enabled radical policy corrections throughout the second half of the twentieth century and beyond. In some cases, authoritarian policy alternation may work similarly to democratic policy alternation, but with authoritarian institutions setting additional boundaries and limits to the extent of policy change, on top of international pressures and domestic policy preferences. Authoritarian regimes may be better able to keep policy alternation within bounds when full democracy would lead to such strong centrifugal forces that no effective or peaceful policy alternation could exist. But this is only suggested by a few cases. The general rule for authoritarian regimes is slow (often painfully slow) alternation and learning, and the persistence of ineffective policies despite long-standing need for correction.

Democratic policy alternation of the type experienced in East Central Europe—and in the most advanced industrial democracies—is contingent and fragile. It is surprising that Central European countries have made it work so well in the course of a transition that seemed to raise contentious and fundamental policy issues that could have led to democratic breakdown. Accelerated learning has occurred largely because of elite and public consensus on the desirability of a "return to Europe" that has focused policy entrepreneurship and set clear goals and limits. Such conditions are not easily replicable. They also may not be sustainable in Central Europe as the realities of EU membership become more widely known. Instances of broad economic policy consensus are not common in the recent history of Central

Europe, nor in West European countries for that matter. The current consensus reflects specific features of the international system at this point in time, including support for democracy and the emergence of a standard range of economic policies that define membership in Western economic clubs. Democracy in transition countries therefore may be heavily reliant on specific features of the contemporary global capitalist system.

Conclusions

When countries seek to advance their fortunes in the present global economy, democratic policy alternation can provide a powerful method of sorting out technical methods of building capitalism while serving the interests of a substantial proportion of the population. Despite concern about globalization, countries still have a range of policy choices in the global economy (Garrett 1998). Different choices may work better for some groups and for a nation as a whole. And the stakes are high. Divergent performance of developing country economies during the 1980s and 1990s suggests that countries that make good policy choices can prosper, while others continue to suffer from low growth and high poverty rates. Therefore the struggle to find effective mechanisms for making decisions about economic policy is far from futile, even though many important decisions are made outside a developing country's boundaries.

And under certain conditions, democracy presents a powerful way forward. In situations of rapid change and policy uncertainty, democratic institutions can help to quickly overturn mistaken policies, accelerate policy learning, and encourage policy entrepreneurship, while maintaining the best policies of past governments in the spirit of pragmatism.

All of these strengths of democratic decision-making, though often unrecognized, have helped the countries of East Central Europe move out of the red and into a freer and more prosperous place in the global political-economic system. These countries have done so not by adherence to any economic orthodoxy or blueprint, but by a process of policy learning accelerated by democratic competition.

Notes

Introduction

1. Use of the term *liberal* throughout this book may be confusing to some American readers because this term has an almost opposite meaning in the domestic politics of the United States. When I refer to *liberal* or *neoliberal,* I am referring to the philosophy of economic liberalism expounded by Adam Smith, David Ricardo, and others, who emphasized the benefits of limited government intervention in free markets, and were thus "liberal." In the United States, however, *liberal* has come to be identified solely with cultural liberalism, or cultural laissez-faire. "Liberals" in the United States are commonly criticized by cultural conservatives who are themselves economic liberals or neoliberals.

Chapter 1

1. Elster, Offe, and Preuss make a similar argument in *Institutional Design in Post-communist Societies* (1998, 32–34). They state that regime consolidation, and hence the establishment of strong, institutionalized centers of power, depends on a new regime's founders accepting self-binding rules and limits on their individual power. To consolidate and institutionalize a new regime, they need to invest their power in creating and allocating "rules, resources, and recognition" to new and relatively independent institutional locations, which necessarily limit their power to achieve individual or momentary goals.

Chapter 2

1. There are some interesting terminological issues here regarding the proper name for this strategy. Western neoliberals prefer to speak of a "jump" rather than a "leap" to the market in Poland (cf. Jeffrey Sachs, *Poland's Jump to the Market Economy,* 1993), probably mostly because Mao Tse-tung ruined the idea of a "great leap forward." Although a jump sounds less elegant than a leap, for political reasons, it appears a safe compromise. On the other hand, "shock therapy," a term derived from a dubious medical practice ("the treatment of certain psychotic conditions by injecting drugs or by passing an electric current through the brain to produce convulsions or coma") is considered pejorative by some, while the metaphor of a "big bang" ("a cosmological theory postulating that all the matter of the universe was hurled in all directions by a cataclysmic explosion and that the universe is still expanding") is preferred by its proponents (definitions from Collins dictionary). I use *shock therapy* because the term has entered such widespread usage and I think that the metaphor of a medical procedure on a live subject is more appropriate than that of creation from scratch.

2. Shock therapy was first tried in Bolivia in 1985–86, where Sachs fashioned this new approach in cooperation with Bolivian government economists (Conaghan 1995).

Bolivia conquered 10,000 percent inflation in a matter of weeks and at the same time introduced a wide-reaching program of economic transformation, including privatization, deregulation, and amendments to the system of labor relations that set it on a path of long-term recovery, if not dynamic growth. The reputation Sachs built in Bolivia helped sell his novel ideas on economic development to Polish reformers in 1989 (Kuroń 1991, 13).

3. On works councils, see Federowicz and Levitas 1995. Federowicz and Levitas (283–84) argue that "periodically elements within the Party promoted the creation of councils either as a way to legitimate Communist power on the shop floor or to improve the flexibility of the economy as a whole." Biezenski (1994, 59) argues that "the driving force behind self-management was not the working class but rather the intelligentsia, who took advantage of workers' revolts to push forward their own interests." Stefancic (1992) takes yet another perspective, arguing that self-management was a constant element in working-class demands from the Second World War until it was abandoned by Solidarity in 1989.

4. Blejer and Coricelli 1995 provides a notable and important primary source for this study. The book consists of interviews conducted with Leszek Balcerowicz, Václav Klaus, and Peter Bod, leading reformers in Poland, the Czech Republic, and Hungary, respectively. The authors asked each of these three reformers the same set of questions on the initiation and continued pursuit of reform, including its political aspects, and hence provide an important data set for analyzing differences between the views of leading reformers in each country.

5. Economic reformers in Poland did not see themselves as career politicians. Balcerowicz wished to stand above politics, following an interwar Polish tradition of politically independent ministers of finance. This was consistent with the technocratic political strategy of shock therapy—the leading cadres should not get involved in politics, lest they begin to place special interests above the "common good." Though many people tried to persuade Balcerowicz and other reformers to form a political party in 1990 and 1991, they refused. Balcerowicz did not join a reform-oriented political party until 1995, when he became a member of the Freedom Union and was soon thereafter elected its president. By that time, however, Freedom Union (created out of a merger between Mazowiecki's Democratic Union and Bielecki's Liberal Democratic Congress) had been reduced to a party of the urban intelligentsia that commanded less than 10 percent of the vote.

6. Wałęsa had always performed a charismatic function in the Solidarity movement, and increasingly after 1989 he became the one man able to bridge the growing gap between Solidarity's working-class base and its liberal governmental leaders. Wałęsa performed this role not only symbolically, as a worker president, but in concrete crisis situations that arose periodically. Wałęsa was often the tool of last resort for a government besieged by wildcat strikes, such as the railway strike in Słupsk that threatened to bring the transport system to a halt in May 1990 (Boyes 1994, 224). Solidarity's liberal intellectual leadership had grown used to relying on Wałęsa's authority.

7. Wałęsa appointed Zdzisław Najder in 1990 to head the Solidarity civic committees for the sole purpose of destroying them or at least wrecking plans to turn them into the kernel of a Solidarity political party (Boyes 1994, 214–15). Wałęsa resented the fact that the committees were becoming a political base for Mazowiecki, independent of Gdansk. Wałęsa then attempted to sack Henryk Wujec, the secretary of the civic committees, in June, along with Adam Michnik, the editor of *Gazeta Wyborcza*.

8. Wałęsa had already been planning to run for president in early 1990, when he was reelected Solidarity chairman, although he played down his ambitions at the Solidarity congress in order to convince the delegates he would work full time throughout the year for the interests of the union. He also fought to postpone the presidential elections until he had won election to the Solidarity chairmanship. In using the trade union as a base for his presidential campaign, rather than building up institutional capacity that was badly damaged during martial law, Wałęsa impeded the development of Solidarity as a trade union and an opponent of the government reform effort. Wałęsa was dismissed as Solidarity chairman at the 1991 congress and replaced by a then unknown Silesian academic, Marian Krzaklewski. See Boyes 1994, 220–21.

9. The statement was signed by Ryszard Bugaj, Wojciech Lamentowicz, Jan Józef Lipski, Karol Modzelewski, Jerzy Szacki, Włodzimierz Wesełowski, and Jan Mujżel, among others.

10. The three amendments were on April 7, 1989, December 29, 1989, and March 8, 1990. The April 1989 amendment, arising from the roundtable compromise, replaced the Council of State with a president vested with significant powers and created a second legislative chamber, the Senate, empowered to review and amend laws originating in the Sejm.

11. At least two government coalition parties opposed decree powers for the government, the Polish Peasant Party (PSL), which issued a strong statement against changing the system of government (PAP, June 28, 1993) and the Christian National Union (ZChN), which believed that once such legislation passed, it would be jettisoned from the government coalition (Inter Press Service, June 22, 1993). Both parties, and other rural parties, thought their interests would be violated by economic decrees.

Chapter 3

Portions of this chapter first appeared as "Václav Klaus: Revolutionary and Parliamentarian," in East European Constitutional Review 7:1 (Winter 1998). Reprinted with permission.

1. William Henry Beveridge's Report on Social Insurance and Allied Services (1942) formed the basis of the British welfare state. His name is often associated with the idea of state-guaranteed minimum standards for all citizens.

2. It must be noted that many people question the accuracy of these figures, like all statistics from East Central Europe. Neoliberals often argue that unemployment and poverty statistics are overstated, while growth rates are understated. Nonetheless, the fact that the multiple Polish studies reviewed in Schwartz (1994) produce poverty figures ten times the Czech ones seems significant.

3. In the Vienna parliament, the Czechs developed a reputation for argumentative and annoying speeches that were a thorn in the side of the Habsburg monarchy. First Republic president T. G. Masaryk made his name in the Vienna parliament as the sole representative of the Realist Party.

4. A fascinating insight into the mentality and policies of Czechoslovak Agrarianism can be gained from the biography of Martin Švehla, chairman of the Agrarian Party during the First Republic.

5. Schweik was a character created by the novelist Jaroslav Hašek (1946) in his world-famous novel The Good Soldier Schweik. Schweik was a seeming idiot who con-

stantly defied and outwitted his master, a lieutenant in the Austrian army during the First World War, by misinterpreting his commands and acting stupid. Strangely, Schweik became an unofficial Czech hero, symbolizing the small nation's resistance to its powerful neighbors, and other national traits.

Chapter 4

1. The first wave of voucher privatization was conducted before the division of Czechoslovakia into two separate countries, the Czech Republic and Slovakia in January 1993. In the first wave, the Czechoslovak Ministry of Privatization approved 1,491 privatization projects, of which 988 involved Czech companies. After the split of Czechoslovakia in 1993, Slovakia canceled its second wave of voucher privatization, while the Czech Republic conducted one in 1994–95.

2. Spicer, McDermott, and Kogut (2000) argue that "Gradual property reform based on joint negotiation and compromise leads to more industrial restructuring than rapid mass privatization based on voucher auctions and exchange. . . . Rapid mass privatization does not lead to the formation of transparent security markets. . . . Mass privatization erodes potentially productive network ties by transforming collective assets into private goods. . . . Negotiated property reform better incorporates institutional experimentation and learning into the process of privatization than does rapid mass privatization policy."

3. *Nomenklatura* is the common name for the group of Communist bureaucrats and officials who were deemed eligible for high-level service and whose names were entered on special party lists, hence the party nomenclature.

4. In Czechoslovakia, the voucher privatization process was managed by a private company, PVT, which actually made a handsome profit from the thirty-five-dollar registration fees. Multiplied by 8.5 million participants in the first wave alone, revenues totaled nearly $300 million. Money to finance program costs in the start-up phase was borrowed at commercial rates of credit against the future fee income.

5. Some advocates of mass voucher privatization still believe that the program was a qualified success, but their defense of the program is weak. Shleifer and Treisman's bottom line, for instance, is that "privatization in Russia worked considerably better than its politically feasible alternative: doing nothing" (2000, 38). It should be noted that Shleifer was an author of the controversial Russian voucher privatization scheme. Jeffrey Sachs, architect of a mass privatization program for Poland in 1990, admitted error at conferences attended by this author starting in 1997.

References

Newspapers, Journals, and Wire Services

BBC. *BBC Summary of World Broadcasts,* London.
CBOS. Center for Public Opinion Research, Warsaw.
The Economist, London.
Ekonom, Prague.
Facts on File, electronic database.
FT. *Financial Times,* London.
Gazeta Wyborcza, Warsaw.
HN. *Hospodářské noviny,* Prague.
Inter Press Service, electronic database.
Lidové Demokracie, Prague.
LN. *Lidové Noviny,* Prague.
MFD. *Mladá Fronta Dnes,* Prague.
Nowe Życie Gospodarcze, Warsaw.
PAP. Polish Press Agency, Warsaw.
Práce, Prague.
Polityka, Warsaw.
Respekt, Prague.
RFE/RL (Radio Free Europe/Radio Liberty). *RFE/RL Research Report on Eastern Europe.*
RP. *Rudé Právo,* Prague.
Rzeczpospolita, Warsaw.
Svobodné Slovo, Prague.
Trend, Bratislava.
Transition, Open Media Research Institute, Prague.
Transition, World Bank, Washington, D.C.
Warsaw Voice.
Życie Gospodarcze, Warsaw.

Books and Articles

Ackerman, Bruce. 1992. *The Future of Liberal Revolution.* New Haven: Yale University Press.
Adam, Jan. 1989. *Economic Reforms in the Soviet Union and Eastern Europe since the 1960s.* London: Macmillan.
———. 1993a. *Planning and Market in Soviet and East European Thought, 1960s–1992.* New York: St. Martin's Press.
———. 1993b. Transformation to a Market Economy in the Former Czechoslovakia. *Europe-Asia Studies* 45, no. 4: 627–45.
Alesina, Alberto, and Nouriel Roubini, with Gerald D. Cohen. 1997. *Political Cycles and the Macroeconomy.* Cambridge: MIT Press.
Amsden, Alice H., Jacek Kochanowicz, and Lance Taylor. 1994. *The Market Meets Its*

Match: Restructuring the Economies of Eastern Europe. Cambridge: Harvard University Press.

Appel, Hilary, and John Gould. 2000. Identity Politics and Economic Reform: Examining Industry-State Relations in the Czech and Slovak Republics. *Europe-Asia Studies* 52, no. 1: 111–32.

Aslund, Anders, Peter Boone, and Simon Johnson. 1996. How to Stabilize: Lessons from Post-Communist Countries. Brookings Papers on Economic Activity, 1:217–313.

Balcerowicz, Ewa. 1995. Struktura Wlasnosciova "Listy 500." *Życie Gospodarcze,* January 1.

Balcerowicz, Leszek. 1994. Understanding Postcommunist Transitions. *Journal of Democracy* 5, no. 4:75–89.

———. 1995. *Socialism, Capitalism, Transformation.* Budapest: Central European University Press.

Balcerowicz, Leszek, with Jerzy Baczyński and Jerzy Komiński. 1992. *800 Dni: Szok Kontrolowany.* Warsaw: Polska Oficyna Wydawnicza BGW.

Batt, Judy. 1988. *Economic Reform and Political Change in Eastern Europe.* London: Macmillan.

———. 1991. *East-Central Europe from Reform to Transformation.* London: Royal Institute of International Affairs, Pinter Publishers.

Berg, Andrew, and Olivier Jean Blanchard. 1992. Stabilization and Transition: Poland, 1990–91. In *The Transition in Eastern Europe,* vol. 1, ed. Olivier Jean Blanchard, Kenneth A. Froot, and Jeffrey D. Sachs. Chicago: University of Chicago Press.

Berg, Andrew, and Jeffrey Sachs. 1992. Structural Adjustment and International Trade in Eastern Europe: The Case of Poland. *Economic Policy* 14:117–73.

Berger, Peter. 1993. The Uncertain Triumph of Democratic Capitalism. In *Capitalism, Socialism, and Democracy Revisited,* ed. Larry Diamond and Marc F. Plattner. Baltimore: Johns Hopkins University Press.

Biezenski, Robert. 1994. Workers' Self-Management and the Technical Intelligentsia in People's Poland. *Politics and Society* 22, no. 1: 59–88.

Blanchard, Olivier, Rudiger Dornbusch, Paul Krugman, Richard Layard, and Lawrence Summers. 1991. *Reform in Eastern Europe.* Cambridge: MIT Press.

Błaszczyk, Barbara. 1999. Moving Ahead: Privatization in Poland. *Economic Reform Today* (Center for International Private Enterprise, Washington, D.C.), no. 4.

Błaszczyk, Barbara, and Marek Dąbrowski. 1993. The Privatization Process in Poland. Typescript, Warsaw.

———. 1994. The Privatization Process in Poland. In *Privatization in the Transition Process: Recent Experiences in Eastern Europe.* Geneva: United Nations Conference on Trade and Development.

Blazyca, George. 1995. Monitoring Economic Transformation. In *Monitoring Economic Transition: The Polish Case,* ed. George Blazyca and Janusz M. Dabrowski. Aldershot, UK: Avebury.

Blazyca, George, and Ryszard Rapacki. 1996. Continuity and Change in Polish Economic Policy: The Impact of the 1993 Election. *Europe-Asia Studies* 48, no. 1: 85–100.

Blejer, Mario I., and Fabrizio Coricelli. 1995. *The Making of Economic Reform in Eastern Europe: Conversations with Leading Reformers in Poland, Hungary, and the Czech Republic.* Aldershot: Edward Elgar.

Böhm, Andreja, and Vladimir Kreacic. 1991. *Privatization in Eastern Europe.* Ljubljana, Slovenia: International Center for Public Enterprises in Developing Countries.

Boone, Peter, Stanisław Gomułka, and Richard Layard, eds. 1998. *Emerging from Communism: Lessons from Russia, China, and Eastern Europe.* Cambridge: MIT Press.

Boyes, Roger. 1994. *The Naked President: A Political Life of Lech Wałęsa.* London: Secker and Warburg.

Bresser Pereira, Luiz Carlos, José María Maravall, and Adam Przeworski. 1993. *Economic Reforms in New Democracies: A Social-Democratic Approach.* Cambridge: Cambridge University Press.

Brom, Karla, and Mitchell Orenstein. 1994. The Privatised Sector in the Czech Republic. *Europe-Asia Studies* 46, no. 6:893–928.

Bruno, Michael. 1994. Stabilization and Reform in Eastern Europe: A Preliminary Evaluation. In *The Transition in Eastern Europe,* vol. 1, ed. Olivier Jean Blanchard, Kenneth A. Froot, and Jeffrey D. Sachs. Chicago: University of Chicago Press.

Burda, Michael. 1992. Unemployment, Labor Market Institutions, and Structural Change in Eastern Europe. Paper presented at the Economic Policy Panel, London, October 15–16.

———. 1994. Structural Change and Unemployment in Central and Eastern Europe: Some Key Issues. Centre for Economic Policy Research Discussion Paper Series 977.

———. 1995. Labor Market Institutions and the Economic Transformation of Central and Eastern Europe. In *Unemployment, Restructuring, and the Labor Market in Eastern Europe and Russia,* ed. Simon Commander and Fabrizio Coricelli. Washington, D.C.: Economic Development Institute of the World Bank.

Calda, Miloš. 1996. The Round-table Talks in Czechoslovakia. In *The Round-table Talks and the Breakdown of Communism,* ed. Jon Elster. Chicago: University of Chicago Press.

Center for Public Opinion Research (CBOS). 1993. Opinia Spoleczna o Prywatyzacji, Powszechnej Prywatyzacji i Projeckcie "Sieci." Warsaw: CBOS.

Coffee, John C., Jr. 1996. Institutional Investors in Transitional Economies: Lessons from the Czech Experience. In *Corporate Governance in Central Europe and Russia: Banks, Funds, and Foreign Investors,* ed. Roman Frydman, Cheryl W. Gray, and Andrzej Rapaczynski. Budapest: Central European University Press.

Cohen, Michael D., James G. March, and Johan P. Olsen. 1972. A Garbage Can Model of Organizational Choice. *Administrative Science Quarterly* 17:1–25.

Collier, David, ed. 1979. *The New Authoritarianism in Latin America.* Princeton, N.J.: Princeton University Press.

Conaghan, Catherine M. 1995. Reconsidering Jeffrey Sachs and the Bolivian Economic Experiment. In *Money Doctors, Foreign Debts, and Economic Reforms in Latin America from the 1890s to the Present,* ed. Paul W. Drake. Wilmington, Del.: Scholarly Resources Books.

Dahrendorf, Ralf. 1990. *Reflections on the Revolutions in Europe.* New York: Random House, Times Books.

Dangerfield, Martin. 1997. Ideology and the Czech Transformation: Neoliberal Rhetoric or Neoliberal Reality? *East European Politics and Societies* 11, no. 3:436–69.

Desai, Raj M., and Vladěna Plocková. 1997. The Czech Republic. In *Between State and*

Market: Mass Privatization in Transition Economies, ed. Ira W. Lieberman, Stilpon S. Nestor, and Raj M. Desai. Washington, D.C.: World Bank.

Dewatripont, Mathias, and Gérard Roland. 1996. Transition as a Process of Large-Scale Institutional Change. *Economics of Transition* 4, no. 1:1–30.

Dlouhý, Vladimir, and Václav Klaus. 1990. *Strategie radikální ekonomické reformy* (Strategy of radical economic reform). Prague: State Planning Commission and Federal Ministry of Finance.

Dominguez, Jorge. 1997. Introduction to *Technopols: Freeing Politics and Markets in Latin America in the 1980s,* ed. Jorge Dominguez. University Park: Pennsylvania State University Press.

Drabek, Zdenek. 1993. Institutional Structure, Supervision, and the Main Contested Areas in the Czech and Slovak Privatization Process. In *Trends and Policies in Privatisation* (Organisation for Economic Cooperation and Development, Paris), 1, no. 2.

Dyba, Karel, and Jan Svejnar. 1994. Stabilization and Transition in Czechoslovakia. In *The Transition in Eastern Europe,* vol. 1, ed. Olivier Jean Blanchard, Kenneth A. Froot, and Jeffrey D. Sachs. Chicago: University of Chicago Press.

———. 1995. A Comparative View of Economic Developments in the Czech Republic. In *The Czech Republic and Economic Transition in Eastern Europe.* San Diego: Academic Press.

Earle, John S. 1997. Mass Privatization, Distributive Politics, and Popular Support for Reform in the Czech Republic. Institute of Sociology, Academy of Sciences of the Czech Republic Working Papers [Pracovní texty] 97, no. 4.

Earle, John S., Roman Frydman, Andrzej Rapaczynski, and Joel Turkewitz. 1994. *Small Privatization: The Transformation of Retail Trade and Consumer Services in the Czech Republic, Hungary, and Poland.* Budapest: Central European University Press.

East, Roger, and Jolyon Pontin. 1997. *Revolution and Change in Central and Eastern Europe.* London: Pinter.

Ekiert, Grzegorz, and Jan Kubik. 1999. *Rebellious Civil Society: Popular Protest and Democratic Consolidation in Poland.* Ann Arbor: University of Michigan Press.

Elster, Jon, Claus Offe, and Ulrich K. Preuss. 1998. *Institutional Design in Post-Communist Societies: Rebuilding the Ship at Sea.* Cambridge: Cambridge University Press.

Estrin, Saul, and Robert Stone. 1997. A Taxonomy of Mass Privatization. In *Between State and Market: Mass Privatization in Transition Economies,* ed. Ira W. Lieberman, Stilpon S. Nestor, and Raj M. Desai. Washington, D.C.: World Bank.

Etzioni, Amitai. 1988. *The Moral Dimension: Towards a New Economics.* New York: Free Press.

Eurobarometer. 1995. *Central and Eastern Eurobarometer 5.* Brussels: European Commission.

European Bank for Reconstruction and Development (EBRD). 1994. *Transition Report.* London: EBRD.

———. 1999. *Transition Report.* London: EBRD.

Federowicz, Michał, and Anthony Levitas. 1995. Poland: Councils under Communism and Neo-Liberalism. In *Works Councils: Consultation, Representation, and Cooperation in Industrial Relations,* ed. Joel Rogers and Wolfgang Streek, 283–312. Chicago and London: University of Chicago Press.

Filar, Dariusz. 1994. A jednak Wałęsa. *Przegląd Polityczny* 26, nos. 2–4.

Filipowicz, Leszek. 1993. The Institutional Aspects of the Privatisation Process in Poland. In *Trends and Policies in Privatisation* (Organisation for Economic Co-operation and Development, Paris), 1, no. 2.

Fish, M. Steven. 1998. The Determinants of Economic Reform in the Post-Communist World. *East European Politics and Societies* 12, no. 1:31–78.

Frydman, Roman. 1995. Is Privatization in Central and Eastern Europe Succeeding? An Interview with Roman Frydman. *Economic Reform Today* (Center for International Private Enterprise, Washington, D.C.), 4.

Frydman, Roman, Kenneth Murphy, and Andrzej Rapaczynski. 1998. *Capitalism with a Comrade's Face.* Budapest: Central European University Press.

Frydman, Roman, and Andrzej Rapaczynski. 1994. *Privatization in Eastern Europe: Is the State Withering Away?* Budapest: Central European University Press.

Frydman, Roman, Andrzej Rapaczynski, John S. Earle, et. al. 1993. *The Privatization Process in Central Europe.* Vol. 1. Budapest: Central European University Press.

Gadomski, Witold. 1993. Poland: A Confused Public, a Divided Parliament. *Economic Reform Today* (Center for International Private Enterprise, Washington, D.C.), 2.

Garlicki, Leszek. 1992. The Development of the Presidency in Poland: Wrong Institutions or Wrong Persons? In *Poland in a World in Change,* ed., Kenneth W. Thompson. Lanham, Md.: University Press of America.

Garrett, Geoffrey. 1998. *Partisan Politics in the Global Economy.* Cambridge: Cambridge University Press.

Garton Ash, Timothy. 1983. *The Polish Revolution: Solidarity.* London: Granta Books.

———. 1990. *The Magic Lantern: The Revolution of '89 Witnessed in Warsaw, Budapest, Berlin, and Prague.* New York: Vintage.

———. 1999. The Puzzle of Central Europe. *New York Review of Books,* March 18, 18–23.

Geddes, Barbara. 1995. Challenging the Conventional Wisdom. In *Economic Reform and Democracy,* ed. Larry Diamond and Marc F. Plattner. Baltimore: Johns Hopkins University Press.

Gomułka, Stanisław. 1998. Output: Causes of the Decline and the Recovery. In *Emerging from Communism: Lessons from Russia, China, and Eastern Europe,* ed. Peter Boone, Stanisław Gomułka, and Richard Layard. Cambridge: MIT Press.

Gomułka, Stanisław, and Piotr Jasiński. 1994. Privatization in Poland, 1989–1993: Policies, Methods, and Results. In *Privatization in Central and Eastern Europe,* ed. Saul Estrin. London: Longman.

Góra, Marek. 1997. Employment Policies and Programs in Poland. In *Employment Policies and Programmes in Central and Eastern Europe,* ed. Martin Godfrey and Peter Richards. Geneva: International Labour Office.

Grabowski, Tomek. 1995. From a Civic Movement to Political Parties: The Rise and Fall of the Solidarity Committees in Poland, 1989–1991. Paper presented to the Annual Meeting of the American Political Science Association, Chicago, Ill.

Graham, Carol. 1994. *Safety Nets, Politics, and the Poor.* Washington, D.C.: Brookings Institution.

Greskovits, Béla. 1998. *The Political Economy of Protest and Patience: East European and Latin American Transformations Compared.* Budapest: Central European University Press.

Grootaert, Christian. 1995. Poverty and Social Transfers in Poland. World Bank Working Paper Series 1440. Washington, D.C.: World Bank.

Gross, Jan T. 1992. Poland: From Civil Society to Political Nation. In *Eastern Europe in Revolution*, ed. Ivo Banac. Ithaca, N.Y.: Cornell University Press.

Haggard, Stephan, and Robert Kaufman. 1992. Economic Adjustment and the Prospects for Democracy. In *The Politics of Economic Adjustment*, ed. Stephen Haggard and Robert Kaufman. Princeton, N.J.: Princeton University Press.

———. 1995. *The Political Economy of Democratic Transitions*. Princeton, N.J.: Princeton University Press.

Ham, John, Jan Švejnar, and Katherine Terrell. 1993. Explaining Unemployment Dynamics in the Czech and Slovak Republics. Center for Economic Research and Graduate Education–Economic Institute (CERGE-EI) Discussion Paper 23.

Hartl, Jan. 1995. Social Policy: An Issue for Today and the Future. *Czech Sociological Review* 3, no. 2: 209–19.

Hašek, Jaroslav. 1946. *The Good Soldier Schweik*. Trans. Paul Selver. New York: Penguin.

Havrylyshyn, Oleh, and Donal McGettigan. 1999a. Privatization in Transition Countries: A Sampling of the Literature. International Monetary Fund Working Paper, January.

———. 1999b. Privatization in Transition Countries: Lessons of the First Decade. *Economic Issues* (International Monetary Fund) 18 (August).

Hellman, Joel. 1998. Winners Take All: The Politics of Partial Reform in Postcommunist Transitions. *World Politics* 50, no. 2:203–34.

Hinich, Melvin J., and Michael C. Munger. 1994. *Ideology and the Theory of Political Choice*. Ann Arbor: University of Michigan Press.

Hirschman, Albert O. 1988. A Dissenter's Confession: The Strategy of Economic Development Revisited. In *The Strategy of Economic Development*. Boulder, Colo.: Westview Press.

Honajzer, Jiří. 1996. *Občanské Fórum: Vznik, Vývoj a Rozpad* (Civic Forum: Rise, development, and collapse). Prague: Orbis.

Huntington, Samuel. 1968. *Political Order in Changing Societies*. New Haven: Yale University Press.

Institute for Public Opinion Research (IVVM). 1994. Názory občanů na privatizaci státního majetku (Opinions of citizens on the privatization of state property). Prague: IVVM.

International Monetary Fund (IMF). 1999a. Czech Republic—1999 Article IV Consultation Mission Concluding Statement, April 16.

———. 1999b. *Czech Republic: Selected Issues*. IMF Staff Country Report No. 99/90, August.

———. 2000. *Republic of Poland: Selected Issues*. IMF Staff Country Report No. 00/60, April.

Jessop, Bob. 1990. *State Theory*. University Park: Pennsylvania State University Press.

Ježek, Tomáš. 1997. Supplement: Privatization in Practice. *Journal of International Affairs* (Winter).

Johnson, Simon, and Gary W. Loveman. 1995. *Starting Over in Eastern Europe: Entrepreneurship and Economic Renewal*. Cambridge: Harvard Business School Press.

Kamiński, Bartłomiej. 1991. *The Collapse of State Socialism: The Case of Poland*. Princeton, N.J.: Princeton University Press.

Kitschelt, Herbert. 1992. The Formation of Party Systems in East-Central Europe. *Politics and Society* 20, no. 1:7–50.

Kitschelt, Herbert, Zdenka Mansfeldova, Radoslaw Markowski, and Gábor Tóka. 1999.

Post-Communist Party Systems: Competition, Representation, and Inter-party Cooperation. Cambridge: Cambridge University Press.

Klaus, Václav. 1993. *Rok Málo Či Mnoho v Dějinách Země?* Prague: Repro-Media.

———. 1994. *Česká Cesta.* Prague: Profile.

———. 1997. *Renaissance: The Rebirth of Liberty in the Heart of Europe.* Washington, D.C.: Cato Institute.

Kolarska-Bobinska, Lena. 1994. *Aspirations, Values, and Interests.* Warsaw: IFiS Publishers.

Kołodko, Grzegorz. 1994. Dear Reader. In *Privatization Update* 23. Polish Ministry of Privatization.

———. 1999. Ten Years of Post-Socialist Transition Lessons for Policy Reform. World Bank Policy Research Working Paper 2095, April.

Kołodko, Grzegorz, and D. Mario Nuti. 1997. *The Polish Alternative: Old Myths, Hard Facts, and New Strategies in the Successful Transformation of the Polish Economy.* Helsinki: (United Nations University/World Institute for Development Economics Research (UNU/WIDER).

Komárek, Valtr. 1993. Czech and Slovak Federal Republic: A New Approach. In *Economic Transformation in Central Europe: A Progress Report,* ed. Richard Portes. London: Centre for Economic Policy Research and Office for Official Publications of the European Communities.

Kornai, János. 1990. *The Road to a Free Economy.* New York: Norton.

———. 2000. The Road to a Free Economy—Ten Years After. *Transition: The Newsletter about Reforming Economies* 11, no. 2 (April):3–5.

Kotrba, Jozef, Evžen Kočenda, and Jan Hanousek. 1999. The Governance of Privatization Funds in the Czech Republic. In *The Governance of Privatization Funds: Experiences of the Czech Republic, Poland, and Slovenia,* ed. Marko Simoneti, Saul Estrin, and Andreja Böhm. Cheltenham, U.K.: Edward Elgar.

Kowalik, Tadeusz. 1993. Can Poland Afford the Swedish Model? *Dissent* (winter), 88–96.

———. 1994. The Great Transformation and Privatization: Three Years of Polish Experience. In *The New Great Transformation?* ed. Christopher G. A. Bryant and Edmund Mokrzycki. London: Routledge.

Kruk, Maria. 1994. *Mała Konstytucja z Komentarzem.* Warsaw: Wydawnictwo AWA.

Kuroń, Jacek. 1991. *Moja Zupa.* Warsaw: Polska Oficyna Wydawnicza BGW.

Layard, Richard. 1998. Why So Much Pain? An Overview. In Peter Boone, Stanisław Gomułka, and Richard Layard, *Emerging from Communism: Lessons from Russia, China, and Eastern Europe.* Cambridge: MIT Press.

Leff, Carol Skalnik. 1997. *The Czech and Slovak Republics: Nation versus State.* Boulder, Colo.: Westview Press.

Levitas, Anthony. 1994. Rethinking Reform: Lessons from Polish Privatization. In *Changing Political Economies: Privatization in Post-Communist and Reforming Communist States,* ed. Vedat Milor. London: Lynne Rienner.

Lewandowski, Janusz, and Roman Szyszko. 1999. The Governance of Privatization Funds in Poland. In *The Governance of Privatization Funds: Experiences of the Czech Republic, Poland, and Slovenia,* ed. Marko Simoneti, Saul Estrin, and Andreja Böhm. Cheltenham, U.K.: Edward Elgar.

Lewis, Paul G. 1994. Party Development in Post-Communist Poland. *Europe-Asia Studies* 46, no. 5: 779–99.

Lieberman, Ira W. 1994. Mass Privatization: A Comparative Analysis. In *Investment Funds as Intermediaries of Privatization,* ed. Marko Simoneti and Dusan Tříska. Ljubljana, Slovenia: Central and Eastern European Privatization Network.

————. 1997. Introduction: Mass Privatization in Comparative Perspective. In *Between State and Market: Mass Privatization in Transition Economies,* ed. Ira W. Lieberman, Stilpon S. Nestor, and Raj M. Desai. Washington, D.C.: World Bank.

Lindblom, Charles. 1965. *The Intelligence of Democracy: Decision Making through Mutual Adjustment.* New York: Free Press.

Linz, Juan, and Alfred Stepan. 1996. *Problems of Democratic Transition and Consolidation: Southern Europe, South America, and Post-Communist Europe.* Baltimore: Johns Hopkins University Press.

Lipset, Seymour Martin. 1960. *Political Man.* Garden City, N.Y.: Doubleday.

Lipton, David, and Jeffrey Sachs. 1990. Creating a Market Economy in Eastern Europe: The Case of Poland. *Brookings Papers on Economic Activity,* no. 1. Washington, D.C.: Brookings Institution.

Maravall, José María. 1995. The Myth of the Authoritarian Advantage. In *Capitalism, Socialism, and Democracy Revisited,* ed. Larry Diamond and Marc F. Plattner. Baltimore: Johns Hopkins University Press.

Michnik, Adam. 1985. *Letters from Prison and Other Essays.* Berkeley and Los Angeles: University of California Press.

Milanovič, Branko. 1998. *Income, Inequality, and Poverty during the Transition from Planned to Market Economy.* Washington, D.C.: World Bank.

Millard, Frances. 1994. *The Anatomy of the New Poland: Post-Communist Politics in Its First Phase.* Aldershot: Edward Elgar.

Ministry of Ownership Transformation. 1991. *Mass Privatization: Proposed Programme.* Warsaw: Ministry of Ownership Transformation.

Modzelewski, Karol. 1993. *Dokąd od Kominizmu?* Warsaw: Polska Oficyna Wydawnicza "BGW." Excerpt translated as What Happened to Solidarity? *Uncaptive Minds,* winter–spring 1994, 63–72.

Moore, Barrington, Jr. 1966. *Social Origins of Dictatorship and Democracy.* Boston: Beacon Press.

Morales, Juan Antonio, and Jeffrey D. Sachs. 1990. Bolivia's Economic Crisis. In *Developing Country Debt and Economic Performance,* vol. 2, ed. Jeffrey D. Sachs. Chicago: University of Chicago Press.

Murrell, Peter. 1992a. Conservative Political Philosophy and the Strategy of Economic Transition. *East European Politics and Societies* 6, no. 1: 3–16.

————. 1992b. Evolutionary and Radical Approaches to Economic Reform. *Economics of Planning* 25.

————. 1993. What Is Shock Therapy? What Did It Do in Poland and Russia? *Post-Soviet Affairs* 9, no. 2: 111–40.

————. 1995. Reform's Rhetoric-Realization Relationship: The Experience of Mongolia. In *The Evolutionary Transition to Capitalism,* ed. Kazimierz Z. Poznanski. Boulder, Colo.: Westview Press.

Myant, Martin. 1993. *Transforming Socialist Economies: The Case of Poland and Czechoslovakia.* Aldershot: Edward Elgar.

Naím, Moisés. 1995. Latin America: The Second Stage of Reform. In *Economic Reform and Democracy,* ed. Larry Diamond and Marc F. Plattner. Baltimore: Johns Hopkins University Press.

————. 2000. Washington Consensus or Washington Confusion? *Foreign Policy* (spring), 87–101.

Nellis, John. 1999. Time to Rethink Privatization in Transition Economies? *Finance and Development* 36, no. 2 (June): 16–19.

Nelson, Joan. 1993. The Politics of Economic Transformation: Is Third World Experience Relevant in Eastern Europe? *World Politics* 45:433–63.

————. 1995. Linkages between Politics and Economics. In *Economic Reform and Democracy*, ed. Larry Diamond and Marc F. Plattner. Baltimore: Johns Hopkins University Press.

Nuti, Domenico Mario. 1999. Employee Ownership in Polish Privatizations. In *Reconstituting the Market: The Political Economy of Microeconomic Transformation*, ed. Paul Hare, Judy Batt, and Saul Estrin. Amsterdam: Harwood Academic Publishers.

Nuti, Domenico Mario, and Richard Portes. 1993. Central Europe: The Way Forward. In *Economic Transformation in Central Europe: A Progress Report*, ed. Richard Portes. London: Centre for Economic Policy Research and Office for Official Publications of the European Communities.

O'Donnell, Guillermo. 1996. Delegative Democracy. In *The Global Resurgence of Democracy*. Larry Diamond and Marc F. Plattner, eds. Baltimore: Johns Hopkins University Press.

Offe, Claus. 1984. *Contradictions of the Welfare State*, ed. John Keane. Cambridge: MIT Press.

————. 1991. Capitalism by Democratic Design? Democratic Theory Facing the Triple Transition in East-Central Europe. *Social Research* 58, no. 4: 865–92.

Olson, Mancur. 1992. The Hidden Path to a Successful Economy. In *The Emergence of Market Economies in Eastern Europe*, ed. Christopher Clague and Gordon C. Rausser. Cambridge, Mass.: Basil Blackwell.

Orenstein, Mitchell. 1994. The Czech Tripartite Council and Its Contribution to Social Peace. Budapest University of Economics Working Paper Series 99.

————. 1998. A Genealogy of Communist Successor Parties in East-Central Europe and the Determinants of their Success. *East European Politics and Societies* 12, no. 3: 472–99.

Organisation for Economic Cooperation and Development (OECD). 1996. *Country Reports: Poland, 1997*. Paris: OECD.

Ost, David. 1993. The Politics of Interest in Post-Communist East Europe. *Theory and Society* 22:453–86.

Pistor, Katharina, and Andrew Spicer. 1997. Investment Funds in Mass Privatization and Beyond. In *Between State and Market: Mass Privatization in Transition Economies*, ed. Ira W. Lieberman, Stilpon S. Nestor, and Raj M. Desai. Washington, D.C.: World Bank.

PlanEcon. 1993. *PlanEcon Report* 9, nos. 7–8 (March 22).

Pollert, Anna. 1997. The Transformation of Trade Unionism in the Capitalist and Democratic Restructuring of the Czech Republic. *European Journal of Industrial Relations* 3, no. 2: 203–28.

Potůček, Martin. 1999. *Not Only the Market: The Role of the Market, Government, and Civic Sector in the Development of Postcommunist Societies*. Budapest: Central European University Press.

Poznanski, Kazimierz Z. 1995. Introduction to *The Evolutionary Transition to Capitalism*, ed. Kazimierz Z. Poznanski. Boulder, Colo.: Westview Press.

Průsa, Ladislav. 1993. Životní minimum—základní prvek záchranné sociální sítě. *Národni hospodářství* 4.

Przeworski, Adam. 1991. *Democracy and the Market.* Cambridge: Cambridge University Press.

————. 1993. Economic Reforms, Public Opinion, and Political Institutions: Poland in the Eastern European Perspective. In Luiz Carlos Bresser Pereira, José María Maravall, and Adam Przeworski, *Economic Reforms in New Democracies: A Social-Democratic Approach.* Cambridge: Cambridge University Press.

Przeworski, Adam, with Pranab Bardhan, Luiz Carlos Bresser Pereira, László Bruszt, Jang Jip Choi, Ellen Turkish Comisso, Zhiyuan Cui, Torcuato di Tella, Elemer Hankiss, Lena Kolarska-Bobińska, David Laitin, José María Maravall, Andranik Migranyan, Guillermo O'Donnell, Ergun Ozbudun, John E. Roemer, Philippe C. Schmitter, Barbara Stallings, Alfred Stepan, Francisco Weffort, Jerzy J. Wiatr. 1995. *Sustainable Democracy.* Cambridge: Cambridge University Press.

Reschová, Jana, and Jindřiška Syllová. 1994. The Legislature in the Czech Republic: Year 1993. Paper presented at a conference on New Parliaments of Central Europe, IEWS Zamek Štiřín, August 14–17.

Rosati, Dariusz K. 1992. The Stabilization Program and Institutional Reform in Poland. In *The Transformation of Socialist Economies, Symposium 1991,* ed. Horst Siebert. Tübingen, Denmark: J. C. B. Mohr.

Rostowski, Jacek. 1998. *Macroeconomic Instability in Post-Communist Countries.* Oxford: Clarendon Press.

Rueschemeyer, Dietrich. 1999. Left Parties and Policies in Eastern Europe after Communism: An Introduction. In *Left Parties and Social Policy in Postcommunist Europe,* ed. Linda J. Cook, Mitchell A. Orenstein, and Marilyn Rueschemeyer. Boulder, Colo.: Westview Press.

Rueschemeyer, Dietrich, Evelyne Huber Stephens, and John D. Stephens. 1992. *Capitalist Development and Democracy.* Cambridge: Polity Press.

Rueschemeyer, Marilyn, and Sharon L. Wolchik. 1999. The Return of Left-Oriented Parties in Eastern Germany and the Czech Republic and Their Social Policies. In *Left Parties and Social Policy in Postcommunist Europe,* ed. Linda J. Cook, Mitchell A. Orenstein, and Marilyn Rueschemeyer. Boulder, Colo.: Westview Press.

Rutland, Peter. 1992. Thatcherism, Czech Style: Transition to Capitalism in the Czech Republic. *Telos* 94.

Sachs, Jeffrey D. 1993. *Poland's Jump to the Market Economy.* Cambridge: MIT Press.

Saxonberg, Steven. 1999. A New Phase in Czech Politics. *Journal of Democracy* 10, no. 1 (January): 96–111.

Schipke, Alfred. 1994. The Political Economy of Privatization. In *The Economics of Transformation,* ed. Alfred Schipke and Alan M. Taylor. Berlin: Springer-Verlag.

Schumpeter, Joseph. 1942. *Capitalism, Socialism, and Democracy.* New York: Harper and Row.

Schwartz, Gerd. 1994. Social Impact of the Transition. In *Poland: The Path to a Market Economy.* Washington, D.C.: International Monetary Fund.

Shleifer, Andrei, and Daniel Treisman. 2000. *Without a Map: Political Tactics and Economic Reform in Russia.* Cambridge: MIT Press.

Simoneti, Marko, and Dusan Tříska, eds. 1994. *Investment Funds as Intermediaries of Privatization.* Ljubljana, Slovenia: Central and Eastern European Privatization Network.

Slay, Ben. 1991. The "Mass Privatization" Program Unravels. *RFE/RL Report on Eastern Europe,* November 1.

———. 1994. *The Polish Economy.* Princeton, N.J.: Princeton University Press.

Smith, Karen E. 1999. *The Making of EU Foreign Policy: The Case of Eastern Europe.* New York: St. Martin's Press.

Sobótka, Elźbieta. 1993. The "Pact on State-Owned Enterprise under Transition" and the Development of Collective Labour Relations in Poland. Warsaw: Ministry of Labor and Social Affairs.

Sokolweicz, Wojciech. 1992. The Polish Constitution in a Time of Change. *International Journal of the Sociology of Law* 20, no. 1: 29–42.

Solidarity. 1990. Program Statement. Typescript, Gdansk (April 25).

Spicer, Andrew, Gerry McDermott, and Bruce Kogut. 2000. Entrepreneurship and Privatization in Central Europe: The Tenuous Balance between Destruction and Creation. *Academy of Management Review* (July) 25, no. 3: 630–49.

Staniszkis, Jadwiga. 1991. *The Dynamics of the Breakthrough in Eastern Europe: The Polish Experience,* trans. Chester A. Kisiel. Berkeley and Los Angeles: University of California Press.

Stark, David, and László Bruszt. 1998. *Postsocialist Pathways: Transforming Politics and Property in East Central Europe.* Cambridge: Cambridge University Press.

Stefancic, David R. 1992. *Robotnik: A Short History of the Struggle for Worker Self-Management and Free Trade Unions in Poland, 1944–1981.* Boulder, Colo.: East European Monographs, distributed by Columbia University Press, New York.

Stein, Jonathan. 1994. Internal Opposition and the Development of Parties in the Czechoslovak Federal Assembly. Paper presented to the Workshop of Parliamentary Scholars and Parliamentarians, International Political Science Association, Berlin, August 19–20.

———. 1995. The Politics of Retrospective Justice in Germany and the Czech Republic. Cambridge: Program on Central and Eastern Europe Working Paper Series 35. Center for European Studies, Harvard University.

Stein, Jonathan, and Mitchell Orenstein. 1995. Dilemmas of Democratic State-Building in Slovakia. Typescript, Institute for EastWest Studies, Prague.

Svejnar, Jan. 1995. Introduction to *The Czech Republic and Economic Transition in Eastern Europe.* San Diego: Academic Press.

Szacki, Jerzy. 1994. *Liberalizm po Komunizmie.* Warsaw: Społeczny Instytut Wydawniczy Znak, Fundacja Im. Stefana Batorego.

———. 1995. *Liberalism after Communism.* Trans. Chester A. Kisiel. Budapest: Central European University Press.

Szomburg, Jan. 1991. The Social and Political Barriers to Privatization in Poland. In *The Social and Political Consequences of Decentralization and Privatization.* Workshop Report, Gdansk, April 10–12, 1991. Cambridge: Project Liberty, John F. Kennedy School of Government, Harvard University.

Teichova, Alice. 1988. *The Czechoslovak Economy, 1918–1980.* London: Routledge.

Thieme, Jerzy. 1994. A Comparison of Mass Privatization Programs in Poland and the Czech Republic. In *Investment Funds as Intermediaries of Privatization,* ed. Marko Simoneti and Dušan Tříska. Ljubljana, Slovenia: Central and Eastern European Privatization Network.

Torańska, Teresa. 1994. *My.* Warsaw: Oficyna Wydawnicza MOST.

Tucker, Aviezer, Jana Balharová, Ivo Losman, Ján Němec, Ján Němeček, David

Ondračka, Zdeněk Polak, Roman Skyva, Martina Vyrková, and Marketa Židková. 1997. The Czech Transition: Politics before Economics. *Journal of Social, Political, and Economic Studies* 22:4 (winter).

Tuveri, Jean-Pierre, and Johannes F. Linn. 1997. Foreword to *Between State and Market: Mass Privatization in Transition Economies,* ed. Ira W. Lieberman, Stilpon S. Nestor, and Raj M. Desai. Washington, D.C.: World Bank.

United Nations Children's Fund (UNICEF). 1994. *Crisis in Mortality, Health, and Nutrition.* Economies in Transition Studies Regional Monitoring Report 2.

Večerník, Jiří. 1996. *Markets and People: The Czech Reform Experience in a Comparative Perspective.* Aldershot: Avebury.

Večerník, Jiří, and Petr Matějů. 1999. *Ten Years of Rebuilding Capitalism: Czech Society after 1989.* Prague: Academia.

Weber, Max. 1994. The Nation State and Economic Policy. In *Weber: Political Writings,* ed. Peter Lassman and Ronald Speirs. Cambridge: Cambridge University Press.

Wedel, Janine. 1998. *Collision and Collusion: The Strange Case of Western Aid to Eastern Europe, 1989–1998.* New York: St. Martin's Press.

Williamson, John. 1990. What Washington Means by Policy Reform. In *Latin American Adjustment: How Much Has Happened?* ed. John Williamson. Washington, D.C.: Institute for International Economics.

———. 1997. The Washington Consensus Revisited. In *Economic and Social Development into the XXI Century,* ed. Louis Emmerij. Washington, D.C.: Inter-American Development Bank.

Winczorek, Piotr, and Jan Majchrowski. 1993. *Ustrój panstwowy Rzeczypospolitej Polskiej.* Warsaw: Wydawnictwa Szkolne i Pedagogiczne.

Winiecki, Jan. 1992. Privatization in East-Central Europe: Avoiding Major Mistakes. In *The Emergence of Market Economies in Eastern Europe,* ed. Christopher Clague and Gordon C. Rausser. Oxford: Basil Blackwell.

———. 1994. East-Central Europe: A Regional Survey—the Czech Republic, Hungary, Poland, and Slovakia in 1993. *Europe-Asia Studies* 46, no. 5: 709–34.

———. 1997. Introduction: Seven Years' Experience. In *Institutional Barriers to Poland's Economic Development: The Incomplete Transition,* ed. Jan Winiecki. London: Routledge.

Wolchik, Sharon L. 1995. The Politics of Transition and the Break-Up of Czechoslovakia. In *The End of Czechoslovakia,* ed. Jiří Musil. Budapest: Central European University Press.

World Bank. 1996. *From Plan to Market: World Development Report, 1996.* Washington, D.C.: World Bank.

Young, S. David. 1997. The Demand Side of Voucher Privatization in Central and Eastern Europe. In *Between State and Market: Mass Privatization in Transition Economies,* ed. Ira W. Lieberman, Stilpon S. Nestor, and Raj M. Desai. Washington, D.C.: World Bank.

Žák, Václav. 1995. The Velvet Divorce—Institutional Foundations. In *The End of Czechoslovakia,* ed. Jiří Musil. Budapest: Central European University Press.

Zubek, Voytek. 1994. The Reassertion of the Left in Post-Communist Poland. *Europe-Asia Studies* 46, no. 5: 801–37.

———. 1995. The Phoenix Out of the Ashes: The Rise to Power of Poland's Post-Communist SdRP. *Communist and Post-Communist Studies* 28, no. 3: 275–306.

Index

Page numbers in italics refer to tables or figures.

Polonia - neoliberalii / guvern contra grassroot
worker - management buy-outs
preferences -

Cehia - neoliberalo fără reglementări ⇒
discreția acoliților guvernului
și dispariția rapidă a
micilor investitori.